America's Most Wanted Recipes

**Recreate Your Favorite Restaurant
Meals in Your Own Backyard!**

AT THE GRILL

Also by Ron Douglas

America's Most Wanted Recipes

More of America's Most Wanted Recipes

America's Most Wanted Recipes Without the Guilt

America's Most Wanted Recipes Just Desserts

Get Even More Restaurant Recipes!

Join Our Recipe Secrets Online Community at
www.RecipeSecrets.net/join

AMERICA'S MOST WANTED RECIPES

**Recreate Your Favorite Restaurant
Meals in Your Own Backyard!**

AT THE GRILL

RON DOUGLAS

ATRIA PAPERBACK
New York   London   Toronto   Sydney   New Delhi

ATRIA PAPERBACK
A Division of Simon & Schuster, Inc.
1230 Avenue of the Americas
New York, NY 10020

Copyright © 2014 by RonDouglas.com

First Atria Paperback edition May 2014

ATRIA PAPERBACK and colophon are trademarks of Simon & Schuster, Inc.

For information about special discounts for bulk purchases, please contact Simon & Schuster Special Sales at 1-866-506-1949 or business@simonandschuster.com.

The Simon & Schuster Speakers Bureau can bring authors to your live event. For more information or to book an event contact the Simon & Schuster Speakers Bureau at 1-866-248-3049 or visit our website at www.simonspeakers.com.

Interior design by Davina Mock-Maniscalco
Cover design by Janet Perr
Cover photographs by Bob Ingelhart/Getty Images; Liza McCorkle/Getty Images

Manufactured in the United States of America

10   9   8   7   6   5   4   3   2   1

Library of Congress Cataloging-in-Publication Data
   Douglas, Ron.
      America's most wanted recipes at the grill : recreate your favorite restaurant meals in your own backyard! / Ron Douglas.
         pages   cm
      Includes index.
      1. Barbecuing. 2. Cooking, American. I. Title.
      TX840.B3D68 2014
      641.5'784—dc23   2013041957

ISBN 978-1-4767-3489-7
ISBN 978-1-4767-3490-3 (ebook)

To my original inspiration behind the grill—
Maston Murphy (aka "Pop")

CONTENTS

INTRODUCTION

As I write this, it's 10°F on Long Island, New York, where I live with my wife and two kids. Not one green sprig of grass to be found. I can't even see the wood surface of my backyard deck, which is covered in snow. But soon, it will be grilling season, and even those of us in the northeast will be back outside, firing up the grill on warm weekend afternoons. And we'll do it up big—not just a few burgers on the grill. I'm talking steaks, seafood, corn on the cob, and, of course, our favorite restaurant remakes.

It's my hope that *America's Most Wanted Recipes At the Grill* will liven up your grilling experience, just as it has for my family. If you've ever wondered how to make grilled dishes from your favorite restaurants, you're in for a treat. Inside, you'll find more than 150 copycat recipes from the most popular restaurants in the United States, which you can easily prepare on your home grill.

If this is your first book in the *America's Most Wanted Recipes* series, welcome! Back in 2003, I founded an online community called Recipe Secrets.net. Since then, with the help of our contributing chefs, we've unlocked the recipes to some of the most popular dishes served at the most popular restaurants around the country. What began as a hobby has grown into a website with more than 1.2 million members.

The main thing that keeps us going is the wonderful feedback we've received from thousands of our followers who have saved money by making their favorite restaurant dishes at home. But besides just the savings, this cookbook will enable you to:

- Impress your family and friends, and have fun comparing your meals with the restaurant versions.
- Prepare the recipes to your liking, perhaps making them healthier, because you can control the ingredients and the cooking method, unlike when you're eating out.

- Enjoy dishes from several different restaurants in one setting. For example, a starter from TGI Fridays, an entrée from Outback Steakhouse, and a dessert from The Cheesecake Factory.
- Challenge yourself in the kitchen by discovering some of the special techniques that go into re-creating some of the most popular dishes in the world.

We've included a special grilling guide to help you become the grill master that your guests will be raving about all year long.

Each recipe in *America's Most Wanted Recipes At the Grill* has been tested and tweaked to taste just like the original. We encourage you to use the website guide at the back of the book to find a restaurant near you, then compare the recipes in this book to the restaurant versions. Although we can claim only to offer copycat versions of these famous dishes, I am confident that if you follow the instructions, you won't be able to tell the difference.

Get ready to fire up the grill. Bon appétit!

Ron Douglas
RecipeSecrets.net
Find us on Facebook: www.facebook.com/LikeRecipeSecrets

AMERICA'S MOST WANTED RECIPES

Recreate Your Favorite Restaurant Meals in Your Own Backyard!

AT THE GRILL

GRILLING GUIDELINES

Grilling is an ancient method of cooking meat and fish by dry heat. The first grills were in the fireplace of the home, where cooking could be controlled by moving the meat closer or farther away from the flame. It was very basic cooking, which hasn't changed much in centuries. From restaurant chefs to backyard barbecue kings, the goal is a piece of meat, chicken, or fish that is browned and richly colored outside and succulent, moist, and flavorful inside.

The tradition of barbecuing is the closest to the original method of cooking. Whether the heat comes from above, as in broiling, or from beneath, as in grilling, the technique needs to be mastered. With all the different grills and barbecues in the marketplace, it's important to realize that the very finest equipment in the world will not save a steak that's being grilled so close to red hot coals that the melting fat catches fire, and your finest porterhouse gets incinerated. A waste of time, money, and good meat. So, first the basics.

Grilling 101

Required Equipment

The Grill—There are a number of options, but, primarily, there are two to consider—charcoal or gas. The decision depends on what you need in terms of cooking temperature, ease of cleanup, and the ability to impart a smoky flavor. Charcoal grills guarantee a smoky flavor, and may double as a smoker. Gas grills make it easy to cook delicate foods such as chicken, fish, shellfish, and vegetables. Smoke boxes for wood chips can achieve some of the smokiness of a charcoal grill; there are several types to choose from.

Charcoal Grills—As with any outdoor equipment, maintenance is a key issue. Manufacturers recommend cleaning the grill grate after every

1

use. A clean grate heats up in the way it was intended to, therefore creating the ability to sear and grill. A grate with leftover particles of food can affect the cooking temperature. A clean grate will do the proper job; a grate caked with carbon will not. Use your steel grill brush to clean the grate while you're cooking and immediately afterward. Brush the grate and coat it with vegetable oil before every use. The consistency of your grilling depends on the condition of your grill.

Learn to use the vents on a kettle grill to control heat and air circulation. Vents are located on the top of the lid and under the fire box. Fire needs air to burn and keep the coals hot. Opening the vents will allow air to be drawn into the barbecue. If the food is cooking too quickly, or you need less heat, close the vents a bit. To raise the heat, open them. Keep the bottom vents open while the coals are preheating to help them get fired up. If your grill or barbecue has a lever to sweep ashes off the vents, be sure to use it while cooking. Ash-clogged vents will not respond properly. Try to keep the airflow even during cooking; unlike a gas grill, you can't turn the heat up and down with the twist of a knob, so try to keep your charcoal grill in optimum condition.

Along with maintaining a clean cooking surface, be sure to discard spent ashes after they have cooled. Ashes collect the juices, fats, and oils used during cooking—letting grease build up in a grill just means a bigger cleaning job down the road. Give the fire box a good brushing down or wipe with a damp cloth, just to get any lingering particles. Try to start every barbecue session with as clean a grill as possible. Keep the grill covered or put away if weather in your area does not allow year-round outdoor grilling. You'll thank yourself in the summer for the great job you did cleaning the grill the previous fall!

Not all charcoal barbecues are big. There are several portable models that can sit on a picnic table or be packed up and taken camping. Just remember that the size of your grill will determine how much you can cook at one time. Small grills and hibachis are excellent choices for a single steak or a couple of burgers. Don't expect to make lunch or dinner for a dozen people on a tabletop barbecue. Using a competition-sized grill for a burger once a week is most likely a waste of fuel. Choose the appropriate grill for your lifestyle. When your family expands or you move into your dream home, then get a new grill. Having an oversized grill on an apartment terrace doesn't give it the room to get the air it needs. Make sure there is plenty of clearance on all sides of your barbecue, for safety as well as optimal cooking conditions. Keep a spray bottle of water handy at all times.

The true beauty of a charcoal grill is its versatility. Your grill can become a smoker just by arranging the charcoal. Depending on what you're cooking, your next biggest decision after choosing your type of fuel is how to lay it in. From the most basic to advanced, follow these guidelines:

1. **Direct Heat**—All the charcoal or briquettes are spread out evenly over the coal grate. This is crowd cooking—burgers, hot dogs, sausages, and thinner steaks. All the same temperature coals, all hot briquettes. This fire burns hot enough that the continuous addition of cold meat doesn't cool it down.

2. **Double Direct**—Arrange the coals in separate areas. Pile most of them to one side of the bottom grate, and a few, just enough, to cover in a single layer on the other side of the grate. Use this arrangement for thick steaks, pork or lamb chops, and chicken breasts, when you need a quick sear on the outside, and a longer time over lower heat to finish cooking.

3. **Indirect**—For long, slow, low temperature grilling. Pile all the coals to one side of the grate, and leave the other side completely empty. This is how to cook a turkey, a large roast, and ribs. The lid of the grill comes down, and your only job is to rotate the food regularly so it is evenly exposed to the hotter side.

4. **Indirect Split**—The coals are banked at opposite ends of the grate, leaving the middle area empty. Smaller roasts and poultry, such as a whole boneless pork loin and whole chicken. Be sure to put a drip pan on the cooler side to catch juices and fat as they drip down.

Once you determine how the charcoal will be arranged, you will need to be able to gauge heat. There are no thermostats on barbecues, so, depending on what you'll be grilling, you will need different heat levels; charcoal barbecues can run a lot hotter than gas grills. You can use a grill thermometer, but, with some practice, you can use your open palm to determine if your grill is ready to go. Use these temperatures as guidelines for recipes that refer to high, medium, and so on.

1. **High Heat**—450° to 650°F. In this range, foods will sear on the outside in just seconds, which is perfect for rare steaks, shrimp in the shell, and thinly pounded chicken breasts.
2. **Medium High**—375° to 450°F. You will still char the outside, but this heat will allow the food to stay on the grill a little longer. Perfect for blistering the skins of peppers and tomatoes, as well as hamburgers and salmon.
3. **Medium**—325° to 375°F. This is the range where you will do most of your indirect grilling. Whole turkey and rib roasts will cook gently but thoroughly while being rotated to heat exposure.
4. **Medium Low**—250° to 325°F. Good for long, slow cooking, frequent turning, or just finishing meat and pork roasts that need cooking all the way through.
5. **Low**—225° to 250°F. This is ribs and brisket heat. Since these items will take a long time to cook, make sure the charcoal doesn't burn out. Have some hot coals ready in a chimney when it looks like time to add a little heat.

Gas Grills—Stand-alone gas grills have become as much a feature of backyards as decks and patios. Outdoor cooking is a year-round activity in many parts of the country; the health benefits of simply grilled meats and vegetables have taken their place in everyday menu planning. The proliferation of the many types and sizes of gas grills has made grilling easier, cleaner, and more affordable. The thought of having to wheel out the kettle grill, pour in messy charcoal, wait for the coals to get hot, and then start cooking has been a weekend-only event for years. With modern gas grills, there are no more excuses for not getting dinner on the grill in the same time it would take to cook on a stove.

Again, the key is to find a grill that suits the space you have, as well as how much you plan on using it. While most stand-alone or built-in gas grills tend to be larger than charcoal grills, the expense is also greater. Whether your grill is moveable with propane tanks or on a gas line, it is more expensive to purchase and costlier to operate. A single person or couple does not need a grand deluxe model for regular use. A two-burner grill is a good starter size and will be more economical in the long run.

The maintenance issues that were covered for charcoal barbecues apply to gas grills as well. A clean and well-seasoned grate is the key to consistent results. Keep carbon from building up by using the grill brush before, during, and after cooking. One advantage to a gas grill over coal is that you can turn up the burners and cover the grill to burn the carbon off, in much the same way that oven interiors are cleaned with high heat. Brush the grate after the burn and coat it with a bit of vegetable oil on a clean rag. Brush it and rub it down with oil before each use as well. Attention to maintenance will protect your investment for years to come.

If you're still undecided as to which type of grill to use, visit your local home goods store and browse the barbecue section. Manufacturers start their annual sales push in early spring and, while the latest models are being shown up front, last year's inventory has likely gone on sale. Take a look at the brochures that come with each model: try to find one that not only fits your culinary skills but also comes with customer support and a warranty.

Find a cookbook or website that has food that interests you. Try to envision more than just burgers and brats—well-grilled food doesn't just happen. Steaks and shrimp on the barbie don't cook themselves. Follow the charts and guidelines for cooking times and heat control. Learn how to build a fire for indirect heat or how to get wood-smoke flavor from a gas grill. These simple tools may not make you the next master chef, but they will help you to learn the art of the grill or enhance the skills you already have.

The cooking areas for gas grills are the same as for charcoal but, rather than mounding coal, you adjust the second burner.

1. **Direct Heat**—Both burners at medium high to high. The grill is essentially at full blast, so be sure to avoid hot spots right over the burners.
2. **Double Direct**—Reduce the temperature on one of the burners to low.
3. **Indirect**—Turn the second burner completely off.
4. **Indirect Split**—Not as effective as with charcoal, but can work for whole chickens and small roasts; it takes careful watching.

Types of Fuel—The charcoal grill or barbecue depends on charcoal briquettes or hardwood coals for its fuel. Charcoal briquettes are the most commonly used, and often come match ready, as they are saturated with lighter fluid. They are made from charcoal composite and burn evenly. Hardwood charcoal is made from woods such as mesquite, hickory, oak, or alder. Each of these woods will impart a different flavor and smoke. Hickory has the heaviest smoke flavor, and is one of the most popular woods used, either as charcoal, logs, or wood chips. Alder is a medium wood, and mesquite is on the lighter side.

Gas grills are most commonly supplied with propane tanks or have a source directly from the home gas line, if it is the built-in in a permanent location. Gas grills allow you to cook several items at different temperatures on different parts of the grill. Gas grills are easier to adjust for the indirect heat required by smoking, where temperatures must remain low and regulated. Startup is quick and easy; cleanup is less time consuming with no leftover ashes to discard. They come in many styles and sizes, often with convenient little extras.

Coal Starter—Unless you have a gas grill, your next piece of equipment should be some type of starter. Lighter fluid is the starter of choice for many people but does come with some warnings. Remember to never add more lighter fluid once the fire has started, to avoid hazardous flare-up. Once the charcoal is ready, let the lighter fluid burn off, about 30 or 45 minutes, before adding food to the grill to avoid an unpleasant chemical taste.

Briquettes and hardwoods can be started with a **chimney starter,** an inexpensive item that works in all types of barbecues, from jumbo kettle grills to small hibachis. Briquettes or coals are stacked inside on top of kindling—a couple of sheets of newspaper works well. The coals will be ready to use within 30 minutes, as they turn from dark to ash white. Simply pour the hot coals into the bottom grate of the grill and spread them out with a long-handled metal implement. A chimney starter does not require lighter fluid and can be used repeatedly for years. It's the starter of choice for most people who have invested in hardwood coals, and don't want the chemical fumes of lighter fluid masking the wood's natural smoke.

Long Handled Tongs—Long metal tongs with blunt or square grippers will keep you from having to reach over burning hot coals to turn a piece of meat. Tongs come in various lengths, but a 12- to 16-inch length is suitable for most people. Light aluminum types are best, as they won't conduct the heat of the grill to your hands as fast as steel or iron. Many now come with rubber handles, but run the chance of melting if left too close to the heat source. Invest in a hot mitt or hot pad to protect hands from the heat. Removing metal jewelry and watches is a good idea, as they can retain enough heat to burn the skin.

Metal Spatula—A long handled spatula with a sturdy turner is perfect for heavy items and burgers. A wide, flexible turner is best for fish and scallops, as the flexibility will allow you to slip the spatula under a delicate fillet without jamming it. A vented or perforated style of either type will let juices and fat drip through, keeping hot oils from splattering.

Instant-Read Thermometer—For precision and safety, nothing succeeds as well as a small instant-read thermometer that can give you a temperature within seconds. While beef is regularly cooked to temperature by touch only, chicken and pork should not be left to chance. Chicken and other poultry need thorough cooking, and an instant-read thermometer will let you take a number of reads in several locations to give you the information you need about its doneness. Most well-made thermometers last for years, and come with either a gauge dial that registers temps from 0° to 220°F or with a digital readout. Some of the best are quite inexpensive, and will become your most trusted cooking device, whether you're grilling, baking, or using any technique that is dependent on accurate timing.

Knives—A set of appropriate knives is a valuable asset that can last for decades. Top-of-the-line professional-grade show pieces are not required. What you must have is an 8- to 10-inch chef's knife, a flexible boning knife, and a paring knife. Slicers are a bonus, and a honing steel is essential for keeping those edges sharp.

Skewers—Sometimes called *brochettes* or *kabobs*, small pieces of meat or seafood and often vegetables are threaded on skewers for grilling. Bamboo skewers must be soaked for at least 15 minutes before setting them on the grill to keep from burning. They must be discarded after use. Metal skewers are available in several lengths and only need a light oiling before use. Look for a square or flattened shape, as round skewers may not hold foods in place, causing them to spin.

Planks—Cedar or other wood planks have been used for centuries to cook fish evenly and slowly to retain moisture and flavor. Planks have become another staple for home grilling, and come in a wide variety of price ranges. The important thing to remember is that a reusable wood plank, whether it be the traditional cedar—or alder, maple, cherry, oak, or apple—must be seasoned before using for the first time. Like bamboo skewers, planks must be soaked in water for at least an hour before using. By absorbing water, the plank will provide an even source of indirect heat, and the fish will have the time it needs to cook through. As the plank sits on the grill and heats up, it will smolder a little, which will impart the wood flavor to the fish as it cooks. Lightly brush it with a little vegetable oil to seal the porous wood, and remove from the grill to cool down. A disposable plank must also be soaked, then lightly oiled to keep the fish from sticking.

Grill Brush—A steel-bristled grill brush with a long wooden handle should have a permanent place by your barbecue, whether gas or coal, to keep food particles from sticking and carbonizing on the grate.

What's on the Grill?

Meat, Seafood, and Vegetables

With the grill selected and accessories in place, it's time to start cooking. Charts for times and temperatures will follow, but first a discussion about what to know, look for, and ask about at the meat and seafood counter and produce section.

Beef—Because grilling is a brief exposure to dry heat, it's primarily suitable for meat that is naturally tender. Beef steaks are the ideal cut for grilling. Rib steaks, tenderloin, flank, sirloin, porterhouse, and rib eye all benefit from grilling. What should you know before you buy?

USDA grades are assigned at an early stage of butchering and are stamped and labeled accordingly. The top grade is Prime, after which comes Choice, then Select. These three grades are judged the best for human consumption. Grading is determined by the measureable amount of fat and marbling in a steer carcass. The more marbling, the greater the tenderness and flavor. There are fewer Prime grades given, which is one reason for its higher cost.

Before you spend money on steak, know the source. Ask if the market is selling grain- or grass-fed beef. Is it locally raised, or was it shipped from another state? Find out if the meat has been frozen, and how long it was in transit. Antibiotics and growth hormones are mainstays of the industry, but some ranchers are offering natural beef raised on organic feed. Even if you're not buying Prime, the taste and texture of your steak can be affected by any or all of these issues.

Boneless steaks are generally easier to cook to your preferred doneness than steaks with the bone in. **Porterhouse, T-bone,** and beef **rib chops** such as **rib eye** can come off the grill at various stages of cooking. Many restaurants and butcher shops sell steaks with part of the bone still attached, as this can affect the flavor of the steak. Beef **tenderloin** fillet steaks and **New York** strip steaks bone-in are popular in restaurants, and you can try them at home. Just be aware that your steak may be cooked the way you want it at the edge but much less near the bone. The steak is thicker and colder at the bone and will take longer to cook. Always check a spot near the bone with your thermometer or by touch to determine its doneness. **Flank** and **sirloin** are not technically steak cuts, but are large pieces that can be cut into pieces called steaks.

To get the best from your steak, bring it to room temperature at least 30 minutes before grilling. Keep the meat covered while it sits. A cold steak will cook unevenly, as the center stays colder than the outside. Moisture escapes from cold meat as soon as it starts heating, making it dry and tough. There are separate schools of thought regarding seasoning steaks. Meat is usually seasoned on both sides with a minimum of at least salt and pepper. Some steakhouses have developed proprietary blends of spices to season their meat. Some grill experts maintain that only one side be seasoned, as salt draws out moisture. And there are those who don't season meat at all until it comes off the grill. The hot meat is then sprinkled with kosher salt and ground black pepper that is absorbed as the steak rests after cooking. Try any or all of these methods to see which one works best for you.

Ground Beef

Most people don't question what's in their ground beef until a news story breaks about contamination and illness. Some of the same questions asked about prime steaks should be asked about ground meat. Most of the ground beef comes from dairy cattle at the end of their productive milk years. Unless your beef is labeled differently, most ground beef comes from all parts of the cow that can be salvaged.

There is a certain percentage of fat that's allowed in ground beef, which can account for the shrinkage in grilled burgers. To cut down on saturated fat, choose ground beef that is at least 20% lean—this ration can be even higher in some cases.

Save regular ground beef for meat loaf or tacos—it can be pretty flavorless. For juicy hamburgers, choose ground **chuck** or **sirloin**. Chuck is a little fattier, but has more flavor. Sirloin is naturally leaner and benefits from adding seasonings before forming burgers. You can also choose beef ground from **Angus** and **Kobe** beef, which offer their own unique flavors and textures.

Don't overmix ground beef when making burger patties. Use your hands and gently mix in any ingredients you're blending in. Overworking ground beef can make it tough. You also should let the patties refrigerate for 30 minutes or so to let the fat firm up—the fat gets warm from contact with your hands. When the cold burgers hit the hot grill, the fat should start sizzling and take a few minutes to start melting, leaving its flavor behind.

Watch cooking temperatures on ground beef patties. Overcooked regular ground beef is dry and flavorless. The plump, juicy burgers you hope for need to be grilled slightly less than your preferred doneness. Take the patties off the grill before they reach their final temperature—the internal heat will continue to cook through and you will end up with it where you want it. By waiting to take it off the grill at the exact temp you've chosen, that same carryover cooking will take place, and you will have an overdone burger.

Ground Chicken and Turkey

Freshness is the key to ground poultry. Make sure you check the **use by** dates on all packages. Make sure what you buy is fresh, never thawed. Buying it frozen and thawing it yourself would be the better option.

Poultry is highly susceptible to bacteria and must be kept below 40°F at all times. The longer it has been in a refrigerator case at a market, the less control there is over the temperatures. If you see blood running in the bottom of a package of ground turkey or chicken, be very careful. It may have spent too much time over the 40°F limit and might be harboring **pathogens**. If it has been frozen once and thawed, conditions at the market may not have been strictly controlled.

Most ground turkey and chicken is a blend of **white and dark meat,** often in a range of 70% white meat to 30% dark. While all breast meat is available, it is usually better to add moisture in some form, such as chutneys or relishes. A blend of white and dark meat holds up better on the grill because of the higher fat content of dark meat.

Avoid using preformed patties for your burgers—they generally have some flavorings already added and may have had preservatives included as well. **Premade patties** are formed mechanically and the rough treatment decreases their crumbly texture. Always buy bulk ground turkey or chicken that is nicely pink. Avoid any meat that has blotches of white or gray—it may have been mixed with older meat.

If you can't make your chicken or turkey burgers within a day of purchase, it's best to freeze the package and carefully thaw them overnight in the bottom of the refrigerator. Never rush the thawing process. Always thaw out frozen poultry in the refrigerator where it can stay **under 40°F.**

Chicken

Chicken takes wonderfully to outdoor cooking, whether it's the whole bird or cut-up parts. Skin on or off, chicken flourishes under marination, hosting flavors both strong and delicate. There are lots of options to cooking chicken on the grill, each with its own advantages. Using a grill lets you barbecue flattened halves or **whole birds** quickly. A rotating spit enables you to **roast** or **smoke** whole chickens and turkeys at a slower pace.

Using a charcoal fire of **fruit wood,** such as cherry or apple, gives poultry a subtly smoky flavor. Chicken and other poultry cooks best over moderate heat, and timing is essential. Unlike beef that is grilled to a preferred doneness, poultry needs to be cooked to an internal temperature of **165°F.**

If the chicken has been in a marinade, be sure to shake off any excess and pat the chicken down with paper towels. If you are grilling **bone-in pieces,** place the bone side down on the grill first. The bones will actually diffuse the heat throughout the rest of the piece as it cooks. Cook the pieces until the bottom is well browned, then turn them over, only once, and grill the skin side until browned and crispy.

If you are basting chicken pieces, or using barbecue sauce for flavoring, grill the skin side only until it is a light golden color. Brush sauce all over the bone side, then, when it is set, turn the pieces over and generously douse the skin side. Keep saucing and turning until the chicken is cooked through.

Grilling **boneless skinless chicken breasts** is a good way to give the mildly flavored cut some depth. To avoid dry, tough pieces, grill them over moderate heat and turn them over only once to ensure even cooking throughout. Take the breasts off the grill when they are no longer pink in the center and let them rest before carving them into slices or chunks. **Marinating** chicken breasts helps them retain their moisture longer, and pounding them to a ¼-inch thickness helps them cook faster. Oiling the grate before cooking will help keep the lean meat from sticking to the grill, or you can give them a thin coating of vegetable oil.

Once cooked through, chicken can be eaten hot, room temperature, or cold. Its popularity in salads is enormous, and grilled chicken is a favorite at picnics and barbecues. Chicken that has already been cooked, cooled, and refrigerated can be refreshed on the grill the next day, making do-ahead preparations a breeze. Chicken **wings** have become a national best seller, and it's hard to find a cuisine anywhere in the world that doesn't feature chicken in one way or another.

Pork

Well-prepared pork can be the juiciest meat of all. Pork comes by its moisture naturally, benefiting from a thick rind or layers of fat. Pork cuts from the **loin, hind leg,** and **belly** have the most flavor and can be grilled to perfection. Because pork must be cooked completely, an instant read thermometer is essential to have on hand.

Grilling pork will generally take longer to cook than beef, lamb, or chicken. Thus, it's good to grill it over medium to medium-low heat. A light covering of vegetable oil will help it withstand the length of time it needs to cook through. A technique called **barding** often accomplishes two tasks; it provides a covering of fat for moisture and adds additional flavor. This extra fat can come in the form of a **rind** or **fatback** from the butcher shop, but the easiest form of extra fat is layers of thick-cut bacon. Smoke-cured or wood-glazed bacon strips wrapped around a boneless pork loin preserves the moisture of the roast and can be served, crisped on the grill, alongside, tossed with vegetables, or on top of a salad or side dish.

The many uses for pork are evident in recipes from around the world. With the exception of regions governed by religious or cultural standards, pork is widely used in every country. There are more parts of the **whole hog** that can be used for food than any other animal. Picture a standard supermarket without sausage, salami, pepperoni, bacon, breakfast links, ham and ham hocks, lard, ribs, roasts, chops, cutlets, or even bags of chicharones.

Ribs

Perhaps the king of the summertime grill is ribs—baby backs, spareribs, riblets, country style, whatever they're called—all benefitting from careful preparation, indirect heat, smoking, or lots of highly seasoned rubs or barbecue sauces. They deserve their own discussion for selection, preparation, and cooking. Here's what you should know.

Spareribs—These slabs come from the belly, the same as bacon. They are large and meaty, having a little more fat than loin ribs, but with more flavor, and are often grilled plain, with only salt and pepper. Because of their greater weight and size, you need fewer of them for a meal. They are often marketed as whole or **St. Louis style**. The whole slab is just that—it has part of the breast bone with a strip of meat attached, plus a flap known as a **skirt**. If the bone, strip, and skirt are trimmed away, it's called a St. Louis style. The strip of attached meat that gets trimmed in this process, often called **rib tips** or **finger ribs** are sometimes called **riblets** on menus. On average, you'll get 2 to 4 servings per slab of spareribs.

Loin rib—These come from the loin area of the hog, as are pork chops. Most are marketed as **baby back ribs** if they weigh less than 1½ to 1¾ pounds per slab. Over that weight they are called **back ribs**. They have less meat and fat than spareribs, but are also more tender and require less time to cook. Plan on 1 to 2 servings per slab of loin ribs.

Both styles are sold in slabs, numbering 11 to 14 bones each. Many markets cut the slabs in half and sell them as half racks, but true rib lovers prefer whole slabs to keep the ribs from drying out during cooking, as the end ribs sometimes have to be sacrificed if they cook too fast. **Country-style ribs** are either split pork chops from the loin or cut from the area of the shoulder closest to the loin. Very good eating, but not really ribs.

What to look for—Choose slabs that are well covered with flesh, with no bones sticking out or flesh peeling away. Avoid those with large areas of surface fat, which has to be trimmed, and you are paying by the pound. As with all meat, try to buy fresh, never frozen. Look for packages that have been sealed in shrink wrap to keep the air out. The labeling on the package should let you know if the product has been **enhanced,** meaning whether it has been treated with a solution of water, salt, and flavorings. Producers feel that consumers will prefer this treatment as they often overcook the ribs, and this process keeps them from drying out. Unfortunately, this also affects their flavor, and you will have to modify how you season your barbecued ribs.

Both back and spareribs need to be prepared for successful grilling. Having a sharp boning knife will make the steps easy and go quickly.

1. Removing the **membrane** from the bone side of the slab is the most important step for tender ribs. All the sauce and spices you rub on ribs won't penetrate this tough layer. For both back and spareribs, slip the tip of your boning knife under the membrane at the smaller end of the slab and cut a small tab. Grab the tab with a kitchen towel and carefully start pulling it away from the bones. You may get it off in a single strip, but this takes practice. Pull up all the pieces of membrane carefully and you're done.
2. Next, trim away any little pieces of meat or vessels hanging off the end bones, as they will burn during cooking.
3. Finally, trim off any large areas of fat. Leave any small patches attached; they will slowly melt during cooking. Your ribs are prepped and ready to cook. Although some recipes call for **washing** and

drying the slabs, this is not necessary. Neither is giving them a **vinegar bath**. Some of these instructions are left over from days when the pork industry was less structured and pork was considered a trap for trichinosis. Modern processing has all but eliminated this threat in today's markets.

Sausage and Bacon

No discussion of pork could end without including sausage and bacon. As described earlier, hogs contribute more to the food chain than any other type of meat. Again, there are few world cuisines that don't grind, stuff, cure, smoke, or wrap scraps of pork for sausages or bacon. The variety is too wide to cover in a manual of simple guidelines, but here are some things to look for and names to know.

Sausages come **fresh**—uncooked—or air-dried, **cooked or smoked,** and **dry-cured** salami types, and while there may be a mixture of meats, the most common are of all pork. Some examples follow.

Fresh

American breakfast links	Merguez
Bratwurst	Mexican-style chorizo
British bangers	Panang
Bulgarian loukaniko	Salsiccia
Chipolata	Shawarma
Cotechino	Thai chiang mai
Serbo-Croatian cevapcici	Touloussiane
Linguica	

Cooked or smoked

Andouille	Headcheese
Bockwurst	Hot dogs
Bologna	Kasewurst
Boudin	Kielbasa
Cervelas	Liverwurst
Chinese lop chong	Mortadella
Cotto	Soppressata

Dry-Cured

Ciauscolo

Cottochino

Genoa

Pepperoni

Salami

Soppressata

Spanish salchichon

There is also more than one style of **bacon**. Fresh bacon comes uncured, brined, or smoked. Typically, bacon is salted and smoked. Others, like the incomparable prosciutto of Italy, are seasoned and air-dried for weeks and are technically ham, since it comes from the leg and not the belly.

Basterma

Bressaola

Canadian bacon—smoked pork
    loin, also not from the belly

Capacollo

Guanciale

Lardo

Lonzino

Pancetta

Pepperoni

Prosciutto

Tasso

Fresh pork sausage needs to be just as carefully chosen as any other pork product. Check the **use by** dates, and freeze the package if you are not going to use it within a day or two of purchase. Keep sausages refrigerated below 40°F and either in their original packaging or well wrapped in plastic to seal out air. Even though cooked sausage has a longer shelf life, it should also stay **refrigerated** and sealed. Well-cured dry salamis are often sold on shelves, not in the refrigerated cases, but once opened, they need to be wrapped and refrigerated.

Fresh sausages do best over moderate heat, as they need time to cook completely through. If your recipe calls for chunks or pieces of sausage, make sure you buy a link-type sausage. Some loose bulk sausages, such as **chorizo,** are meant to be pan fried or mixed in with other ingredients and baked or fried.

Use a plain or seasoned bulk breakfast sausage for making your own **pork patties** for the grill. Cook them over moderate heat so that they have time to cook through.

Cooked sausage such as **hot dogs** and **bratwurst** are perfect for grilling. They just need to be heated through, and can pick up extra flavor by being grilled over hardwood charcoal. Butterflied, they have even more surface area for absorbing that good grill flavor.

Salami or other **dry-cured** sausage are not usually grilled, but try some thinly sliced and lightly grilled genoa salami in a sandwich with toasted brioche and smoked mozzarella, for a different take on grilled cheese and ham.

Everyday **bacon** is elevated to incredible when grilled over moderate heat and allowed to slowly render almost all of its fat, turning the lean meat mahogany brown and dense. Use an extra-thick style and turn it over frequently to evenly cook on all sides, then serve hot. Smoked bacon grilled over maple or hickory wood is sublime.

Lamb

Perfectly cooked lamb is richly browned on the outside and rosy pink in the center. The initial searing is done over the hottest part of the grill, then it's moved to a cooler spot to finish. Small parts of lamb are best suited to the grill, such as **loin, rib, sirloin** or **leg steaks,** and **chops**. Cubed pieces of lamb shoulder are perfect for kabobs. Tougher cuts can be ground and formed into patties or sausages, then carefully grilled over moderate heat.

Cooking times should be kept as brief as possible to prevent natural juices from escaping. Look for steaks or chops that are evenly sized to determine how long to cook them and over how much heat. For pieces **1-inch thick** and under, a quick searing on both sides may be all that it needs to cook to the perfect temperature. For pieces from 1 to 3 inches, an initial searing and additional cooking at a lower temperature is required.

Lamb, like other meat, takes longer to cook if cold. Because of the leaner interior and delicate nature of lamb, it's best to bring it to room temperature at least 15 minutes before cooking.

Lamb chops and **blade steaks** with bones attached do better on the grill if bathed in an oil-based marinade for a lengthy period, preferably overnight. The distinct flavor of lamb can withstand the combined effects of fresh herbs, garlic, whole peppercorns, and bay leaves. Just a touch of acid such as red wine or balsamic vinegar is all that's needed to not only flavor the chops but to also protect them from high heat.

Lamb **fat** must be trimmed before grilling. Rendered fat dripping onto hot charcoal or a gas burner can cause flare-ups, leaving a burnt, chemical taste to the meat. In order to achieve a proper **sear,** the grill must be about 3 inches from the source of heat, either charcoal, briquettes, or a burner. If using a charcoal barbecue, arrange the coals in the **Double Direct** method discussed earlier, so that after searing, you can move the chops to the lower-heat side of the grill. If you are grilling the chops over **Direct Heat,** make a cooler spot by raising the grate an additional 2 to 3 inches to finish cooking. Turn down the flame on the burner of a gas grill.

Most recipes will instruct the cook to serve lamb **medium rare**. A temperature past medium in lamb turns it quite tough, no matter how much it has been marinated. If you or your guests will only eat well-done meat, butterfly the chop or steak, give it a thick coating of vegetable oil, and sear it over the hottest part of the grill until the edges char. Move the steak to a cooler part of the grill and let it cook just until it is no longer pink in the center. The meat will have been thoroughly cooked through but should still be somewhat moist and tender.

Fish and Seafood

Fresh or saltwater fish and shellfish present not only the greatest challenge to a cook but possibly also the greatest rewards. **Shrimp,** cooked in the shell or marinated in exotic aromatics such as jerk or curry, is possibly one of the most gratifying finger foods ever. Jumbo sea **scallops** on a skewer between two pieces of pineapple or wrapped in prosciutto is an ultimate dining experience. Wild **salmon** on a cedar plank or teriyaki-glazed **tuna** are restaurant mainstays. Duplicating the fresh fish and shellfish of top restaurants is not impossible, but careful attention to your grill and to the product itself will determine how memorable, good or bad, is the meal your efforts produce.

Fish

A fish fillet with firm, dense flesh, high in natural fats, and a definitive flavor is made for the grill, and the fish that's at the top of that list is **salmon.** Wild caught or farm raised, steaks or fillets, skin on or off, no other fish has so many methods or styles of preparation. Here are some basics:

Pacific—Wild caught Pacific salmon is found in an area that stretches from the Sacramento River to Alaska. Due to overfishing, wild salmon is now strictly regulated to let the species regenerate. Pacific salmon are categorized by size:

King/Chinook—Not only tops in flavor but also in size. These fish can weigh up to 100 pounds, though they average around 20 pounds. The flesh ranges from deep red to white, depending on where they lived and what they ate. **Copper River King** salmon from Alaska has for years been the standard bearer of the highest quality. Salmon are known to be rich in **omega-3 fatty acids,** and doctors have recommended it for its cholesterol-lowering properties. It can be found fresh from early spring to late summer in good supply years, but will be withheld from the commercial market if the numbers of spawning salmon are low.

Silver/Coho—Similar in texture and flavor to King, but smaller and with a shorter life span. They have a slightly longer range of habitat, from Monterey County in California to the Bering Sea near Russia. Higher in omega-3 fats than King, the bright red flesh of Silver salmon is unmistakable, even in the farm-raised variety, which averages about a pound.

    Sockeye salmon has less omega-3 fats than King or Silver, and has the darkest red flesh of all. The texture is very firm and is often used for canning, but can still be grilled with excellent results. For grilling purposes, stay away from chum, pink, or humpbacked.

Atlantic—Wild Atlantic salmon are found north of Maine and into northern Europe. They are usually labeled Norwegian, Scottish, or Irish, although several European countries maintain fish hatcheries for the purpose of raising salmon. They usually have a lighter colored flesh and are more mildly flavored. The salmon labeled **Atlantic** in markets is a **farm-raised** fish produced everywhere from Chile to British Columbia.

Farm-raised Atlantic—As noted earlier, Atlantic farm-raised salmon is the most prevalent on the market today. It allows salmon to be eaten year-round for a fraction of the cost of the wild variety. Just as there are differences in wild salmon, different regions farm raise salmon according to different methods.

    Scotland is the leader in a naturally raised habitat salmon. The fisheries are ladder-stepped to reproduce the instinctive nature of the salmon to swim upstream from the ocean to the freshwater in which it was born. Other countries are paying closer attention to **farming methods** since criticisms were made about the red dye in the feed, meant to color the salmon flesh, as well as the breeding conditions and the effects they had on the fish.

Buy your salmon from markets with information on their products; they should be able to at least let you know the **country of origin**. Fish shipped from farms in Chile in plastic bags have been out of the water for a greater number of days than fresh fillets overnighted from British Columbia.

Salmon can be purchased as **whole sides, fillets,** or **steaks**. Salmon steaks fell out of favor when the market for fresh salmon increased. A center-cut fillet of salmon of 6 ounces is a reasonable size per person as an entrée. Restaurants serving salmon salads, tacos, and chowder can make use of the thinner tail portions, and home cooks can do the same. For grilling, the thicker pieces of salmon cook more evenly than tail pieces, which can cook too quickly and dry out.

Serving salmon **skin on** has gained some popularity, especially with wild fish. The skin gets naturally crispy as the fat is rendered from a slowly cooked piece of salmon. The skin can be easily removed after cooking—it sometimes sticks to the grill and slides right off —or can be removed before grilling and cooked separately. Thinly sliced salmon skin crisps are a wonderful garnish for soups and salads.

Other ocean fish that do well on the grill include the following:

Alaska halibut	Mako shark
Bluefish	Monkfish
Bonito	Rockfish
Flounder	Swordfish
Grouper	Yellow-eye and blue-fin tuna
Mackerel	Yellowtail
Mahimahi	

Buy fish fresh whenever possible. Frozen fillets can be successfully thawed and grilled, but run a high risk of drying out, regardless of the amount of marinade or sauce applied before or after.

Markets generally display their items on **crushed ice,** which can also be drying. Just like meat and chicken, vacuum-sealed packages of fresh fillets should be in a refrigerated case and not have accumulated liquid sloshing around the bottom. When buying fresh fillets or steaks, keep some simple guidelines in mind:

Buy what is in season—This may be the most important thing to remember. Doing so will ensure that you have the best fish available at the best price. If it's the height of salmon season, buy it.

Buy the fish the same day you plan to grill it—Extremely fresh fish will keep another day, but you may not know when the fish was brought in. Fresh fish begins to deteriorate within hours of being caught. Regardless of the methods and care that fishermen use to preserve the flesh, too many days out of the water is never a good sign.

Be flexible—You may have salmon in mind, but if the fishmonger or store is featuring a special on really fresh swordfish, it would be wise to consider it.

1. Perhaps the hardest thing to do from where you stand on the other side of the fish counter is judging freshness. Easiest to judge are **whole fish,** with telltale signs like clear eyes bulging from the head, bright pink or red gills, flesh that is firm to the touch, and smell of the sea. In reality, most people are buying fish already filleted or steaked, making it harder to choose, but not impossible.
2. Make sure that the pieces of fish you want have a **bright flesh**—whether it's salmon, tuna, or halibut—the flesh should look like it was just cut.
3. The flesh should have a **tight grain,** not gaping spaces on the surface.
4. There should not be any brown spots, or any discoloration making the fish look yellowed. Above all else, make sure the fish is **moist,** dried-out fish on sale for a discount is there for a reason, which is that the market needs to get rid of it.
5. If you have any questions, ask the counter employee to put a fillet on a sheet of butcher paper and hold it for you to get a whiff. If it doesn't have **a clean, fresh odor,** go with something else.

It's never a good idea to **freeze fish,** but you may have just been presented a gift of fresh fillets that you can't possibly use all at once. If you know for sure the fish is fresh, and has not been previously frozen and thawed, there are some things to know.

1. The connective tissues in fish are very delicate and easily break down during the freezing and thawing process. No cooking method can restore lost moisture or flavor.
2. Wrap individual fillets in at least two layers of **plastic wrap.** Even if you have a home-version vacuum sealer, wrap the fillets in plastic first. It's the cold air of the freezer that will draw the moisture out, so minimize that contact as much as possible.
3. Lay the wrapped pieces in a **single layer** in the freezer. When they are completely frozen, you may put all the pieces in a resealable bag, but do not freeze the fresh fillets in one large bundle.
4. Most home freezers do not go below 0°F, which means the spoiling process will slow down, but not be eliminated. Be sure to **date** and **label** each piece of fish you freeze and rotate them if necessary to use the oldest pieces first. If it's all the same date, plan a barbecue party and cook it all.
5. **Thawing** is critical with all frozen food, but most critically with fresh fish. Let the wrapped pieces sit on a plate in the bottom part of the refrigerator until thawed out, and keep them there until the grill is ready.

Once you have your fish home, it's time to get them on the grill. Different recipes will have specific instructions, but in general, the following directions can be used for steaks and fillets of most fish.

1. Prepare the charcoal barbecue or gas grill for **Direct Heat.** Clean the grate and coat it with vegetable oil.
2. Lightly coat fish that have not been marinated with vegetable oil on both sides before seasoning.
3. Let the fish warm up just briefly to **room temperature** indoors just before grilling. This allows the heat of the grill to penetrate evenly and get to the center of the fillet more quickly without overcooking it on the outside.

4. Make sure the grill is thoroughly **preheated**. Briquettes or charcoals should be ash white. Hold your hand about 3 inches above the grill surface; if you can only hold it there a couple of seconds, the grill is hot enough.

5. Turn the fish over only once—too much handling increases the chance that the fish will stick to the grill or fall apart. The first side that should be grilled is called the **bone side,** the fleshy part of the fillet where ribs and pin bones have been removed. The other side is referred to as the **skin side,** and should be grilled second. Try to plate the fish with the bone side up for the best presentation. The skin side often reveals the darkened blood line that some people find unappetizing.

Shellfish

This category covers the crustaceans and mollusks we know and love as shrimp, lobster, and scallops. Don't forget crab, crayfish, and clams. Grilling shellfish is so much easier than fresh fish, and is a staple of backyard barbecues all summer long. Modern shrimp farms supply the world with clean, wholesome product frozen within minutes of harvesting. Lobsters are held live in tanks for immediate cooking. Scallops are cleaned and shipped out in refrigerated containers still smelling like the ocean. It's hard not to think of shellfish as a cook's best friend, and just a few simple steps take the worry out of grilling them perfectly.

Shrimp—The terms shrimp and prawns are sometimes used interchangeably. Prawns will generally refer to the larger sizes. Technically, prawns are crustaceans, farm raised primarily in the waters of Malaysia and Indonesia. Most of the shrimp available in the U.S. market is from the Gulf of Mexico and the waters of Baja California. For cooking purposes, use either one.

Most recipes require shrimp to be **deveined**. The vein is the digestive track of the shrimp running from head to tail. Because so much of today's catch is aquacultured, veins don't really affect the flavor. Skipping this step is actually preferred when using very small shrimp.

Most shrimp are sold without heads and are correctly referred to as **shrimp tails**. They are classified by size, according to the number of tails in a pound. The larger the shrimp, the fewer in a pound. Most recipes refer to medium or large, so knowing how many people to feed will probably determine your choice. Keep this chart for reference.

Market name	Shrimp count per pound	Av. shrimp per pound
Extra Colossal	U/10	5–6
Colossal	U/12	8–9
Colossal	U/15	13–14
Extra Jumbo	16/20	17–18
Jumbo	21/25	22–23
Extra Large	26/30	27–28
Large	31/35	33
Medium Large	36/40	38
Medium	41/50	45
Small	51/60	55
Extra Small	61/70	65

The U in the chart above stands for Under, meaning that **U10 shrimp** gives you under 10 shrimp per pound.

Grilling shrimp is fairly straightforward. Peeled and deveined shrimp, whether marinated or not, need little time on the grill. Arrange the barbecue for **Direct Heat,** use tongs to place the shrimp on the grill and turn them over once during cooking. Pick one up and look at the head end—if the flesh is **opaque,** it's time to turn them over. Cook them a little less on the second side; the shrimp are done when the flesh is opaque all the way through, or a solid pink color depending on the shrimp. You want to leave the center just a little **translucent** when taking them off the grill, as the heat of the interior flesh will continue to cook the shrimp all the way through.

Shrimp can use extra moisture while grilling, so **baste** liberally with butter or oil. Barbecue sauce or other thick sauce provides a slight shield to the heat. Marinated shrimp may cook even more quickly if some form of acid, such as lemon juice or wine, has been added.

Many recipes call for shrimp grilled on **skewers,** either by themselves or sandwiched between other ingredients. Basting helps here as well, as it will keep the shrimp moist while the other ingredients cook.

Try not to mix the fast-cooking shrimp with another ingredient, such as steak or a hard vegetable like carrots, and expect everything to cook at the same time. Your shrimp will be terribly overdone by the time the other items are ready, so consider your kabob ingredients carefully. A little blanching or precooking might be the answer.

Metal skewers will cook shrimp more quickly because of the hot metal; **bamboo** might be a better option if other ingredients are sharing the same brochette.

Scallops—Of the two types of scallops, it's the sea scallop that usually finds its way to the grill. Harvested on both coasts, the part we eat is the muscle that opens and closes the shell, although other cultures enjoy the roe as well. **Sea scallops** are produced commercially and are available in a number of sizes. They have a sweet flavor that can stand on its own or blend well with other ingredients. Recipes calling for scallops to be wrapped in bacon and grilled are a favorite of restaurant chefs not only for the delightful combinations of flavors, but also because the fat in the bacon provides moisture.

Like shrimp, scallops benefit from basting, marinating, quick grilling over high heat, and a slight undercooking on the grill. As is the case with all seafood, making sure the grate is properly cleaned and oiled before heating is the key to perfectly grilled shellfish.

Lobster—The king of the crustaceans has no equal. It is also one of the most expensive due to the labor-intensive nature of harvesting them. Though traditionally served boiled or steamed, Maine lobster takes on a different realm of flavors when simply basted with butter and grilled.

The **roe,** or egg sack, of female lobsters is technically called the *coral*, and is prized as an ingredient in and of itself in sauces and compound butters. The *tomalley*, or the liver, is not utilized as much in the United States but is also edible.

Live lobsters should be killed quickly and cleaned of the large intestinal vein. Crack the claws and knuckles and pull out the meat. Remove the flange of cartilage in each claw. It's best to save the knuckle and claw meat for other uses and just concentrate on the tail for the grill.

Lobster tails can be grilled **whole, butterflied,** or cut into **medal-**

lions and skewered on brochettes with other shellfish, meat, or vegetables. Frequent basting is necessary and, as with shrimp and scallops, a little undercooking on the grill will make it less likely that the lobster meat will be tough. Tails can be arranged over the split shells for a dramatic presentation and sauced with a simple butter emulsion or garnished with a *cordon* of salsa or relish.

Lobster tails in varying sizes are **aquafarmed** in different areas and can be found frozen in many markets. Careful thawing in the bottom of the refrigerator is the key to tender tail meat that comes frozen. These tails are often called **slipper meat** or **rock lobster** and are related to the Pacific **Spiny lobster** that can range from 1 to 4 pounds and have no claws to speak of. After removing the head, they are all tail meat.

Follow the guidelines for other shellfish—high heat, basting, grilled quickly, and removed from the grill when slightly underdone. Lobster tails also benefit from being at indoor **room temperature** just prior to being grilled. Pull them out of the refrigerator about 10 to 15 minutes before grilling. Coat them with a little vegetable oil or clarified butter before seasoning and grilling.

Larger tails are often run through with skewers to keep them from curling up from the heat of the grill. Use a **square or flat skewer** to keep the tail meat from rotating. Insert the skewer at the tail end and weave it through the center to the head end. This method is especially effective on large, butterflied tails, and will help keep their shape on the grill and afterward, as they cool down.

Like other shellfish, grilled lobster meat can be served hot, chilled, or at room temperature. It works beautifully not only as an elegant entrée but also as medallions on a salad, cut in chunks for a seafood cocktail, or in delicious lobster tacos!

Other shellfish are perfectly adaptable for grilling. Take advantage of any of the following if found fresh in the market.

Abalone	Oysters on the half shell
Crayfish	Rock shrimp
Dungeness crab claws	Soft shell crab
King crab	Squid
Littleneck clams on the half shell	Stone crab claws

Vegetables

Grilled vegetables, which seem to be on every restaurant menu now, weren't even mentioned in many cookbooks until the late 1970s. What seemed unusual very few years ago is as commonplace today as fish tacos and barbecued pizza. Though rarely the main entrée, grilled vegetables can enhance any weekday dinner or backyard barbecue with a variety of **colors, textures,** and **flavors**. Many vegetables absorb a charcoal grill's smoke surprisingly well, and grills can be used to char or blister the skin of peppers and tomatoes before they're added to other preparations.

Use **firm, solid** vegetables for grilling whole, sliced, cut in pieces, or as part of a brochette of meat, chicken, or fish. Corn on the cob is the classic whole example, but don't rule out fresh summer squash and zucchini, carrots, and parsnips. Once cooled, these colorful vegetables can bet cut into bite-sized pieces, generously seasoned, and served together, separately, or as part of a larger combination.

Although garden fresh is the ideal, the reality is that most vegetables are market bought. Buy what is the freshest and **in season**. If you have a recipe that calls for big ripe tomatoes, the middle of winter is not the time to find the cream of the crop!

Look for vegetables in **spotless condition**—without soft spots, gouges, or other discolorations. Limp vegetables are probably past their prime and may be bitter when grilled.

Most will do well over **medium heat**. Solid, hard roots like fennel take a while to cook through. While a little char is tasty, burnt edges are not. Vegetables that take a longer time to grill can be basted and turned frequently to retain their moisture and cook evenly.

Without listing every variety available, look through the vegetable families below to keep in mind what you might like to have grilled. Don't forget mushrooms and artichokes.

Roots and Tubers	**Pods and Seeds**
Carrots	Green beans
Parsnips	Peas
Potatoes	Snow peas
Sweet potatoes	Yellow and white corn
Yams	

Greens
Belgian endive
Chard, red and green
Kale
Mustard greens
Romaine

Technically Fruits
Chilies
Eggplant
Peppers
Tomatoes

Squash
Acorn
Butternut
Chayote

Pumpkin
Scallop or patty-pan
Yellow crookneck or summer
Zucchini

Stalks
Asparagus
Bok choy
Celery
Fennel

Onion
Garlic
Green or scallions
Maui or sweet
Shallots
Yellow, red, and white

Charts for Times and Temperatures

Following is information from the USDA for meats and poultry. The USDA Guidelines show the maximum temperature allowable; the Professional Kitchens Guideline shows the temperature your steak or poultry would reach in a restaurant before resting. This is the preferred guideline for home cooks as well.

Temperatures: USDA Guidelines for Grilling
www.grillinwoodsandrubs.com/LetsGetGrillin.php

BEEF

Rare
USDA Guidelines (Before Resting): n/a
Professional Kitchens (Before Resting): 115 degrees

Medium Rare
USDA Guidelines (Before Resting): 145 degrees

Professional Kitchens (Before Resting): 120 degrees to 130 degrees

Medium
USDA Guidelines (Before Resting): 160 degrees
Professional Kitchens (Before Resting): 140 degrees

Medium Well
USDA Guidelines (Before Resting): n/a
Professional Kitchens (Before Resting): 150 degrees

Well Done
USDA Guidelines (Before Resting): 170 degrees
Professional Kitchens (Before Resting): 155 degrees to 160 degrees

---

GROUND BEEF

USDA Guidelines (Before Resting): 160 degrees
Professional Kitchens (Before Resting): 160 degrees

PORK

Medium
USDA Guidelines (Before Resting): 160 degrees
Professional Kitchens (Before Resting): 145 degrees

Well Done
USDA Guidelines (Before Resting): 170 degrees
Professional Kitchens (Before Resting): 160 degrees

Ground Pork
USDA Guidelines (Before Resting): 160 degrees
Professional Kitchens (Before Resting): 160 degrees

LAMB

Rare
USDA Guidelines (Before Resting): n/a
Professional Kitchens (Before Resting): 110 degrees to 115 degrees

Medium Rare
USDA Guidelines (Before Resting): 145 degrees
Professional Kitchens (Before Resting): 130 degrees

Medium
USDA Guidelines (Before Resting): 160 degrees
Professional Kitchens (Before Resting): 140 degrees

Medium Well
USDA Guidelines (Before Resting): n/a
Professional Kitchens (Before Resting): 145 degrees to 150 degrees

Well Done
USDA Guidelines (Before Resting): 160 degrees
Professional Kitchens (Before Resting): 150 degrees to 155 degrees

Ground Lamb
USDA Guidelines (Before Resting): 170 degrees
Professional Kitchens (Before Resting): 160 degrees

POULTRY

Whole Bird, Thighs, Legs, Wings, Ground Poultry
USDA Guidelines (Before Resting): 165 degrees
Professional Kitchens (Before Resting): 165 degrees

Boneless Skinless Chicken Breasts
USDA Guidelines (Before Resting): 165 degrees
Professional Kitchens (Before Resting): 160 degrees

Cooking by Steak Size
The following chart gives guidelines for cooking times by thickness of a beefsteak. Some cooks feel that judging time by thickness is easier when cooking more than one steak at a time. These are guidelines; your actual experience is the best judgment for how you prefer your steak cooked.

STEAK TIME COOKING CHART		COOKING METHOD: RED HOT CHARCOAL OR GAS GRILL	
Thickness	Doneness	First Side	After Turning
¾"	Rare	4 minutes	2 minutes
	Medium	5 minutes	3 minutes
	Well	7 minutes	5 minutes
1"	Rare	5 minutes	3 minutes
	Medium	6 minutes	4 minutes
	Well	8 minutes	6 minutes
1¼"	Rare	5 minutes	4 minutes
	Medium	7 minutes	5 minutes
	Well	9 minutes	7 minutes
1½"	Rare	6 minutes	4 minutes
	Medium	7 minutes	6 minutes
	Well	10 minutes	8 minutes
1¾"	Rare	7 minutes	5 minutes
	Medium	8 minutes	7 minutes
	Well	11 minutes	9 minutes

Resting and Carving

All cooked meat, whether steak or chicken, benefit from being allowed to rest before carving or serving. This lets the juices redistribute within the meat before the first cut is made. As cooked meat starts to cool down after the heat of the grill, its fibers start to relax. This allows the moisture in the fibers to mostly stay around the center of the meat. This is usually 10 to 15 minutes, depending on the weight and thickness of the meat. This applies to whole roasts as well as separate pieces.

All cooked protein also goes through what is called **carry-over cooking**. This means that hot meat will continue to cook even after it has been taken off the grill. You know that the center of your steak or fish fillet is hot when you cut into it—that amount of heat is all that's necessary to take a steak from medium rare to medium. The same can happen with chicken and fish, even if boneless. Try to get your meat or fish off the grill before it reaches the temperature you want. The USDA chart indicates the temperatures before resting; don't assume that because your steak registers a few degrees lower than when you pulled it off the grill that it's not cooked. Pull fish or chicken off the grill a few minutes before optimal temperatures are reached to keep them from overcooking on the cutting board.

To keep the meat from getting cold, make a tent of foil just large enough to go over the meat and its cutting board. The foil will deflect the heat escaping from the hot meat and keep the surface warm. A cutting board with a trough around the edges can collect whatever juices escape, which allows you to save it for a sauce or pour it directly over the meat as it's served.

Carving a steak depends on a few factors but, as with any meat or poultry, a sharp knife is essential. The large steaks, such as porterhouse, T-bone, or bone-in rib eye can usually be left whole, unless you want to split the steak. Carve the meat away from the bone with the tip of the knife and cut its side in half. Other steaks, such as flank, should be sliced very thin, and always against the grain. Use a fork to hold the small of the steak down and place the blade of the cutting knife almost perpendicular to the meat. Slice the meat in wide, thin pieces to get tender, chewable pieces.

The grain of the meat should be apparent just by looking. The grain is the linear structure of the meat fiber. Cutting meat the same way the grain runs makes it tough to chew. Cutting the opposite way, against the grain, breaks down the fibers and delivers tender pieces or slices of meat.

While not as crucial to poultry as to meat, carving a large piece of grilled breast is best done against the grain to keep the moisture contained in the meat and not let it escape, as it would if slicing with the grain. Cutting poultry with the grain of the flesh is simply separating the fibers, and doing so releases the moisture which had been resting there.

Observing these few guidelines will ensure that your shopping, storing, preparation, and cooking will not be undone by a slipup just before serving.

A&W
Deluxe Grilled Chicken Sandwich

WITH FRESH TOMATO SLICES AND TANGY RANCH DRESSING, THIS FRESH CHICKEN BREAST SANDWICH IS A HEALTHY CHOICE FOR LUNCH OR DINNER AND IS JUST AS TASTY AS IT IS NUTRITIOUS.

1 (8-ounce) boneless skinless chicken breast
½ teaspoon seasoned salt, such as Lawry's
¼ teaspoon pepper
2 whole wheat hamburger buns, split in half

2 teaspoons unsalted butter, melted
2 tablespoons ranch dressing
6 slices dill pickle
2 thick tomato slices
1 leaf iceberg lettuce, halved

1. Light a charcoal barbecue or heat a gas grill to medium. Clean the grate and coat it with vegetable oil.

2. Split the chicken breast and lightly pound each half between 2 pieces of plastic wrap. The chicken should be evenly flattened to ensure proper cooking. Sprinkle both sides with the seasoned salt and pepper

3. Grill the chicken 6 to 7 minutes per side, or until cooked through and no longer pink in the center.

4. While the chicken is cooking, coat each half of the hamburger buns with some of the melted butter. Grill the buns over medium heat, taking care to not let them burn. They should be lightly toasted.

5. Spoon some of the ranch dressing on the bottom of each toasted bun. Layer each half with 3 of the pickle slices.

6. Put the cooked chicken on top of the pickles, then top with a slice of tomato and the iceberg lettuce. Spread the top halves of the buns with the remaining ranch dressing and place them over the assembled sandwich.

7. Serve warm.

Serves 2

Serve this grilled chicken favorite with a cold drink and a side of chips or coleslaw. Customize your sandwich with extra pickles or a slice of cheese.

A&W

Mama Burger

WHEN YOU'RE HUNGRY FOR A SATISFYING BURGER, THERE'S NONE BETTER THAN THIS CLASSIC OF SEASONED GROUND BEEF WITH ALL THE TRADITIONAL TOPPINGS. BE SURE TO USE THE FRESHEST BEEF AVAILABLE, NEVER FROZEN.

8 ounces fresh ground beef or chuck
½ teaspoon seasoned salt, such as Lawry's
¼ teaspoon pepper
2 sesame seed hamburger buns, split in half
2 teaspoons unsalted butter, melted

1 tablespoon ketchup or chili sauce
1 tablespoon yellow mustard
6 slices dill pickle
2 slices yellow onion, thickly sliced
2 tablespoons tartar sauce

1. Combine the ground beef with the seasoned salt and pepper. Mix gently by hand, just until the seasonings are blended in. Don't overmix the meat or the burgers will be tough.

2. Separate the meat into 2 patties. Shape them into equal sizes then lightly and evenly flatten them. Cover the patties with waxed paper and refrigerate for at least 30 minutes.

3. Light a charcoal barbecue or heat a gas grill to medium. Clean the grate and coat it with vegetable oil.

4. Grill the patties 3 to 4 minutes per side, or until they are cooked to the desired doneness, turning them over only once.

5. While the burgers are cooking, coat each half of the hamburger buns with some of the melted butter. Grill the buns over medium heat, taking care not to burn them. They should be lightly toasted.

6. Combine the ketchup and mustard. Spoon a tablespoon of the mixture on the bottom of each toasted bun. Layer each half with 3 of the pickle slices, then top them with a slice of onion.

7. Put the hot burger patty on top of the onion. Spread the top halves of the buns with a tablespoon of tartar sauce each and place them over the assembled sandwich.

8. Serve warm.

Serves 2

Don't use the leanest ground meat in the market. Burgers with little or no fat can be dry and tasteless. Use a ratio of 80% meat and 20% fat for a juicy hamburger. Most of the fat will melt during the grilling, leaving its wonderful flavor behind.

A&W

Mozza Burger

NOTHING SAYS, "LET'S HAVE LUNCH!" LIKE A HAMBURGER WITH BACON AND CHEESE. TRY THIS LONG-TIME FAVORITE THE NEXT TIME HUNGER STRIKES.

8 ounces fresh ground beef or chuck
½ teaspoon seasoned salt, such as Lawry's
¼ teaspoon pepper
2 sesame seed hamburger buns, split in half
2 teaspoons unsalted butter, melted
2 tablespoons ketchup or chili sauce
2 tablespoons tartar sauce
2 slices mozzarella cheese, regular or skim
4 slices hickory smoked bacon, cooked crisp
2 thick slices tomato
1 leaf iceberg lettuce, halved

1. Combine the ground beef with the seasoned salt and pepper. Mix gently by hand, just until the seasonings are blended in. Don't overmix the meat or the burgers will be tough.

2. Separate the meat into 2 patties. Shape them into equal sizes, then lightly and evenly flatten them. Cover the patties with waxed paper and refrigerate for at least 30 minutes.

3. Light a charcoal barbecue or heat a gas grill to medium. Clean the grate and coat it with vegetable oil.

4. Grill the patties 3 to 4 minutes per side, or until they are cooked to the desired doneness, turning them over only once.

5. While the burgers are cooking, coat each half of the hamburger buns with some of the melted butter. Grill the buns over medium heat, taking care not to burn them. They should be lightly toasted.

6. Combine the ketchup and tartar sauce. Spoon a tablespoon of the mixture on the bottom of each toasted bun.

7. Put a slice of mozzarella on each patty just a few seconds before you remove them from the grill. Place 2 strips of the crisply cooked bacon on top of the cheese, then carefully move the patties to the prepared buns.

8. Top each burger with a slice of tomato and a piece of lettuce. Spread the remaining sauce on the top halves of the buns and place them over the assembled sandwich.

9. Serve warm.

Serves 2

Topping the patties while they are still on the grill gives the cheese a few moments to melt slightly and to absorb the flavors of the beef and the bacon. If your bacon has gotten cold, lay the strips on the grill for just a few seconds to crisp them up again, turning them over once or twice as needed.

A&W
Spicy Chipotle Chubby Chicken Burger

GET YOUR TASTE BUDS READY FOR THE SPICY HEAT OF CHIPOTLE PEPPERS IN A
SPECIAL BLEND OF MAYONNAISE AND OLD BAY SEASONING. THIS RECIPE MAKES
EXTRA, SO YOU CAN LIVEN UP OTHER DISHES WITH A JOLT OF FLAVOR.

Spicy Chipotle Sauce
- 1 chipotle pepper, mashed or finely minced
- 1 teaspoon adobo sauce
- 1½ teaspoons Old Bay Seasoning
- 1½ teaspoons Dijon mustard
- 1 tablespoon fresh lemon juice
- ½ cup mayonnaise, regular or reduced fat
- ¼ teaspoon kosher salt
- ¼ teaspoon pepper

- 1 (8-ounce) boneless skinless chicken breast
- ½ teaspoon seasoned salt, such as Lawry's
- ¼ teaspoon pepper
- 2 large ciabatta rolls, halved
- 2 teaspoons unsalted butter, melted
- 4 slices hickory smoked bacon, cooked crisp
- 2 thick slices tomato
- 1 leaf iceberg lettuce, halved

1. Do ahead: To make the Spicy Chipotle Sauce, whisk together the chipotle, adobo sauce, Old Bay, mustard, lemon juice, and mayonnaise. Stir in the salt and pepper, then cover the sauce and refrigerate until ready to use.

2. Light a charcoal barbecue or heat a gas grill to medium. Clean the grate and coat it with vegetable oil.

3. Split the chicken breast and lightly pound each half between 2 pieces of plastic wrap. The chicken should be evenly flattened to ensure proper cooking. Sprinkle both sides with the seasoned salt and pepper.

4. Grill the chicken 6 to 7 minutes per side, or until cooked through and no longer pink in the center.

5. While the chicken is cooking, coat each half of the ciabatta rolls with the melted butter. Grill the rolls over medium heat, taking care to not let them burn. They should be lightly toasted.

6. Spoon 1 or 2 tablespoons of the Spicy Chipotle Sauce over the bottom halves of the toasted rolls. Put the freshly grilled chicken on each of the prepared rolls and top each with 2 slices of the crisply cooked bacon.

7. Top each piece of chicken with a slice of tomato and a piece of lettuce. Spread more sauce on the top half of each ciabatta roll and place it on the assembled sandwich.

8. Serve warm.

Serves 2

Chipotle peppers are jalapeños that have been smoked. They are packed in adobo, which is a mixture of tomatoes, chilies, and spices. After opening the can, store leftover chipotles and their sauce in a tightly sealed glass container to maintain freshness and keep refrigerated.

A&W

Teen Burger

8 ounces fresh ground beef or chuck

½ teaspoon seasoned salt, such as Lawry's

¼ teaspoon black pepper

2 sesame seed hamburger buns, split in half

2 teaspoons unsalted butter, melted

1 tablespoon ketchup or chili sauce

1 tablespoon yellow mustard

6 slices dill pickle

1 thick slice yellow onion, chopped

2 slices Cheddar or American cheese

4 slices hickory smoked bacon, cooked crisp

2 thick slices tomato

1 leaf iceberg lettuce, halved

2 tablespoons tartar sauce

1. Do ahead: Combine the ground beef with the seasoned salt and pepper. Mix gently by hand, just until the seasonings are blended in. Don't overmix the meat or the burgers will be tough.

2. Separate the meat into 2 equal pieces. Shape them into patties, then lightly and evenly flatten them. Cover the patties with waxed paper and refrigerate for at least 30 minutes.

3. Light a charcoal barbecue or heat a gas grill to medium. Clean the grate and coat it with vegetable oil.

4. Grill the patties 3 to 4 minutes per side, or until they are cooked to the desired doneness, turning them only once.

5. While the burgers are cooking, coat each half of the hamburger buns with some of the melted butter. Grill the buns over medium heat, taking care not to burn them. They should be lightly toasted.

6. Combine the ketchup and mustard. Spoon a tablespoon of the mixture on the bottom of each toasted bun. Layer each half with 3 of the pickle slices and cover with some of the chopped onion.

7. Put a slice of the cheese on each patty just a few seconds before you remove them from the grill. Place 2 strips of the crisply cooked bacon on top of the cheese, then carefully move the patties to the prepared buns.

8. Top each burger with a slice of tomato and a piece of lettuce. Spread a tablespoon of tartar sauce on the top halves of the buns and place them over the assembled sandwich.

9. Serve warm.

Serves 2

For times when even this filling burger isn't quite enough, make your own version of a double-double: Cook 2 patties for each burger, and layer each one with a slice of cheese, either the same kind or a combination of whatever you have on hand, such as Cheddar and mozzarella. Serve with plenty of napkins!

APPLEBEE'S
Broiled Salmon with Garlic Butter

WHEN LOOKING FOR A DINNER THAT'S HEALTHY, QUICK, AND MEMORABLE, LOOK NO FURTHER THAN THIS APPLEBEE'S FAVORITE. GRILLING OR BROILING FISH IS NOT ONLY A MORE HEALTHFUL WAY TO COOK, BUT IT IMPARTS A SMOKY ESSENCE THAT CAN ONLY COME FROM THE GRILL.

½ teaspoon kosher salt
¼ teaspoon pepper
¼ teaspoon granulated garlic

4 tablespoons unsalted butter, softened
4 (5-ounce) salmon fillets
I teaspoon fresh lemon juice

1. Light a charcoal barbecue or heat a gas grill to medium. Clean the grate and coat it with vegetable oil.

2. Blend the salt, pepper, and garlic with the butter.

3. Using the back of a teaspoon, spread about a tablespoon of the seasoned butter over each fillet. Refrigerate the salmon until ready to use, or until the butter on each piece has chilled.

4. Put the remaining butter and the lemon juice in a small skillet or saucepan and set it on the side of the grill to melt.

5. Grill the salmon 3 to 4 minutes, butter side down. Using a wide, flexible spatula, turn the fish over and grill the other side for 3 to 4 minutes. Baste occasionally with the lemon butter while grilling.

6. The salmon is done when it is just slightly translucent in the center. You can take it off the grill a bit underdone and it will finish cooking on a warmed platter.

7. Baste the top of the salmon one last time before serving.

8. Serve hot.

Serves 4

Cooking times will depend on the thickness of the fish. Try to buy salmon from a market that offers individual pieces rather than packaged. You'll be able to select fillets of equal size and weight. Thicker, center cut pieces of salmon are generally easier to grill, although the thinner tail pieces will cook faster and are great for sandwiches.

APPLEBEES'S
Cajun Grilled Tilapia with Mango Salsa

. . . .

TILAPIA IS A WHITE-FLESHED FISH THAT HAS GAINED POPULARITY IN THE PAST FEW YEARS. BECAUSE OF ITS FIRM TEXTURE, IT HOLDS UP WELL TO GRILLING. IT'S A PERFECT CHOICE FOR THE HEAT OF CAJUN SPICES AND THE BRIGHT FLAVORS OF THE MANGO SALSA.

. . . .

Mango Salsa
1 cup chopped tomato
½ cup chopped red onion
½ small jalapeño, seeded and minced
2 tablespoons finely chopped cilantro
1 teaspoon olive oil
1 teaspoon apple cider vinegar
½ teaspoon kosher salt
½ teaspoon granulated garlic
¼ teaspoon pepper
½ cup chopped mango

1 tablespoon olive oil
4 (6-ounce) tilapia fillets
2 tablespoons Cajun seasoning
Steamed white rice and mixed vegetables, optional
2 cups Mango Salsa

1. Do ahead: Combine all of the ingredients for the Mango Salsa except for the chopped mango. Gently fold in the mango just before serving.

2. Light a charcoal barbecue or heat a gas grill to medium. Clean the grate and coat it with vegetable oil.

3. Spread a little of the olive oil over both sides of each tilapia fillet, then cover evenly with the Cajun seasoning.

4. Grill the fillets 2 to 3 minutes per side, depending on the thickness of each piece. Turn over only once, using a wide, flexible spatula, to keep the fish from breaking.

5. Center a portion of the steamed rice, if using, on warmed dinner plates and place a fillet on top. Surround the rice with the mixed vegetables, and spoon a portion of the salsa over the fish.

Fresh mangos are not in season year-round and may be hard to find in some regions. Frozen mango is sold in some specialty stores and many major markets. Let the chunks thaw out in a colander, then chop them to the same size as the rest of the salsa ingredients.

APPLEBEE'S
Chicken Fajita Rollup

LET A PREPARED FAJITA SEASONING DO THE MIXING FOR YOU. CHOOSE A CHIPOTLE BLEND FOR A SMOKY ESSENCE AND LASTING FLAVOR. OLD EL PASO, McCORMICK, AND FRENCH'S ARE WIDELY AVAILABLE.

2 ounces fajita seasoning mix
1 (8-ounce) boneless skinless chicken breast
1 large poblano pepper
1 tablespoon olive oil
1 large red bell pepper, seeded and thinly sliced
1 large yellow onion, thinly sliced
2 medium Roma tomatoes, cut in thick strips
1 teaspoon kosher salt

½ teaspoon pepper
4 (8-inch) flour tortillas
½ cup pico de gallo or other salsa
1 cup shredded Cheddar and Monterey Jack blend
½ cup sour cream
1 cup shredded iceberg lettuce
1 small jalapeño, seeded and diced, optional

1. Light a charcoal barbecue or heat a gas grill to medium. Clean the grate and coat it with vegetable oil.

2. Rub the fajita seasoning into the chicken breast. Grill the chicken 6 to 7 minutes per side, turning once, or until cooked through and no longer pink in the center. Let it rest for 10 minutes, then slice it into long strips.

3. Put the poblano pepper on the grill at the same time as the chicken, and turn it frequently until charred. Peal the skin or rub it off, then remove the stem and seeds. Cut into long slices.

4. Heat the olive oil in a large skillet and sauté the bell pepper and onion. When the vegetables have softened, add the strips of tomato and season with the salt and pepper.

5. Put the tortillas on the grill until warmed. Lay them on a flat service and spoon the chicken and vegetables into the center of each one. Top with

spoonfuls of pico de gallo, cheese, sour cream, lettuce, and the jalapeño, if desired.

6. Roll up the tortillas and serve.

. . . .

Serves 4

. . . .

Applebee's also serves this as a chicken fajita entrée. You can do the same. Just serve the tortillas on the side.

APPLEBEE'S
Classic Patty Melt

WHAT MAKES THIS PATTY MELT SPECIAL IS THE ROASTED GARLIC MAYONNAISE USED ON THE TOASTED ITALIAN BREAD. ONIONS, CHEESE, AND QUALITY GROUND BEEF MAKE THIS AN EASY ANSWER TO THE WHAT'S FOR LUNCH QUESTION.

1 tablespoon olive oil	½ teaspoon kosher salt
1 large clove garlic, finely minced	¼ teaspoon pepper
1 large yellow onion, sliced	¼ teaspoon granulated garlic
1 tablespoon yellow mustard	2 tablespoons unsalted butter
4 tablespoons mayonnaise	4 slices Italian bread
12 ounces fresh ground beef or chuck	4 slices Swiss cheese
	4 slices Cheddar cheese

1. Heat the olive oil in a medium skillet over medium-low heat. Add the minced garlic and sauté until completely softened and lightly browned. Remove with a slotted spoon and let cool.

2. Add the sliced onion to the skillet and sauté over medium heat until soft and golden.

3. Add the cooked garlic and mustard to the mayonnaise and blend in a food processor or blender. Set aside.

4. Light a charcoal barbecue or heat a gas grill to medium. Clean the grate and coat with vegetable oil.

5. Divide the beef into 2 equal pieces and form into patties. Season with the salt, pepper, and granulated garlic. Grill the patties 4 to 5 minutes per side, or until cooked to desired doneness, then set aside.

6. Melt 1 tablespoon of the butter in a large skillet and toast 2 pieces of bread on one side. Spread the other side of the bread with a teaspoon of the garlic mayonnaise. Put 2 slices of Swiss cheese on one piece of bread and 2 slices of Cheddar on the other piece of bread.

7. Remove the toasted bread from the skillet and add the remaining tablespoon of butter. When it has melted, add the remaining 2 pieces of bread and toast them as before. Top with some of the garlic mayonnaise and the remaining slices of cheese.

8. Place a patty on a piece of toasted bread and smother it with the sautéed onion. Cover with the additional toasted bread and cheese and heat through.

9. Slice the sandwiches in half and serve warm.

Serves 2

Make sure when you assemble the patty melts that each one has slices of Swiss and slices of Cheddar. For garlic lovers, roast whole peeled cloves in a hot oven with a little olive oil and add an extra clove or two when making these sandwiches.

APPLEBEE'S
Grilled Oriental Chicken Salad

APPLEBEE'S SERVES THIS SALAD WITH FRIED CHICKEN. THE GRILLED OPTION HAS FAR FEWER CALORIES AND IS JUST AS FLAVORFUL—MAYBE EVEN MORE SO!

Oriental Salad Dressing
¼ cup mayonnaise, regular or reduced fat
¼ cup rice wine vinegar
2 tablespoons golden brown sugar
1 teaspoon sesame oil
1 teaspoon yellow mustard
2 tablespoons soy sauce

1 (8-ounce) boneless skinless chicken breast
½ teaspoon kosher salt
¼ teaspoon pepper
3 cups shredded green cabbage
3 large carrots, julienned
1 cup rice noodles, such as La Choy
⅓ cup sliced almonds, lightly toasted

1. Do ahead: To make the Oriental Salad Dressing, whisk the mayonnaise and vinegar until smooth and well blended. Stir in the brown sugar, sesame oil, mustard, and soy sauce. Whisk the dressing briskly until well blended. Cover and refrigerate until needed.

2. Split the chicken breast and pound lightly between 2 sheets of plastic wrap. Season on both sides with the salt and pepper. Cover and refrigerate until ready to use.

3. Light a charcoal barbecue or heat a gas grill to medium. Clean the grate and coat it with vegetable oil.

4. Grill the chicken 5 to 7 minutes per side, or until cooked through, and no longer pink in the center. Let the chicken rest, lightly covered, for at least 10 minutes before slicing into bite-sized pieces.

5. To assemble the salad, toss the cabbage with half the salad dressing and arrange it on chilled plates. Layer the carrots on top, then sprinkle the rice noodles and toasted almonds over the carrots. Top the salads with the sliced chicken pieces.

6. Drizzle a little more of the salad dressing over the salad, and serve any remaining dressing on the side.

Serves 2

Chow mein noodles and chopped cashews are alternative ingredients that can add crunch to this salad. If raw cabbage is not a family favorite, substitute your favorite mix of lettuces, such as iceberg and romaine. A little shredded red cabbage adds color and texture.

APPLEBEE'S
Quesadilla Burgers

A SPICY HERB MIXTURE GIVES THE GROUND BEEF A SATISFYING LATIN FLAVOR IN THIS DISH. MAKE A DOUBLE BATCH OF THE SOUTHWEST SEASONING MIX TO ADD TO OTHER FAVORITES, SUCH AS TACOS OR BURRITOS.

Southwest Seasoning Mix
2 teaspoons ground cumin
2 teaspoons chili powder
1 teaspoon kosher salt
1 teaspoon dried oregano
½ teaspoon black pepper
½ teaspoon red pepper flakes
¼ teaspoon cayenne pepper

8 ounces fresh ground beef or chuck
½ cup chopped red onion
½ cup chopped tomato
2 tablespoons red wine vinegar

2 tablespoons chopped fresh cilantro
½ teaspoon kosher salt
1 small jalapeño, seeded and finely diced
2 leaves iceberg lettuce, thinly sliced
2 tablespoons unsalted butter
2 (10-inch) flour tortillas
½ cup shredded pepper Jack cheese
½ cup shredded Cheddar cheese
4 slices thick-cut bacon, diced and cooked crisp

1. Do ahead: Combine all the ingredients for the Southwest Seasoning Mix and mix with the ground beef. Form into a large, flat patty, cover, and refrigerate for at least 30 minutes.

2. In a small bowl, gently mix the red onion, tomato, red wine vinegar, cilantro, salt, jalapeño, and lettuce. Cover and refrigerate until ready to use.

3. Light a charcoal barbecue or heat a gas grill to medium. Clean the grate and coat it with vegetable oil.

4. Grill the beef patty 3 to 4 minutes per side, or until cooked to your preferred doneness.

5. Melt 1 tablespoon of the butter in a 12-inch skillet and swirl it around to coat the pan evenly. Add one of the tortillas.

6. Combine the cheeses and spread them evenly over the tortilla, leaving 1 inch around the edge. Layer half the salsa over the cheese and add half the cooked bacon.

7. Place the cooked beef patty on the cheese and salsa, then cover with the remaining cheese, salsa, and bacon. Cover with the last tortilla.

8. When the bottom tortilla is browned, cover the skillet with a large plate and flip the quesadilla over. Melt the remaining tablespoon of butter in the skillet, swirling to evenly cover the bottom of the pan.

9. Slide the quesadilla back into the skillet and cook over medium-low heat until the cheese is warmed through and the bottom tortilla is browned and crisp.

10. Remove the quesadilla from the skillet and cut into 4 to 8 wedges. Serve warm.

Serves 4 to 6

If you're not in the mood to grill, pan fry and crumble the ground beef before assembling the quesadilla. Spread it evenly with the cheese and salsa and cut into 10 to 12 wedges to serve as an appetizer. Sour cream and guacamole make great accompaniments.

APPLEBEE'S
Riblets with Honey Barbecue Sauce

EVERYONE LOVES RIBS, AND THESE ARE SOME OF THE BEST. RESTAURANTS ARE ABLE TO BUY CUTS NOT OFTEN SEEN IN MARKETS, AS IS THE CASE WITH THESE RIBLETS. TO MAKE AT HOME, USE PORK RIB TIPS OR A FULL RACK OF BABY BACK RIBS.

2½ pounds pork rib tips or a rack of baby back ribs
1 tablespoon kosher salt
1 teaspoon pepper
¼ teaspoon liquid smoke flavoring

Honey Barbecue Sauce
1 cup ketchup or chili sauce
½ cup light corn syrup
½ cup honey
¼ cup apple cider vinegar
¼ cup water
2 tablespoons molasses or dark maple syrup
2 teaspoons dry mustard
2 teaspoons granulated garlic
1 teaspoon onion powder
1 teaspoon chili powder

1. Light a charcoal barbecue or heat a gas grill to medium-low. Clean the grate and coat with vegetable oil.

2. Season the pork with the salt and pepper. Cook on the grill, turning occasionally, until the meat begins to pull away from the bones.

3. Preheat the oven to 275°F.

4. Combine the liquid smoke with enough water to cover the bottom of a roasting pan. Set a rack over the liquid and arrange the ribs in a single layer, making sure the meat does not touch the water, as the liquid smoke would alter its flavor.

5. Cover the roasting pan with foil and bake for 2 to 3 hours, or until the meat is fork tender and easily falls away from the bones.

6. The ribs can be prepared ahead up to this point, then cooled, wrapped in plastic and refrigerated.

7. Whisk together all the ingredients for the Honey Barbecue Sauce in a medium saucepan and simmer for 20 minutes.

8. To serve, grill the cooked ribs over a hot grill or heat them in a hot oven. The ribs should be heated just to sizzling—don't let them cook, or they will dry out.

9. Brush the ribs with some of the Honey Barbecue Sauce and serve the remainder on the side.

10. Serve the ribs hot.

Serves 4

If you don't have corn syrup and don't want to purchase it to use such a small amount, replace it with a simple solution of 1 cup sugar dissolved in ¼ cup hot water. When the sugar is completely dissolved, let the syrup cool, then use ½ cup for the sauce. You can save the remaining syrup for other uses if kept refrigerated in a tightly sealed container.

APPLEBEE'S
Southwest Skillet Steak

SMOTHERED WITH SAUTÉED PEPPERS AND ONIONS, THESE SIRLOIN STEAKS ARE TOPPED WITH CHEDDAR AND MONTEREY JACK CHEESE. THEY ARE SEASONED WITH A SPECIAL STEAK SEASONING, THEN BLACKENED ON THE GRILL. SERVE ON A SIZZLING HOT CAST IRON SKILLET TO COMPLETE THE RESTAURANT THEME.

Blackened Steak Seasoning
1 tablespoon chili powder
1 teaspoon kosher salt
1 teaspoon onion powder
1 teaspoon granulated garlic
½ teaspoon ground white pepper
½ teaspoon black pepper
½ teaspoon dried thyme
½ teaspoon dried oregano, crushed

2 (5½-ounce) sirloin steaks
2 tablespoons unsalted butter

1 medium yellow onion, thinly sliced
1 large clove garlic, minced
1 small green bell pepper, seeded and thinly sliced
1 small red bell pepper, seeded and thinly sliced
½ teaspoon kosher salt
¼ teaspoon pepper
1 slice Cheddar cheese, halved
1 slice Monterey Jack cheese, halved

1. Light a charcoal barbecue or heat a gas grill to medium-high. Clean the grate and coat with vegetable oil.

2. Combine all the ingredients for the Blackened Steak Seasoning. Dredge the steaks in the seasoning and sear on the grill.

3. When the steaks are charred on both sides, move them to a cooler part of the grill to finish cooking to the doneness you like. Let the meat rest, lightly covered, for about 15 minutes before serving.

4. Heat the butter in a large skillet over medium heat. Sauté the onion and garlic until soft, then add the bell peppers. Season with the salt and pepper. Keep warm, while the steaks are finishing.

5. Just before serving, put the steaks back on the grill and top each one with a piece of each cheese. Plate the steaks and spoon a portion of the sautéed vegetables over each steak.

6. Serve hot.

Serves 2

Sirloin steaks take well to grilling over high heat, but not for an extended period of time, as this cut is very lean, with very little protective fat. The steaks can be put into a hot oven to finish cooking if you want them cooked past medium. Be sure to turn them regularly, so that they cook evenly on both sides.

APPLEBEE'S
Steakhouse Salad

APPLEBEE'S USES SIRLOIN STEAK FOR THEIR VERSION AND DOESN'T SKIMP ON THE BEEF. NEITHER SHOULD YOU.

Blue Cheese Vinaigrette
½ cup extra virgin olive oil
2 large cloves garlic, minced
¾ cup blue cheese
⅓ cup white wine vinegar
1 tablespoon water
1 teaspoon sugar
½ teaspoon Tabasco sauce
½ teaspoon kosher salt
¼ teaspoon pepper
1 tablespoon shredded fresh basil

16 ounces sirloin steak
1 teaspoon kosher salt
½ teaspoon pepper
1 large head romaine lettuce
4 slices red onion, sliced ¼-inch thick
4 thick slices tomato
¼ cup blue cheese

1. Do ahead: To prepare the Blue Cheese Vinaigrette, heat 1 tablespoon of the olive oil in a small saucepan. Add the garlic and sauté until lightly golden brown. Remove the pan from the heat and add the remaining oil to let it become infused with the garlic flavor.

2. Put the blue cheese, vinegar, water, sugar, Tabasco, salt, pepper, and the garlic oil into a blender and pulse until well blended. Stir in the basil and set the dressing aside. If you are not using it right away, it may be refrigerated in an airtight container for 3 days.

3. Light a charcoal barbecue or heat a gas grill to medium. Clean the grate and coat it with vegetable oil.

4. Season the steak with the salt and pepper, then cook 4 to 5 minutes per side, turning once, or until it's cooked to your preferred doneness. Let the steak rest for 10 minutes, then slice it into ¼-inch strips and set aside.

5. Take 3 or 4 of the outer leaves of romaine from the head and arrange them on the bottom of a large platter. Quarter the remaining romaine from stem end to the top, then slice it crosswise into 1½-inch squares.

6. Toss the chopped romaine with ¾ cup of the Blue Cheese Vinaigrette and place it on the platter with the whole leaves. Arrange the sliced steak over the salad, then top with the rings of red onion and sliced tomatoes.

7. Crumble the blue cheese over the top and serve.

Serves 2

Crisp iceberg lettuce or mixed greens can be substituted for the romaine.

ARBY'S
Grilled Chicken Pecan Salad Sandwich

NOT YOUR USUAL CHICKEN SALAD SANDWICH. IF THE RECIPE SOUNDS TOO FILL-
ING, LEAVE THE BREAD OUT AND HAVE A VERY FLAVORFUL SALAD, CRUNCHY WITH
PECANS AND APPLES, AND SIZZLING WITH JUICY CHICKEN HOT OFF THE GRILL.

4 (6-ounce) boneless skinless chicken breasts
1½ teaspoons kosher salt
¼ teaspoon pepper
1 large red or green apple
1 tablespoon fresh lemon juice
1 cup halved seedless red or green grapes
1 large stalk celery, chopped
1 cup pecan pieces
½ cup mayonnaise, regular or reduced fat
8 slices whole wheat or whole grain bread
8 green leaf lettuce leaves

1. Light a charcoal barbecue or heat a gas grill to medium. Clean the grate and coat it with vegetable oil.

2. Season the chicken with half of the salt and pepper. Grill until cooked through and no longer pink in the center. Let the chicken rest at least 10 minutes before slicing into bite-sized pieces.

3. Core the apple and cut it into chunks. Toss with the lemon juice to keep from browning.

4. Combine the apple, grapes, celery, and pecans. Fold in the mayonnaise, and season with the remaining salt and pepper.

5. Gently stir in the cooked chicken.

6. Line 4 slices of bread with 2 lettuce leaves and spoon on a portion of the chicken salad. Top with the remaining slices of bread.

Serves 4

Toasting the bread first adds a little extra crunch to these tasty sandwiches. If you decide to serve as a salad only, line chilled plates with the lettuce leaves, then pile on the chicken mixture. You could also grill a few slices of the bread and cut them into wedges to make toast points to serve with your salad.

BAHAMA BREEZE
Bahamian Grilled Steak Kabobs

THE BAHAMA BREEZE RESTAURANT CHAIN FEATURES FOODS COOKED OVER A WOOD GRILL. YOU MAY BE ABLE TO DUPLICATE THE FLAVOR BY USING HARDWOOD CHARCOAL AND WOOD CHIPS OR LOGS IN YOUR BARBECUE OR GRILL. IT MAKES ALL THE DIFFERENCE TO HOW THEIR FRESH FISH ITEMS CARRY THAT WONDERFUL, SMOKY ESSENCE TO THE TABLE.

8 ounces beef sirloin or tenderloin, cubed
½ cup teriyaki sauce
2 (1-inch) pieces each of zucchini, red bell pepper, mushroom, and red onion
4 metal or bamboo skewers (if bamboo, soak in water before use)
1 teaspoon kosher salt
½ teaspoon pepper

Kabob Basting Sauce
½ cup spicy barbecue sauce or Pickapeppa Sauce
¼ cup orange juice concentrate, thawed
1 tablespoon golden brown sugar
2 tablespoons chopped fresh cilantro

1. Mix the cubed beef with the teriyaki sauce and marinate for at least 4 hours in the refrigerator.

2. Light a charcoal barbecue or heat a gas grill to medium. Clean the grate and coat it with vegetable oil.

3. Thread skewers with the meat, alternating with the vegetables. Season the meat and vegetables with the salt and pepper. Leave a little room between each of the ingredients to ensure even cooking.

4. Make the Kabob Basting Sauce by whisking together all the ingredients in a small bowl. Use a pastry brush to evenly coat the kabobs with the sauce.

5. Cook the kabobs on the grill, basting regularly with the basting sauce, turning them on all sides to develop a crispy char. Grill until the beef is cooked to your preferred doneness.

Serves 2

Use additional vegetables or substitute others that you may prefer. Eggplant, fennel, cherry tomatoes, or even fruits, such as pineapple, make good additions to kabobs.

BAHAMA BREEZE
Chicken Santiago

OFTEN SERVED WITH PLANTAINS OR RICE, THE BAHAMA BREEZE VERSION COMES WITH YOUR CHOICE OF SIDES AND CHIMICHURRI SAUCE, THE DELECTABLE OLIVE OIL— AND PARSLEY-BASED HERB SAUCE USED IN SOUTH AMERICA ON GRILLED MEATS.

Chimichurri Sauce
½ cup olive oil
¼ cup white wine vinegar
¼ cup fresh lemon juice
2 teaspoons kosher salt
½ teaspoon pepper
½ cup finely chopped parsley
3 tablespoons minced cilantro
½ teaspoon dried oregano
4 green onions, green part only, thinly sliced
2 large cloves garlic, finely minced

Roasted Red Pepper Sauce
1 tablespoon olive oil
1 small yellow onion, chopped
2 small cloves garlic, minced

1 large red bell pepper, seeded and chopped
1½ cups whipping cream
½ teaspoon ground cumin
1 teaspoon paprika
½ teaspoon kosher salt
¼ teaspoon pepper
2 tablespoons cornstarch
2 tablespoons cold water

2 (8-ounce) boneless skinless chicken breasts
½ teaspoon kosher salt
¼ teaspoon pepper
½ cup Chimichurri Sauce
½ cup Roasted Red Pepper Sauce

1. Do ahead: To make the Chimichurri Sauce, whisk together the olive oil, vinegar, lemon juice, salt, and pepper. Stir in the remaining ingredients and mix until well blended. Cover and refrigerate until ready to use.

2. Do ahead: To make the Roasted Red Pepper Sauce, heat the olive oil in a medium saucepan and simmer the onion and garlic until soft.

3. Add the red bell pepper, whipping cream, cumin, paprika, salt, and pepper. Bring the mixture to a boil, then reduce the heat and simmer for 20 minutes.

4. Whisk together the cornstarch and water. Stir this mixture into the saucepan and whisk until the sauce is thickened.

5. Ladle the sauce into a blender and puree. Taste the sauce and add additional seasoning, if desired. Return the blended sauce to the pan and keep warm.

6. Light a charcoal barbecue or heat a gas grill to medium. Clean the grate and coat it with vegetable oil.

7. Season the chicken breasts with the salt and pepper. Grill 6 to 7 minutes per side, or until cooked through and no longer pink in the center. Baste occasionally with some of the Chimichurri Sauce.

8. Serve the chicken breasts in a pool of the Roasted Red Pepper Sauce, drizzled with more Chimichurri Sauce. Serve warm.

Serves 2

Steamed rice or mashed potatoes would be perfect side dishes with this chicken. They would easily pick up the flavors of both the red bell pepper and Chimichurri Sauce. Any leftover sauce can be used with fish or beef, either grilled or broiled. The Chimichurri Sauce is better if made 1 or 2 days in advance, and refrigerated in an airtight container.

BAHAMA BREEZE
Grilled Fish Tostada Salad

THIS RECIPE CALLS FOR USING FRESH MAHIMAHI, WHICH MAY NOT BE AVAILABLE IN YOUR MARKET. CONSIDER USING SWORDFISH, YELLOWTAIL, OR ANOTHER FIRM-BODIED FRESH FISH.

Tomato Salsa

6 large plum tomatoes, diced
1 small red onion, chopped
2 small cloves garlic, minced
2 tablespoons chopped fresh
  cilantro
1 small jalapeño, seeded and
  minced
1½ teaspoons chili powder
½ teaspoon cumin
½ teaspoon onion powder
½ teaspoon kosher salt
¼ teaspoon pepper

Citrus Vinaigrette

¼ cup olive oil
⅔ cup white wine vinegar
1 tablespoon Dijon mustard
½ cup orange juice concentrate
1 tablespoon honey
2 medium cloves garlic, minced
1 medium shallot, diced
½ teaspoon Creole or Cajun
  seasoning mix
2 tablespoons chopped fresh
  cilantro

Chimichurri Sauce

½ cup olive oil
¼ cup white wine vinegar

¼ cup fresh lemon juice
2 teaspoons kosher salt
½ teaspoon pepper
½ cup finely chopped parsley
3 tablespoons minced cilantro
½ teaspoon dried oregano
4 green onions, green part only,
  thinly sliced
2 large cloves garlic, finely minced

4 (6-ounce) mahimahi fillets
½ teaspoon kosher salt
1 tablespoon Creole or Cajun
  seasoning mix
½ cup Chimichurri Sauce
8 (6-inch) flour tortillas, lightly
  oiled
1½ cups shredded Mexican blend
  cheese
6 cups mixed lettuces
½ cup Citrus Vinaigrette
½ cup frozen corn kernels,
  thawed 1 small red bell pepper,
  seeded and chopped
1 cup Tomato Salsa
1 medium avocado, pitted and
  quartered

1. Do ahead: To make the Tomato Salsa, gently toss the tomatoes and onion, then add the remaining ingredients. Stir well to blend and refrigerate until ready to use.

2. Do ahead: To make the Citrus Vinaigrette, combine the olive oil, vinegar, and mustard in a blender. Pulse just until blended, then add the remaining ingredients. Pulse until well mixed, then refrigerate until ready to use.

3. Do ahead: To make the Chimichurri Sauce, whisk together the olive oil, vinegar, lemon juice, salt, and pepper. Stir in the remaining ingredients and mix until well blended. Cover and refrigerate until ready to use.

4. Light a charcoal barbecue or heat a gas grill to medium. Clean the grate and coat it with vegetable oil.

5. Preheat the oven to 400°F.

6. Season the fish fillets with the salt and Creole or Cajun mix.

7. Grill 3 to 4 minutes per side, depending on the thickness of the fillet. Use a wide, flexible spatula to turn the pieces over. Remove from the grill when just cooked through and no longer translucent in the center. Baste with some of the Chimichurri Sauce.

8. While the fish is cooking, lay the prepared tortillas on a baking sheet and use a fork to poke several holes in each one. Bake until lightly browned, about 4 minutes.

9. Overlap 2 tortillas to form one large, double-sized tostada. Sprinkle each tostada with a portion of the shredded cheese, then return them to the oven and bake 1 more minute, or until the cheese is melted.

10. Place each tostada on a plate.

11. Toss the lettuce with the Citrus Vinaigrette and corn and chopped bell pepper. Spoon a portion of the salad onto each of the prepared tortillas. Spoon a portion of the tomato salsa over the salads.

12. Place a piece of the mahimahi on each salad and drizzle the fish with the Chimichurri Sauce. Top each fillet with a quarter of the avocado.

Serves 4

Make the Tomato Salsa, Citrus Vinaigrette, and Chimichurri Sauce a couple of days ahead of time. Keep the sauces refrigerated in airtight containers. Any leftovers can be used with other dishes or served with the tostada salad on the side.

BAHAMA BREEZE
Guava Glazed Double Pork Chops

DOUBLE PORK CHOPS CAN BE ORDERED FROM YOUR BUTCHER. THEY ARE TWICE THE THICKNESS OF A SINGLE CHOP, AND CAN DRY OUT IF OVERCOOKED. THE JAMAICAN MARINADE USED IN THIS RECIPE WILL NOT ONLY TENDERIZE THE PORK BUT ALSO HELP MAINTAIN ITS MOISTURE WHILE GRILLING.

Jamaican Marinade
(see page 68)

Guava Glaze
1 cup frozen guava fruit pulp
2 cups barbecue sauce
1 teaspoon Cajun Seasoning mix

½ teaspoon kosher salt

4 (10- to 12-ounce) double cut
   pork chops
1 cup Jamaican Marinade
½ cup Guava Glaze

1. Do ahead: To make the Jamaican Marinade, see page 68. Refrigerate until ready to use.

2. Do ahead: To make the Guava Glaze, whisk together the guava pulp, barbecue sauce, Cajun mix, and salt. Refrigerate until ready to use.

3. Marinate the pork chops in a cup of the marinade for at least 4 hours in the refrigerator, making sure the marinade completely covers the meat.

4. Light a charcoal barbecue or heat a gas grill to medium. Clean the grate and coat it with vegetable oil.

5. Shake the excess marinade from the pork chops and grill them, turning once, until cooked through. It is acceptable to cook the chops to medium rare, which leaves them still pink in the center. If you want well-done pork, it's best to butterfly the chops before you marinate them.

6. Baste the chops frequently with the Guava Glaze as they cook. Let the chops rest for at least 10 minutes before serving.

7. Serve hot.

Be very careful when handling hot chilies. The habañero, also known as the Scotch bonnet, is one of the hottest peppers on the market. Use disposable gloves while preparing the marinade and use care to keep the juices and seeds away from you.

BAHAMA BREEZE
Jamaican Marinade

THE ABSOLUTE TOP ISLAND FLAVORS ALL COME TOGETHER IN THIS MARINADE/
BARBECUE/BASTING/DIPPING COCKTAIL, WHICH YOU WILL FIND ADDICTIVE.
SWEET FRUIT JUICES AND FIERY SCOTCH BONNET PEPPERS ARE COMPETING WITH
DARK RUM FOR YOUR TASTE BUDS' ATTENTION. MAKE A BIG BATCH; YOU'LL BE
FINDING ALL SORTS OF THINGS TO GO WITH THIS MARINADE.

¼ cup canola oil
2 tablespoons Jamaican jerk spice
¼ cup orange juice concentrate
¼ cup light soy sauce
¼ cup rice wine vinegar
2 tablespoons Jamaican dark rum
I tablespoon lime juice

I teaspoon Creole seasoning mix
I Scotch bonnet (habañero),
   seeded and minced
2 large cloves garlic, minced
I medium red onion, diced
2 green onions, green part only,
   chopped

1. Whisk together the oil and jerk spice. When the spice is dissolved, stir in the remaining ingredients.

2. Refrigerate in a glass container with a tight fitting lid. The marinade will last up to 4 days.

3. To use as a sauce, bring the marinade to a boil in a small saucepan, lower the heat, and simmer 5 minutes. This will cook off the alcohol to keep the vegetables from spoiling.

Makes about 1½ cups

This amount of marinade should be enough for about 3 pounds of chicken wings or 3 full rib racks.

BAHAMA BREEZE
Wood-Grilled Chicken Breast

TO GET THE SMOKIEST FLAVOR IN YOUR GRILLED CHICKEN, CLOSE THE LID OF YOUR BARBECUE OR GRILL WHILE THE MEAT IS COOKING. SOAK THE WOOD CHIPS, SO THAT THEY DON'T BURN UP RIGHT AWAY.

1 cup hickory wood chips
2 (8-ounce) boneless skinless
   chicken breasts
1 teaspoon kosher salt
½ teaspoon pepper

Orange Glaze
¼ cup orange marmalade
¼ cup orange juice concentrate

Citrus Butter
1 small shallot, minced
¼ cup dry white wine
¼ cup orange juice concentrate
1 tablespoon fresh lemon juice
½ teaspoon kosher salt
¼ teaspoon ground white pepper
¼ cup (half stick) unsalted butter,
   cubed

1. Soak the wood chips in cold water for at least 15 minutes before using.

2. Light a charcoal barbecue or heat a gas grill to medium. Clean the grate and coat it with vegetable oil. Sprinkle the wood chips over the charcoal or set a burner ring with the chips in the heated grill just before you are ready to start cooking the chicken.

3. Season the chicken breasts with the salt and pepper. Cook about 6 to 7 minutes per side, turning once, until cooked through and no longer pink in the center.

4. To make the Orange Glaze, combine all the ingredients in a blender and pulse until smooth. Baste the chicken occasionally while cooking to develop a light char. Glaze once or twice more just before serving.

5. Make the Citrus Butter while the chicken is cooking and keep warm. Combine the shallot, wine, juices, salt, and pepper in a small saucepan and reduce by ¾ over medium heat. Remove the pan from the heat and whisk in the cold butter, a piece at a time, until it is all incorporated. Set aside until ready to serve.

6. Let the chicken rest about 10 minutes before serving. Spoon some of the Citrus Butter over the cooked chicken and serve the rest on the side.

Serves 2

The Orange Glaze can easily be made 2 or 3 days ahead of time and refrigerated in a tightly sealed container. You may want to make a double or triple amount to use with other meals, such as grilled shrimp or broiled vegetables.

BAJA FRESH
BBQ Salsa Loco

THIS SALSA TAKES A LITTLE MORE TIME TO PUT TOGETHER, BUT IT'S WORTH EVERY BITE.

4 large cloves garlic
1 tablespoon olive oil
10 Roma tomatoes, halved
5 large jalapeños
1 large yellow onion, quartered

½ teaspoon kosher salt
½ teaspoon pepper
1 tablespoon lime juice
½ cup finely chopped fresh cilantro

1. Light a charcoal barbecue or heat a gas grill to medium. Clean the grate and coat it with vegetable oil.

2. Cut a square of aluminum foil and make a pouch. Add the whole garlic cloves and olive oil, then wrap the pouch tightly and set it on the grill.

3. Put the tomatoes, skin side down, on the grill and cook until the skins are blackened and slip off easily. Flip them over and move them to a cooler area of the grill.

4. Put the jalapeños and the onion on the grill and cook until charred. When the skins on the jalapeños are blackened, slip them off and remove the stems and as many of the seeds as possible.

5. Unwrap the garlic and combine it with the oil, the jalapeños, half the onions, and tomatoes in a blender. Add the salt, pepper, and lime juice. Pulse until the mixture is well ground. Add a little more oil, lime juice, or water if the salsa is too thick. Chop the remaining onion and add it with the cilantro to the salsa and pulse only a couple of seconds to blend the ingredients.

6. Check for seasoning and add more salt and pepper if necessary. Let the salsa cool, then store in an airtight container.

Serves 8

This salsa is not only perfect to serve with chips but also as a condiment or sauce with grilled fish, chicken, and burgers.

BENIHANA

Hibachi Chateaubriand with Garlic Butter Glaze

Garlic Butter Glaze
½ cup (1 stick) unsalted butter
2 large cloves garlic, minced
2 tablespoons finely chopped
   parsley
1 tablespoon lemon juice
½ teaspoon kosher salt

2-pound piece beef tenderloin
1 teaspoon kosher salt
½ teaspoon pepper
½ cup chopped watercress

1. Do ahead: For the Garlic Butter Glaze, melt the butter in a small sauce-pan and add the garlic. Stir in the parsley, lemon juice, and salt. Pour the mixture into a small container and refrigerate until it hardens.

2. Light a charcoal grill or heat a gas grill to medium. Clean the grate and coat it with vegetable oil.

3. Season the tenderloin with the salt and pepper. Melt 2 tablespoons of the garlic butter and brush it over the beef.

4. Grill the tenderloin about 4 minutes per side, or until seared on all sides. Move the meat to a cooler part of grill until it reaches your desired done-ness. Let the meat rest for about 10 minutes before serving.

5. Carve the tenderloin into ½-inch slices. Garnish it with the chopped watercress and the garlic butter.

Serves 4

Save the remaining Garlic Butter Glaze for other recipes, such as the Grilled Shrimp on page 74. You can also reheat the butter and use it as a sauce to serve with the tenderloin and your favorite side dish.

BENIHANA
Hibachi Meat Marinade

USE THIS MARINADE FOR BEEF TENDERLOIN, SIRLOIN, AND OTHER LEAN CUTS.

2 tablespoons apple cider vinegar

2 tablespoons soy sauce

2 large cloves garlic, finely minced

1 teaspoon sesame oil

1 tablespoon sesame seeds

1. Whisk all the ingredients until well blended.

2. Store in an airtight container until ready to use.

3. Steaks should be marinated for at least 30 minutes before grilling.

Makes ½ cup

Try this marinade on all types of cuisine. Just because it contains soy sauce doesn't mean it should be used only in Asian dishes!

BENIHANA
Grilled Shrimp

INSTEAD OF A SIMPLE DINNER FOR TWO, GO BIG AND HAVE A FEAST. DOUBLE THE RECIPE FOR THE GARLIC BUTTER GLAZE AND USE WITH AS MANY SHRIMP AS YOU THINK YOU CAN FINISH IN A SINGLE SITTING—THIS DISH IS JUST THAT GOOD!

10 large shrimp, peeled and deveined
4 tablespoons Garlic Butter Glaze, melted (see page 72)

1 tablespoon fresh lemon juice
¼ teaspoon kosher salt
¼ teaspoon pepper

1. Light a charcoal barbecue or heat a gas grill to medium. Clean the grate and coat it with vegetable oil.
2. Brush the shrimp with the Garlic Butter Glaze, and grill for a minute or two, until the shrimp are no longer translucent in the center.
3. Brush with more of the garlic butter and sprinkle with the lemon juice. Season with the salt and pepper and serve hot.

Serves 2

BENIHANA
Tsutsumi-Yaki

A COLORFUL ASSORTMENT OF VEGETABLES IS GRILLED THEN GLAZED WITH A SA-
VORY ASIAN-STYLE SAUCE. EASY TO MAKE AHEAD AND REHEAT WHEN NECESSARY.

2 cups broccoli florets
2 cups cauliflower florets
2 large carrots
2 cups green beans, cut in 1-inch
  pieces
1 medium yellow onion, sliced
  into 4 rounds
8 large shiitake mushrooms,
  stemmed
2 tablespoons olive oil
¼ green cabbage, cut into four
  wedges

4 roughly chopped green onions
1 cup bean sprouts
2 tablespoons white miso or
  tahini paste
1 tablespoon brown sugar
1 tablespoon rice wine vinegar or
  sherry
1 teaspoon soy sauce
2 sheets nori, julienned
2 green onions, green part only,
  thinly sliced

1. Blanch the broccoli, cauliflower, carrots, and green beans, then drain and let dry.

2. Light a charcoal barbecue or heat a gas grill to medium. Clean the grate and coat it with vegetable oil.

3. Brush the yellow onion, carrots, and mushrooms with some of the olive oil and grill them on all sides.

4. Cut 4 sheets of foil and center each one with a round of the grilled onion.

5. Cut the carrots diagonally and slice the mushrooms into thick strips. Layer them over the onions in the foil. Top with the blanched vegetables, cabbage, chopped green onions, and bean sprouts.

6. Whisk together the miso, sugar, vinegar, and soy sauce. Brush the mixture over the vegetables in each of the foil sheets.

7. Sprinkle the nori and sliced green onions over each of the bundles and seal the edges to make packets.

8. Place the packets on the hot grill and cook for 10 to 12 minutes, or until the packages are puffed up.

9. Serve the packets at the table and let each diner open his or her own. Serve hot.

Serves 4

Double the size of the packets for a vegetarian dinner, or serve a packet along with grilled shrimp, chicken, or beef.

Nori is dried seaweed and is mostly used for wrapping sushi. Miso is made from fermented rice, other grains, or soybeans and is most often used to flavor sauces and soups. Both can be found in specialty markets or online.

BENNIGAN'S
Bamboo Chicken and Shrimp Skewers

TENDER PIECES OF CHICKEN BREAST AND SHRIMP ARE MARINATED IN SPICY GARLIC, GRILLED, AND SERVED OVER NOODLES BATHED IN A CRUNCHY PEANUT SAUCE. PERFECT HOT OFF THE GRILL AND EXCELLENT FOR A BUFFET OR PICNIC.

Satay Marinade
1 large jalapeño, seeded and minced
3 large cloves garlic, minced
2 teaspoons fresh ginger, peeled and grated
¼ cup rice wine vinegar
½ cup soy sauce
2 teaspoons sesame oil
½ cup brown sugar

Peanut Sauce
¾ cup crunchy peanut butter
1 cup unsweetened coconut milk
¼ cup rice wine vinegar
2 tablespoons soy sauce
2 tablespoons dark brown sugar
1 teaspoon fresh ginger, peeled and grated

2 large cloves garlic, minced
¼ teaspoon cayenne pepper
¼ cup chicken broth

1 (8-ounce) boneless skinless chicken breast, cut into 12 equal pieces
8 large shrimp, peeled and deveined
4 metal or bamboo skewers (if bamboo, soak in water before use)
½ cup Satay Marinade
4 ounces lo mein noodles, cooked according to package directions
½ cup Peanut Sauce
1 green onion, chopped
1 teaspoon black sesame seeds

1. Do ahead: To make the Satay Marinade, combine all the ingredients in a blender and pulse until the mixture is well ground. Add a little water if the mixture is too much like a paste. Refrigerate the marinade in an airtight container until ready to be used.

2. Thread the pieces of chicken and shrimp alternately onto skewers. Cover them with the marinade and refrigerate, covered, for at least 30 minutes.

3. Do ahead: To make the Peanut Sauce, combine the peanut butter, coconut milk, rice wine vinegar, soy sauce, brown sugar, ginger, garlic, and cayenne pepper in a medium saucepan and whisk to blend. Bring the sauce to medium heat and cook, stirring frequently, until the sauce is the consistency of thick cream. Transfer the mixture to a blender and add the chicken broth. Pulse until the sauce is well blended and smooth. Set the sauce aside, or refrigerate in an airtight container until ready to use.

4. Light a charcoal barbecue or heat a gas grill to medium. Clean the grate and coat it with vegetable oil.

5. Remove the skewers from the marinade and shake off any excess. Grill the shrimp and chicken until cooked through and the chicken is no longer pink in the center.

6. Toss the lo mein noodles with the Peanut Sauce and put a portion onto each of four plates. Put a skewer on top of the noodles and sprinkle with the chopped green onions and black sesame seeds.

Serves 4

Bamboo skewers must be soaked before using on a grill.
Submerge them in warm water for at least 15 minutes before
making the chicken and shrimp skewers.

BENNIGAN'S
Smothered Chicken

THE SMOKY FLAVOR OF GRILLED CHICKEN WILL APPEAL TO ALMOST EVERYONE. BENNIGAN'S UPS THE SMOKINESS IN THIS POPULAR ENTRÉE BY ADDING SMOKED BACON UNDER A LAYER OF PROVOLONE CHEESE, TOPPED WITH MUSHROOMS AND ONIONS, AND BROILED UNTIL BUBBLING.

Chicken Marinade
2 large basil leaves, julienned
1 tablespoon granulated garlic
¼ teaspoon hickory smoke liquid
¼ cup dry white wine
¼ cup canola oil
½ teaspoon kosher salt
½ teaspoon pepper
2 tablespoons red wine vinegar

½ cup Chicken Marinade
4 (6-ounce) boneless skinless
   chicken breasts
¼ cup (½ stick) unsalted butter
2 drops hickory smoke liquid
1 large yellow onion, thinly sliced
½ pound large white mushrooms,
   stemmed and sliced
½ teaspoon kosher salt
¼ teaspoon pepper
8 slices smoked bacon, cooked
   crisp
8 slices provolone cheese

1. Do ahead: To make the Chicken Marinade, whisk together the ingredients until well blended. Refrigerate, covered, until ready to use. This marinade may be made up to 3 days before using.

2. Put the chicken breasts into a large resealable plastic bag and pour the marinade over them. Make sure the chicken is well covered and refrigerate for at least an hour, turning occasionally.

3. Heat the butter in a large skillet and add the hickory smoke liquid. Sauté the onion until soft, then add the mushrooms and sauté until cooked through. Season with the salt and pepper.

4. Light a charcoal barbecue or heat a gas grill to medium. Clean the grate and coat it with vegetable oil.

5. Remove the chicken from the marinade and shake off any excess. Grill the breasts for 6 to 7 minutes per side, turning once, or until cooked through and no longer pink in the center.

6. Heat the oven broiler to high.

7. Place the grilled chicken in an oven-proof baking dish and top each one with 2 pieces of bacon. Layer 2 slices of the provolone cheese over each breast, then finish with the mushrooms and onions.

8. Broil under the high heat for just a couple of minutes, until the cheese is slightly toasted and bubbly.

Serves 4

Serve this with a fresh green vegetable or mixed green salad to complement the richness of the dish.

BOB EVANS
BBQ Beer Brat Kabobs

BOB EVANS RESTAURANTS ARE KNOWN FOR THEIR DOWN-HOME STYLE OF COOK-ING. MOSTLY FOUND IN THE MIDWEST, THE CHAIN OFFERS REGULAR AND SEASONAL DISHES IN SATISFYING PORTIONS, AND THEIR PRODUCTS ARE WIDELY AVAILABLE.

1 (19-ounce) package Bob Evans Beer Bratwurst, or other bratwurst, cut into 1-inch pieces

1 medium green bell pepper, seeded and cut into 1-inch pieces

1 medium red bell pepper, seeded and cut into 1-inch pieces

1 medium zucchini, cut into 1-inch pieces

1 medium yellow summer squash, cut into 1-inch pieces

1 medium red onion, cut into 1-inch pieces

6 long metal or bamboo skewers (if bamboo, soak in water before use)

12 ounces large white mushrooms, stemmed

2 cups Bob Evans Wildfire Barbecue Sauce, or other barbecue sauce

1. Light a charcoal barbecue or heat a gas grill to medium. Clean the grate and coat it with vegetable oil.

2. Thread the pieces of sausage and vegetables alternately on skewers.

3. Grill the kabobs 10 to 12 minutes, turning frequently, while basting with the barbecue sauce.

4. Serve hot.

Serves 6

If using bamboo skewers, soak them in warm water at least 15 minutes before using. These kabobs are equally tasty simply seasoned with a little olive oil, salt, and pepper. A sprinkling of your favorite fresh herb will add a delicious twist.

BOB EVANS
Backyard Burgers

THIS IS A WONDERFUL BLEND OF SAUSAGE AND GROUND BEEF. MAKE THE PATTIES
AHEAD OF TIME SO THEY ARE WELL-CHILLED WHEN THEY HIT THE GRILL. IT WILL
KEEP THE PARMESAN CHEESE IN THE MIXTURE FROM MELTING TOO RAPIDLY.

1 pound Bob Evans bulk sausage
1 pound ground beef or chuck
½ cup grated Parmesan cheese
2 tablespoons Worcestershire
   sauce
1 teaspoon kosher salt

½ teaspoon pepper
6 hamburger buns, split in half
3 leaves iceberg lettuce, halved
6 thick slices tomato
6 ¼-inch-thick slices onion

1. Using your hands, combine the sausage, ground beef, cheese, Worcestershire sauce, salt, and pepper. Do not overmix, just blend the ingredients.

2. Form the mixture into 6 patties. Wrap and refrigerate for at least 30
   minutes before cooking.

3. Light a charcoal barbecue or heat a gas grill to medium. Clean the grate
   and coat it with vegetable oil.

4. Grill the burgers 8 to 10 minutes per side, or until cooked to your preferred doneness.

5. Put a cooked patty on the bottom of each bun, then layer with the lettuce, tomato, and onion slices. Top with the remaining bun.

Serves 6

*This mixture makes 6-ounce burgers. If this is too large, make
more patties but smaller patties. The extras can be wrapped
tightly in plastic and frozen individually.*

BOB EVANS
Bratwurst with Tomato Pepper Relish

A SURPRISINGLY LIGHT ANYTIME DISH, QUICK AND EASY TO PREPARE, THIS COM-
BINATION OF SAUSAGE AND TOMATOES, ONIONS, AND HERBS WILL SOON FIND ITS
PLACE IN YOUR ONCE-A-WEEK FILE.

1 (19-ounce) package Bob Evans
   Bratwurst, or other bratwurst
1½ cups halved cherry tomatoes
¼ cup diced sweet onion

1 small green bell pepper, seeded
   and diced
1 teaspoon minced fresh thyme
2 tablespoons Italian dressing

1. Heat ½ cup water in a large skillet over medium heat. When it simmers, add the bratwurst and cook, turning occasionally. Add a little more water, if necessary.
2. Light a charcoal barbecue or heat a gas grill to medium. Clean the grate and coat it with vegetable oil.
3. Grill the bratwurst for 5 to 10 minutes, or until cooked through.
4. Combine the tomatoes, onion, bell pepper, thyme, and dressing. Toss until well combined, and serve with the grilled bratwurst.

Serves 4 to 6

You can alter the vegetables according to what you have on hand or what looks best in the market. Cucumbers, corn, and sweet peppers are good choices. Basil, parsley, and chives are fresh alternatives to thyme.

BOB EVANS
Original Sausage Sandwich

BOB EVANS SELLS THEIR BRANDED SAUCES AT THEIR RESTAURANTS AND ONLINE.
IF YOU CAN'T FIND THE TASTE OF THE FARM OLD ROUTE 35 SAUCE NEAR YOU, USE
YOUR FAVORITE HAMBURGER SAUCE WITH THE ADDITION OF WORCESTERSHIRE.

1 pound Bob Evans bulk sausage
4 hamburger buns, split in half
4 slices American cheese

1 medium red onion, sliced in
¼-inch slices
½ cup Old Route 35 Sauce, or
other burger sauce

1. Light a charcoal barbecue or heat a gas grill to medium. Clean the grate and coat it with vegetable oil.

2. Slice the package of sausage equally into 4 pieces and remove the plastic packaging. Gently press each section into a patty.

3. Grill the sausage patties 4 to 5 minutes per side, or until cooked through and no longer pink in the center.

4. Place a cooked patty on a hamburger bun and top with a slice of cheese and 2 onion rings. Drizzle with sauce.

Serves 4

For an easy, creamy dressing with a touch of tang, which will work with any burger, whisk together:

½ cup mayonnaise
½ cup ketchup
¼ cup yellow mustard
1 ½ tablespoons Worcestershire
sauce
1 tablespoon steak sauce

1 tablespoon brown sugar
½ teaspoon granulated garlic
½ teaspoon onion powder
½ teaspoon kosher salt
½ teaspoon pepper

BOB EVANS
Southwest Burgers

SALSA AND CHILI POWDER FIRE UP THESE SAUSAGE BURGERS JUST A BIT. USING KAISER ROLLS IN PLACE OF A STANDARD BURGER BUN IS A NICE TOUCH TO THESE NEWER ADDITIONS TO THE BOB EVANS MENU.

1 pound Bob Evans Zesty Hot bulk sausage
¼ cup salsa, medium
2 tablespoons finely chopped cilantro
¼ cup diced red onion
2 teaspoons chili powder

½ teaspoon kosher salt
½ teaspoon pepper
½ teaspoon cumin
4 Kaiser rolls, split in half
4 slices Cheddar cheese, regular or smoked

1. Using your hands, mix the sausage with the salsa, cilantro, onion, chili powder, salt, pepper, and cumin. Do not overmix; work the mixture just until all the ingredients are well combined.

2. Form the mixture into 4 patties, cover, and refrigerate at least 30 minutes before using.

3. Light a charcoal barbecue or heat a gas grill to medium. Clean the grate and coat it with vegetable oil.

4. Grill the patties 6 to 7 minutes per side, or until cooked through and no longer pink in the center.

5. Put a patty on the bottom half of each Kaiser roll and top with the cheese. Top with other half of each roll. Serve hot.

Serves 4

While standard Cheddar cheese is fine for this dish, the smoked variety adds a wonderful flavor that you'll want to use in other dishes as well. It makes quite a statement when melted in mashed potatoes and can really perk up your best mac-and-cheese recipe.

BOB EVANS
Wildfire Grilled Corn

WHAT A GREAT WAY TO LIVEN UP CORN ON THE COB! JUST WRAP THE EARS IN FOIL AND LET THEM SOAK UP THE SLATHERED-ON BARBECUE SAUCE AS THEY COOK. IF BOB EVANS PRODUCTS AREN'T AVAILABLE NEAR YOU, USE YOUR OWN OR A SMOKY-SWEET BOTTLED SAUCE.

¼ cup (1 stick) unsalted butter
¼ cup Bob Evans Wildfire Barbecue Sauce

4 ears fresh corn, husk and silk removed

1. Light a charcoal barbecue or heat a gas grill to medium. Clean the grate and coat it with vegetable oil.
2. Melt the butter in a small saucepan over medium-low heat. Whisk in the barbecue sauce.
3. Brush each ear of corn with the sauce, then wrap in heavy-duty foil.
4. Cook on the hot grill 15 to 20 minutes, or until the corn is tender.
5. Serve in the foil, for each diner to unwrap on his or her plate.

Serves 4

This is a great recipe to double or triple to bring to a backyard barbecue or a cookout with family and friends. Make ahead of time and keep refrigerated, ready to toss on the grill.

BONEFISH GRILL
Salmon and Asparagus Salad

THIS RESTAURANT CHAIN COVERS MOST OF THE UNITED STATES WITH ITS SIG-
NATURE CARIBBEAN VIBE. THEIR SALMON AND ASPARAGUS SALAD IS FAMOUS FOR
THE FRESHNESS OF ITS INGREDIENTS AND OUTSTANDING FLAVOR COMBINATIONS.

Citrus Herb Vinaigrette
⅔ cup extra virgin olive oil
¼ cup white wine vinegar
2 tablespoons lime juice
2 tablespoons lemon juice
1 tablespoon Dijon mustard
2 large cloves garlic, minced
2 tablespoons sugar
2 tablespoons minced fresh
  parsley
½ teaspoon dried basil
½ teaspoon dried oregano
1 teaspoon kosher salt
½ teaspoon pepper

2 (6-ounce) salmon fillets
½ teaspoon kosher salt
¼ teaspoon pepper
2 tablespoons sun-dried
  tomatoes, oil-packed, julienned
3 cups mixed greens
4 ounces green beans, halved and
  steamed crisp
½ cup Citrus Herb Vinaigrette
6 spears asparagus, trimmed and
  steamed crisp
1 ounce goat cheese (chevre),
  crumbled
1 tablespoon pine nuts, toasted

1. Do ahead: To make the Citrus Herb Vinaigrette, combine the olive oil, vinegar, lime juice, lemon juice, mustard, garlic, and sugar in a blender and pulse until smooth. Pour the mixture into a small saucepan and simmer over medium heat for a minute. Remove from the heat and whisk in the parsley, basil, oregano, salt, and pepper. Cover and refrigerate at least 30 minutes before using.

2. Light a charcoal barbecue or heat a gas grill to medium. Clean the grate and coat it with vegetable oil.

3. Season the salmon fillets with the salt and pepper. Grill, top side down, for 4 to 5 minutes. Turn the fillets once, using a large, flexible spatula, and grill until just cooked through.

4. Drain the excess oil from the sun-dried tomatoes.

5. Combine the mixed greens with the sundried tomatoes and green beans in a large bowl. Toss with vinaigrette until well coated but not over-dressed.

6. Pile the salad in the center of a plate. Tuck the asparagus underneath the greens and top with the grilled salmon. Sprinkle the crumbled goat cheese and toasted pine nuts over the salad and serve immediately.

Serves 2

Good pine nuts can be costly. As an alternative, use an equal amount of lightly toasted slivered almonds.

BUCA DI BEPPO
Salmon Siracusa

THE SIRACUSA IN THE TITLE REFERS TO THE CITY OF SYRACUSE IN SICILY, A RE-
GION WELL KNOWN FOR RECIPES THAT UTILIZE THE WEALTH OF THE MEDITER-
RANEAN SEA. TRY THIS RECIPE WITH SWORDFISH OR TUNA.

Bruschetta Sauce
4 large Roma tomatoes, seeded
  and chopped
½ cup chopped fresh basil
1 small yellow onion, diced
4 large cloves garlic, minced
1 (16-ounce) can artichoke
  hearts, drained and quartered
1 cup capers, drained
1 cup Kalamata olives, pitted and
  halved
½ cup dry white wine

½ cup fresh lemon juice
3 tablespoons dried oregano
1 teaspoon pepper

Basting Mixture
½ cup olive oil
4 large cloves garlic, minced

6 (5-ounce) salmon fillets
3 teaspoons sea salt
3 teaspoons pepper
½ cup Basting Mixture

1. Do ahead: To make the Bruschetta Sauce, combine the tomatoes,
   basil, onion, and garlic and set aside. In a large saucepan, combine the
   artichoke hearts, capers, olives, wine, lemon juice, oregano, and pepper.
   Bring the sauce to a boil, then lower the heat and simmer for 10 minutes. Remove the sauce from the heat and stir in the tomato mixture. Set
   aside until ready to use.

2. Light a charcoal barbecue or heat a gas grill over medium heat. Clean the
   grate and coat it with vegetable oil.

3. To make the Basting Mixture, whisk together the olive oil and garlic.

4. Season the salmon with the salt and pepper. Brush with some of the
   Basting Mixture and grill, top side down, about 4 to 5 minutes per side.
   Use a wide, flexible spatula to turn the fillets over, only once, then grill
   until just cooked through, or until no longer translucent in the center.

5. To serve, spoon a portion of the Bruschetta Sauce into the center of warmed dinner plates. Place each fillet on top of the sauce and serve immediately.

Serves 6

For days when grilling just isn't an option, simmer or bake the salmon directly in the Bruschetta Sauce until cooked through, then serve as directed. Lemon wedges and chopped parsley as garnishes add a hint of freshness to a baked dish.

BURGER KING
Angry Whopper Sandwich

THIS SANDWICH ISN'T REALLY ANGRY, JUST HOT AND SPICY! BE SURE TO INCLUDE ALL THE INGREDIENTS THAT MAKE THIS BURGER SPECIAL: HABAÑERO JACK CHEESE, FRESH JALAPEÑOS, AND FRANK'S REDHOT HOT SAUCE. ALL ARE GUARANTEED TO BRING NOT ONLY THE HEAT BUT ALSO A WELL-BLENDED SENSE OF BALANCE TO THIS DEVILISH WHOPPER.

1 pound ground beef or chuck
1 teaspoon kosher salt
½ teaspoon pepper
4 sesame seed hamburger buns, split in half
¼ cup Angry Sauce
4 slices habañero Jack cheese
2 medium jalapeños, seeded and sliced
8 slices applewood smoked bacon, cooked crisp
Spicy Onion Rings
4 thick slices tomato
4 leaves iceberg lettuce

Angry Sauce
3 tablespoons ketchup or chili sauce
2 tablespoons yellow mustard
1 tablespoon mayonnaise
3 tablespoons golden brown sugar

1 tablespoon Frank's RedHot Hot Sauce
½ teaspoon cayenne pepper
½ teaspoon chili powder

Spicy Onion Rings
¾ cup all-purpose flour
¼ cup cornstarch
1 tablespoon chili powder
½ teaspoon baking powder
¼ teaspoon baking soda
½ cup dry bread crumbs, unseasoned
1 teaspoon kosher salt
½ teaspoon pepper
1 large egg, well beaten
½ cup milk
2 cups vegetable oil
1 large yellow onion, cut into ½-inch slices

1. Do ahead: Using your hands, combine the ground beef with the salt and pepper. Don't overmix the meat, just blend the ingredients. Form into patties and refrigerate until needed.

2. Do ahead: To make the Angry Sauce, whisk together the ketchup, mustard, and mayonnaise until well blended. Stir in the brown sugar, hot sauce, cayenne, and chili powder. Set aside or refrigerate, covered, until ready to use.

3. Do ahead: Prepare the components for the Spicy Onion Rings so they can be fried as your burger is finishing on the grill. Whisk the flour, cornstarch, chili powder, baking powder, baking soda, bread crumbs, salt, and pepper together until well blended. Whisk the beaten egg with the milk, then stir the dry ingredients into the egg mixture. Beat only until the lumps are dissolved.

4. Heat the vegetable oil in a small saucepan and keep over a low flame while burgers are cooking. Turn the heat to medium-high (375°F) before you fry the onions.

5. Dip the onion rings into the batter, then fry until browned on both sides, turning once. Drain on paper towels and keep warm in a low oven.

6. Light a charcoal barbecue or heat a gas grill to medium. Clean the grate and coat it with vegetable oil.

7. Grill the patties 3 to 4 minutes per side for medium, or until cooked to your preferred doneness.

8. Remove the burgers and keep them warm. Grill the hamburger buns until lightly toasted.

9. Spread a spoonful of Angry Sauce on the bottom bun and top with a grilled patty. Layer with the habañero cheese, sliced jalapeños, 2 bacon slices, 2 onion rings, tomato, and lettuce.

10. Spread some Angry Sauce on the top bun and finish the sandwich.

11. Enjoy immediately!

Serves 4

Go all the way and make a bunch of onion rings to go with your burger. Prepare 1 extra onion as noted above and serve crispy and hot. If you can't find habañero Jack cheese, it is also made with Cheddar. If neither of those are available, use pepper Jack for your Angry Whopper.

BURGER KING
Big King

THE ULTIMATE DOUBLE BURGER! NOW, EVEN BETTER, BECAUSE IT'S PREPARED FRESH AND HOT FROM THE GRILL.

½ cup mayonnaise, regular or
  reduced calorie
2 tablespoons French dressing
1 tablespoon yellow mustard
1 teaspoon sugar
1 tablespoon sweet pickle relish
1 teaspoon white wine vinegar
1½ pounds ground beef or chuck
3 teaspoons kosher salt

1½ teaspoons pepper
4 sesame seed hamburger buns,
  split in half
8 slices American cheese
2 medium onions, sliced ¼-inch
  thick
8 slices dill pickles
1½ cups shredded iceberg
  lettuce

1. Do ahead: To make the sauce, whisk together the mayonnaise, dressing, mustard, and sugar. When the sugar is dissolved, add the pickle relish and vinegar. Stir to blend well and refrigerate, covered, until ready to use.

2. Season the ground beef with the salt and pepper. Using your hands, blend the seasonings into the beef, but do not overwork the meat. Form the meat into 8 patties of about 3 ounces each. Cover and refrigerate until ready to use.

3. Light a charcoal barbecue or heat a gas grill to medium. Clean the grate and coat it with vegetable oil.

4. Grill the patties 2 to 3 minutes per side, or until cooked to your preferred doneness.

5. Grill the hamburger buns until lightly toasted.

6. On the bottom bun, place one patty and follow with one slice of cheese, then another patty and another slice of cheese.

7. Follow with 3 onion slices, 2 pickle slices, and shredded lettuce.

8. Spread the top part of the bun with 2 tablespoons of sauce and finish the burger.

Serves 4

This Big King was one of Burger King's first entries into the famous burger wars with McDonald's. Their current double burger is much the same but includes sliced tomato.

CALIFORNIA PIZZA KITCHEN
BBQ Chicken Salad

THIS CPK FAVORITE IS AN UPDATED VERSION OF THE '80's CLASSIC TOSTADA SALAD. CRISP TORTILLA STRIPS GARNISH A SALAD OF CRUNCHY JICAMA, BEANS, CORN, AND CHEESE UNDER A MOUND OF GARLICKY BARBECUED CHICKEN. THE GARDEN HERB RANCH DRESSING IS GOOD ENOUGH TO DOUBLE OR TRIPLE AND KEEP IN THE FRIDGE TO USE WITH ALMOST ANYTHING.

Tortilla Strips
2 cups vegetable oil
12 corn tortillas, sliced into thin
   strips

Garden Herb Ranch Dressing
1 cup buttermilk
½ cup mayonnaise
½ cup sour cream
1 teaspoon yellow mustard
1 tablespoon white wine vinegar
1 teaspoon Worcestershire sauce
1 large clove garlic, minced
1 tablespoon minced parsley
1 teaspoon minced dill
1 tablespoon minced basil
½ teaspoon dried oregano
1 teaspoon sea salt
½ teaspoon pepper

Salad
2 cups shredded iceberg lettuce
2 cups shredded Romaine lettuce

¼ cup julienned fresh basil
1 cup jicama, cut into thin strips
2 cups shredded Monterey Jack
   cheese
1 cup black beans, rinsed and
   drained
1 cup frozen corn
3 tablespoons chopped cilantro

Chicken Marinade
1 tablespoon olive oil
1 teaspoon granulated garlic
1 tablespoon soy sauce
1 teaspoon kosher salt

4 (5-ounce) boneless skinless
   chicken breasts
¼ cup sweet and smoky
   barbecue sauce
4 large Roma tomatoes, seeded
   and diced
1 green onion, thinly sliced, for
   garnish

1. Do ahead: To make the Tortilla Strips, heat the vegetable oil in a heavy-bottomed saucepan or skillet. When the oil reaches 350°F, fry the sliced tortillas in batches. Remove them with a skimmer or slotted spoon when crispy and drain on paper towels. Set aside until ready to use.

2. Do ahead: To make the Garden Herb Ranch Dressing, combine the buttermilk, mayonnaise, and sour cream in a medium bowl and whisk until smooth and creamy. Stir in the remaining ingredients, mixing until the dressing is well blended and smooth. Refrigerate, covered, until ready to use.

3. Do ahead: Mix together the Salad ingredients. Cover and refrigerate until ready to use.

4. For the Chicken Marinade, whisk together the olive oil, garlic, soy sauce, and salt. Pour over the chicken breasts in a resealable plastic bag and marinate at least 30 minutes.

5. Light a charcoal barbecue or heat a gas grill to medium. Clean the grate and coat it with vegetable oil.

6. Remove the chicken from the marinade and shake off the excess. Grill the chicken 5 to 6 minutes per side, or until cooked through and no longer pink in the center.

7. Let the chicken cool, then refrigerate. When completely chilled, cut the breasts into bite-sized pieces and toss with the barbecue sauce. Cover and refrigerate until ready to use.

8. To assemble the salad, toss half the fried tortilla strips with the salad ingredients. Toss with the Garden Herb Ranch Dressing.

9. Divide the salad onto 4 chilled plates and surround each portion with the chopped tomatoes and the remaining tortilla strips.

10. Top each salad with a portion of the grilled chicken and drizzle with a little more barbecue sauce.

11. Garnish with the chopped green onion and serve.

Serves 4

This recipe can easily be served as an appetizer by making smaller portions, serving up to 8 people. It also makes an excellent buffet salad. Just arrange it on an attractive serving platter and keep refrigerated until the last moment.

CALIFORNIA PIZZA KITCHEN
Carne Asada Pizza

A COMBINATION OF THE BEST OF TWO POPULAR CUISINES, ITALIAN AND MEXICAN. DON'T LET THE LONG LIST OF INGREDIENTS DETER YOU, AS MUCH OF THE PREPARATION CAN BE DONE AHEAD OF TIME.

1 (8-ounce) package refrigerated or frozen pizza dough, divided
1 pound beef in thin slices, such as top round or skirt steak
½ cup Carne Asada Marinade
¼ cup all-purpose flour
½ cup Cilantro Pesto
1 cup Monterey Jack cheese
2 medium white onions, sliced ¼-inch thick
¾ cup Salsa
½ cup roasted green or red chilies, cut in ¼-inch strips
Cilantro (left over from the Pesto)

Carne Asada Marinade
1 tablespoon chopped cilantro
¼ cup lime juice
3 tablespoons vegetable oil
1 tablespoon kosher salt
½ teaspoon red chili flakes
½ teaspoon granulated garlic
¼ teaspoon sweet paprika
¼ teaspoon pepper
½ teaspoon cumin

Salsa
3 large Roma tomatoes, seeded and diced
¼ cup diced white onion
1 small serrano pepper, seeded and minced
1 tablespoon chopped cilantro
3 tablespoons olive oil
1 large clove garlic, minced
1 tablespoon lime juice
½ teaspoon kosher salt

Cilantro Pesto
½ cup chopped cilantro
½ small serrano pepper
1 tablespoon pine nuts
2 large cloves garlic, crushed
1 teaspoon lime juice
½ teaspoon kosher salt
¼ cup olive oil
¼ cup shredded Parmesan cheese

This recipe will come out best when using a pizza stone, as well as a pizza peel to transfer the pizza to the oven. You can also use 1 large or 2 small sheet pans, turned upside down and lightly oiled. If you have a pizza stone, center it in the oven and heat at 500°F for 1 hour before baking the pizzas.

Follow the directions on the pizza dough package so that the pieces are ready to be rolled out and baked about 30 minutes after the marinated beef comes off the grill and the salsa and pesto have been prepared.

1. Do ahead: Make the Carne Asada Marinade by whisking together all the ingredients. Cover and refrigerate until ready to use. It may be made 2 days ahead of time.

2. Do ahead: To make the Salsa, combine the tomatoes, onion, half the minced serrano pepper, and 1 tablespoon of the chopped cilantro in a small bowl. Add the olive oil, garlic, lime juice, and salt. Stir until just blended. Cover and refrigerate until ready to use. It may be made at least 2 days ahead of time.

3. Do ahead: Make the Cilantro Pesto the same day you make the pizza, at least 2 hours ahead of time. Combine ¼ cup cilantro, the remaining serrano pepper, pine nuts, garlic, lime juice, salt, and olive oil in a blender. Pulse until well ground. Add the Parmesan cheese and pulse again until well blended. Cover and refrigerate until ready to use. You should have enough chopped cilantro left over to sprinkle on the pizzas after they are baked.

4. Combine the sliced beef with the Carne Asada Marinade and refrigerate, covered, for 1 hour.

5. Light a charcoal barbecue or heat a gas grill to medium. Clean the grate and coat it with vegetable oil.

6. Grill the beef 3 to 4 minutes per side, depending on how thick the slices are. Let the beef cool, then chill for about 15 minutes. Slice the beef into ¼-inch-thick strips and refrigerate until ready to use.

7. If you are using sheet pans, preheat the oven to 500°F. Spread a little olive oil over the sheet pans and put them in the hot oven 10 minutes before baking the pizzas.

8. Sprinkle a work surface with the all-purpose flour and roll out the balls of dough to form two 9-inch crusts. Pinch the edges with your fingers to keep the toppings from sliding off.

9. Use the back of a large spoon to spread half the Cilantro Pesto over each of the crusts up to the rim.

10. Sprinkle half the Monterey Jack over each crust, then layer the sliced onions over the cheese.

11. Drain any accumulated liquid from the salsa and spoon it over both pizzas. Divide the roasted chilies over the salsa and finish with the grilled strips of beef.

12. Use a pizza peel to slide them onto the pizza stone, or carefully slide them onto the back of the hot sheet pan.

13. Bake until the crust is golden and the cheese is bubbly, 9 to 10 minutes on a stone, 12 to 14 on a sheet pan.

14. Garnish the pizzas with the remaining chopped cilantro, cut into wedges, and serve hot.

Makes 2 pizzas, serving 2 to 4

A number of specialty markets offer fresh or frozen pizza dough. Check out what's available at Trader Joe's, Fresh & Easy, or Sam's Club. You can also buy a Pillsbury crust ready for baking in the freezer section at larger supermarkets. Save yourself some time by buying ready-made salsa and pesto, and use canned chilies, such as Ortega. Also, it's good to know that pine nuts may be omitted, as they are rather expensive.

CALIFORNIA PIZZA KITCHEN
Grilled Vegetable Salad

THIS SALAD IS PERFECT FOR A SPECIAL LUNCHEON WHEN YOU NEED A DISH THAT IS AS GOOD LOOKING AS IT IS GOOD TASTING. FRESH ASPARAGUS, CORN, AND AVO-CADO BLEND WITH GRILLED CHICKEN AND DIJON BALSAMIC VINAIGRETTE—YOU MAY HAVE FRIENDS AND FAMILY BEGGING FOR MORE!

Dijon Balsamic Vinaigrette
¼ cup Dijon mustard
½ cup balsamic vinegar
2 large cloves garlic, minced
1¼ cups olive oil
½ teaspoon sea salt
¼ teaspoon pepper

Vegetable Marinade
½ cup balsamic vinegar
¼ cup extra virgin olive oil
¼ cup minced parsley
¼ cup julienned basil
2 large cloves garlic, minced

1 (8-ounce) boneless skinless chicken breast
1 teaspoon kosher salt

½ teaspoon pepper
1 cup Vegetable Marinade
2 ears corn, husks and silk removed
1 medium Japanese eggplant, split lengthwise
1 medium zucchini, split lengthwise
6 large spears asparagus, trimmed
1 medium avocado, diced
2 tablespoons chopped oil-packed sun-dried tomatoes
2 cups chopped Romaine lettuce
2 cups chopped green leaf lettuce
1 cup Dijon Balsamic Vinaigrette, plus extra, for serving
2 green onions, chopped

1. Do ahead: To make the Dijon Balsamic Vinaigrette, combine the mustard, vinegar, and garlic in a blender. With the motor running, pour the oil in a thin stream and process just until blended. Add the salt and pepper, then set aside.

2. Do ahead: To make the Vegetable Marinade, combine the ingredients in a food processor and pulse until well blended. Cover and refrigerate until ready to use.

3. Do ahead: Season the chicken breast with some of the salt and pepper and put it in a resealable plastic bag. Lightly pound it with a mallet, then add ¼ cup of the Vegetable Marinade. Refrigerate for 30 minutes.

4. Light a charcoal barbecue or heat a gas grill to medium. Clean the grate and coat it with vegetable oil.

5. Put the corn, eggplant, zucchini, and asparagus into a large resealable bag and pour the remaining marinade over them. Refrigerate for 15 minutes.

6. Shake excess marinade from the chicken and grill for 5 to 6 minutes per side, or until cooked through and no longer pink in the center. Let it rest 10 minutes before slicing thinly into strips.

7. Grill the marinated vegetables, turning frequently, until nicely charred and cooked through, but still firm.

8. Cut the kernels from the corn cobs and slice the zucchini, eggplant, and asparagus into ½-inch pieces. Put the grilled vegetables in a medium bowl and toss with the avocado and sun-dried tomatoes.

9. Combine the lettuces and dress them with half of the Dijon Balsamic Vinaigrette. Mound the greens in the center of chilled plates and surround them with the mixed vegetables. Put a portion of the grilled chicken on top of each salad and sprinkle with the chopped green onion. Serve the remaining salad dressing on the side.

Serves 2 as an entrée, 4 as a starter

You can easily make this a tempting steak salad by grilling an 8-ounce cut of sirloin or New York steak after an hour in the marinade. Let the meat rest for about 15 minutes before slicing it into thin strips.

CALIFORNIA PIZZA KITCHEN

Jamaican Jerk Chicken Pizza

JERK SEASONING IS THE KEY TO THIS RECIPE. YOU CAN FIND IT AT SPECIALTY STORES OR LARGER SUPERMARKETS, OR ONLINE FROM SPICE AND HERB RETAILERS.

Caribbean Sauce

½ cup Asian-style sweet red chili sauce

1 teaspoon Jamaican jerk seasoning

1 tablespoon cold water

1 teaspoon cornstarch

1 (8-ounce) package refrigerated or frozen pizza dough, split into 3 pieces

1 (8-ounce) boneless skinless chicken breast

1 tablespoon vegetable oil

1 tablespoon Jamaican jerk seasoning

¼ teaspoon cayenne pepper

1 small red bell pepper, seeded and cut in half

1 small yellow bell pepper, seeded and cut in half

¼ cup all-purpose flour

½ cup Caribbean Sauce

1½ cups shredded mozzarella,

1 small white onion, sliced ¼-inch thick

½ cup diced bacon, about 8 slices, fried crisp

1 green onion, chopped

This recipe will come out best by using a pizza stone and a pizza peel for transferring the pie to the hot oven. Or you can also use 1 large or 2 small sheet pans, turned upside down and lightly oiled. If you have a pizza stone, center it in the oven and heat at 500°F for 1 hour before baking the pizzas.

Follow the directions on the pizza dough package so that the pieces are ready to be rolled out and baked about 30 minutes after the chicken comes off the grill and the vegetables and sauce have been prepared.

1. Do ahead: To make the Caribbean Sauce, combine the sweet chili sauce and jerk seasoning in a small saucepan and bring to a simmer over medium-low heat. Blend the water and cornstarch to make a paste, then whisk it into the simmering sauce and stir until the sauce is thickened. Set aside until ready to use.

2. Light a charcoal barbecue or heat a gas grill to medium. Clean the grate and coat it with vegetable oil.

3. Place the chicken breast between 2 sheets of plastic wrap and pound it gently until it is ½-inch thick. Coat it on both sides with the vegetable oil.

4. Combine the jerk seasoning with the cayenne and sprinkle the mixture on both sides of the chicken.

5. Cook the breast 5 to 6 minutes per side, turning once, or until cooked through and no longer pink in the center. Remove from the grill and let cool, then slice it into ¾-inch pieces. Cover and refrigerate.

6. Put the halves of the red and yellow bell peppers on the grill, skin side down, and char until the skin blisters. When they are cool enough to handle, peel or rub the skin off and cut the peppers into ¼-inch strips and set them aside.

7. If using sheet pans, preheat the oven to 500°F. Spread a little olive oil over the sheet pans and put them in the hot oven 10 minutes before baking the pizzas.

8. Sprinkle a work surface with the all-purpose flour and roll out the balls of dough to form three 9-inch crusts. Pinch the edges with your fingers to keep to toppings from sliding off.

9. Use the back of a large spoon to spread a portion of the Caribbean Sauce over each of the crusts up to the rim.

10. Divide 1 cup of mozzarella over each crust, then layer the sliced white onion over the cheese. Follow with the peppers, bacon, and cooked chicken. Finish with the remaining ½ cup cheese.

11. Use a pizza peel to slide the pizza onto the pizza stone, or carefully slide it onto the back of the hot sheet pan.

12. Bake until the crust is golden and the cheese is bubbly, 9 to 10 minutes on a stone, 12 to 14 on a sheet pan.

13. Garnish the pizzas with the chopped green onion. Cut into wedges and serve hot.

Serves 3 to 6

Sweet red chili sauce can be found online or at specialty food stores. Larger markets with a well-supplied Asian aisle should carry brands from Panda, Annie Chun, Sun Luck, or Roland.

CALIFORNIA PIZZA KITCHEN
Moroccan Chicken Salad

IMPRESS DINNER GUESTS WITH YOUR KNOWLEDGE OF WORLD CUISINES. THIS EXOTIC BLEND OF VEGETABLES AND DRIED FRUIT IS A GRAND BACKDROP TO THE SUBTLY SPICED CHICKEN.

2 (8-ounce) boneless skinless chicken breasts
1 tablespoon vegetable oil
½ teaspoon kosher salt
1 teaspoon ground coriander
1 teaspoon cinnamon
1 large head Romaine lettuce, quartered and shredded
1 cup champagne dressing, such as Girard's
1 cup diced and steamed or baked butternut squash

1 (8-ounce) can diced beets, drained
1 hard-boiled egg, diced
1 medium avocado, diced
2 medium carrots, diced
1 medium red bell pepper, seeded and diced
¼ cup dried cranberries
¼ cup chopped dried apricots
¼ cup lightly toasted slivered almonds

1. Light a charcoal barbecue or heat a gas grill to medium. Clean the grate and coat it with vegetable oil.

2. Coat the chicken breasts with the vegetable oil. Whisk together the salt, coriander, and cinnamon, then sprinkle on both sides of the breasts.

3. Grill the chicken 6 to 7 minutes per side, turning once, or until cooked through and no longer pink in the center. Let the chicken cool, then slice into small cubes.

4. Put the lettuce into a large bowl and toss with half the dressing. Add the squash, beets, egg, avocado, carrots, bell pepper, cranberries, and apricots to the bowl and toss until well coated. Add additional dressing if preferred.

5. Portion the salad onto chilled plates and top each one with some of the grilled chicken and slivered almonds. Serve any remaining dressing on the side.

Serves 4

Acorn squash or sweet potatoes can be used in place of the butternut squash. Since you are only using a small amount, wrap the rest of the squash in plastic and save for another dish, or bake and serve it mashed with butter and the same seasonings used for the chicken.

CARL'S JR.
The Six Dollar Burger

THE COMMERCIAL PROMOTING CARL'S SIX DOLLAR BURGER STARRED PARIS HILTON MUNCHING ON THE SANDWICH AND WASHING A CAR AT THE SAME TIME. IT WAS A TOP SELLER IN THE MALE 18- TO 24-YEAR-OLD AGE BRACKET. EVEN IF YOU'RE NOT A SEXY BLONDE, YOUR GUYS WILL DEFINITELY APPRECIATE THIS EFFORT.

8 ounces Black Angus ground beef
½ teaspoon kosher salt
¼ teaspoon pepper
2 slices American cheese
I sesame seed hamburger bun, split in half
2 tablespoons mayonnaise

4 slices dill or bread and butter pickles
½ slice iceberg lettuce
2 thick slices tomato
3 ¼-inch-thick slices red onion
I teaspoon yellow mustard
I tablespoon ketchup or chili sauce

1. Make a patty from the ground beef that is slightly larger than the hamburger bun. Refrigerate the patty at least 15 minutes before cooking.

2. Light a charcoal barbecue or heat a gas grill to medium. Clean the grate and coat it with vegetable oil.

3. Season both sides of the patty with the salt and pepper. Grill the meat 3 to 4 minutes per side, turning once, or until cooked to your preferred doneness.

4. Put the cheese on the patty and place it on the cooler side of the grill to let the cheese melt slightly.

5. Grill both halves of the hamburger bun until lightly toasted, taking care to not let them burn. Spread a tablespoon of mayonnaise on each half.

6. Arrange the pickles on the bottom bun and top with the lettuce and sliced tomatoes. Layer the red onions over the tomatoes, then finish with the patty and cheese.

7. Spread the top bun with the mustard and ketchup and place it on the burger. Serve hot.

Serves 1

Carl's Jr. has three other Six Dollar Burgers on their menu that would be fun to try at home. The Guacamole and Bacon uses pepper Jack cheese. The Western has fried onion rings and barbecue sauce. The Low Carb is wrapped in iceberg lettuce instead of a bun.

CARL'S JR.
Western Bacon Cheeseburger

THIS CLASSIC IS A TOP SELLER AT THE BURGER CHAIN AND A SERIOUS CHAL-
LENGER IN ANY BURGER WAR.

4 ounces ground beef or chuck
½ teaspoon kosher salt
¼ teaspoon pepper
1 slice American cheese
1 sesame seed hamburger bun,
  split in half

2 tablespoons tangy barbecue
  sauce
2 deep fried or oven-baked onion
  rings (see page 91 for a recipe)
2 slices smoked bacon, cooked
  crisp

1. Make a beef patty and refrigerate it for 15 minutes before cooking.
2. Light a charcoal barbecue or heat a gas grill to medium. Clean the grate and coat it with vegetable oil.
3. Season the patty on both sides with the salt and pepper, then grill 2 to 3 minutes per side, turning once, or until cooked to your preferred doneness.
4. Top the cooked patty with the cheese and move to the cooler side of the grill to let the cheese slightly melt.
5. Grill both halves of the hamburger bun until lightly toasted, taking care to not let them burn. Spread a tablespoon of the barbecue sauce on each half of the bun.
6. Put the onion rings on the bottom bun, then top with the patty and cheese, followed by the bacon. Finish with the top bun and serve hot.

Serves 1

*To make sure the bacon is hot when you make the sandwich,
place the strips of cooked bacon on the grill for a few seconds on
each side. Transfer them to the burger as soon as they sizzle.*

CARINO'S ITALIAN GRILL

Grilled Chicken Bowtie Festival

WHAT STARTED AS A SMALL GROUP OF NEIGHBORHOOD RESTAURANTS NOW HAS 130 LOCATIONS IN THE UNITED STATES. THE CHAIN IS COMMITTED TO QUALITY INGREDIENTS AND DINING SATISFACTION. THIS PASTA WITH GRILLED CHICKEN, CHEESE, AND BACON IN CREAM SAUCE IS AN OUTSTANDING REPRESENTATION OF THEIR MISSION.

Alfredo Sauce
3 cups whipping cream
1 teaspoon kosher salt
1 teaspoon pepper
1 cup grated Parmesan cheese
½ cup milk

1½ teaspoons kosher salt
1 teaspoon granulated garlic
¾ teaspoon pepper
2 (4-ounce) boneless skinless
   chicken breasts

2 tablespoons olive oil
2 large cloves garlic, minced
¼ cup diced yellow onion
2 large Roma tomatoes, diced
2 tablespoons whipping cream
¼ cup grated Asiago cheese
2 strips smoked bacon, diced and
   cooked crisp
8 ounces bowtie pasta, cooked
   according to package directions

1. Do ahead: To make the Alfredo Sauce, bring the whipping cream to a simmer in a medium saucepan. Season with the salt and pepper and reduce the volume by ½ cup. Remove the pan from the heat and stir in the Parmesan cheese. When halfway incorporated, return the pan to a low flame and add the milk. Stir the sauce until the cheese is melted and the sauce is smooth. Set aside. Keep warm.

2. Light a charcoal barbecue or heat a gas grill to medium. Clean the grate and coat it with vegetable oil.

3. Combine ½ teaspoon salt and ½ teaspoon granulated garlic with ¼ teaspoon pepper and season the chicken breasts. Grill 5 to 6 minutes per

side, turning once, or until the chicken is cooked through and no longer pink in the center. Set aside to cool, then cut into bite-sized pieces.

4. Heat the olive oil in a large saucepan and sauté the minced garlic until it is soft. Stir in the onion and tomatoes. When the onion is soft, add the whipping cream, ¼ cup of the Alfredo Sauce and the Asiago cheese. Stir until the cheese is melted. Add the remaining salt, pepper, and granulated garlic. Stir until blended, then add the cooked bacon.

5. Toss the cooked pasta with 2 cups of the Alfredo Sauce. Stir in the vegetable mixture and toss to just combine. Add the cooked chicken pieces and stir until all the ingredients are covered with the sauce and the chicken is warmed through.

Serves 2 to 4

Add a little extra bacon flavor to the vegetable mixture. Instead of sautéing the vegetables in olive oil, fry the diced bacon in the saucepan. When most of the fat has been rendered, add the garlic and continue with the rest of the recipe.

CARINO'S ITALIAN GRILL

Lemon Rosemary Chicken

ROSEMARY AND GARLIC ARE TRADITIONAL FLAVOR MATES FOR CHICKEN. IN THIS RECIPE, THIS COMBINATION IS INTENSIFIED BY THE FRESH CITRUS TANG OF LEMON JUICE AND VINAIGRETTE.

4 (8-ounce) boneless skinless chicken breasts
2 cups Italian vinaigrette
Juice of 1 large lemon
5 large sprigs fresh rosemary
¼ cup extra virgin olive oil
4 large cloves garlic, minced
3 cups fresh baby spinach
½ teaspoon kosher salt
¼ teaspoon pepper

1 pound green beans, trimmed, split and blanched
4 large Roma tomatoes, diced
1 (8-ounce) jar roasted red peppers, drained and diced
10 ounces angel hair pasta, cooked according to package directions
2 tablespoons shredded Parmesan cheese
4 slices lemon, for garnish

1. Do ahead: Butterfly the chicken breasts, cutting through the thick side and leaving the thin side intact. Marinate the chicken for an hour in 1 cup Italian vinaigrette.

2. Light a charcoal barbecue or heat a gas grill to medium. Clean the grate and coat it with vegetable oil.

3. Grill the chicken until cooked through and no longer pink in the center. Give the breasts a quarter turn to create diamond-shaped grill marks. This will be the presentation side of the chicken when it's plated.

4. Heat the remaining vinaigrette, lemon juice, and one sprig of rosemary in a large skillet and add the folded-up chicken breasts. Set the skillet on a back burner over a low flame to slowly reduce and glaze the chicken. Turn the breasts over occasionally so they are evenly coated.

5. Heat the ¼ cup of olive oil in a large skillet and sauté the garlic and spinach. Season it with salt and pepper.

6. Add the green beans, tomatoes, and the roasted red peppers to the skillet and simmer until the vegetables are warmed. Add the cooked angel hair pasta and toss to blend. Use tongs to mound a swirl of pasta on each warmed dinner plate. Open up each grilled breast and place it up against the pasta. Sprinkle shredded Parmesan over the pasta and chicken.

7. Garnish each plate with a sprig of rosemary and a slice of twisted lemon. Serve hot.

Serves 4

This is a lot of chicken. You might want to use only 2 breasts and split them or slice them into bite-sized pieces after they are grilled. Cut pieces of chicken or meat are a little easier to eat when paired with a pasta dish.

CARINO'S ITALIAN GRILL

Spicy Shrimp and Chicken

THIS IS ONE OF CARINO'S SIGNATURE RICH PASTA DISHES. THE PENNE AND VEGE-
TABLES ARE DRENCHED IN A CREAMY CHEESE SAUCE THAT HAS A KICK OF CAYENNE
TO BALANCE IT. SERVE WITH A CRISP WHITE WINE AND FRESH GREEN SALAD.

2 (6-ounce) boneless skinless
chicken breasts

1 cup chopped dry-packed
sun-dried tomatoes

2 tablespoons (¼ stick) unsalted
butter

2 large cloves garlic, minced

3 cups large white mushrooms,
stemmed and sliced

1 cup sliced green onions

2 teaspoons kosher salt

1 teaspoon black pepper

2 cups whipping cream

2 teaspoons cayenne pepper

20 medium shrimp, peeled and
deveined

½ cup grated Pecorino Romano
cheese

1 (16-ounce) box penne rigate,
cooked according to package
directions

1. Light a charcoal barbecue or heat a gas grill to medium. Clean the grate and coat it with vegetable oil.

2. Grill the chicken 6 to 7 minutes per side, turning once, or until cooked through and no longer pink in the center.

3. After the chicken cools, slice it into ¼-inch-thick strips and set aside.

4. Soak the sun-dried tomatoes in warm water until soft, drain, and set aside.

5. Heat the butter in a large skillet and sauté the garlic until soft. Stir in the mushrooms and cook 2 minutes more. Add the sun-dried tomatoes and green onions, then season with salt and pepper.

6. Stir in the 2 cups of whipping cream and cayenne pepper. Reduce the sauce almost by half, over medium-low heat, stirring occasionally.

7. While the cream sauce is reducing, grill the shrimp until just cooked through, about 1 minute per side. Remove them and keep warm.

8. When the sauce is reduced, stir in the cheese and cook 2 minutes more until well blended. Add the cooked chicken and shrimp, then toss with the penne and simmer a minute or two longer to heat through.

9. Serve hot on warmed plates or in shallow pasta bowls.

Serves 4

You may have to judge how much cayenne to use. Those who like really spicy food will want more and those with milder palates would want less. If you're not sure, go with the amount suggested and serve with red pepper flakes on the side for those who prefer more heat.

CARRABBA'S ITALIAN GRILL
Chicken Bryan

CARRABBA'S PRIDES ITSELF ON THE FLAVORS AND INGREDIENTS OF THE FAMILY'S
SICILIAN HERITAGE. BRYAN, TEXAS, WAS THEIR FIRST AMERICAN HOME.

1½ cups chopped dry-packed
  sun-dried tomatoes
2 tablespoons olive oil
3 large cloves garlic, minced
1 medium shallot, minced
½ cup dry white wine
3 tablespoons lemon juice
6 tablespoons (¾ stick) unsalted
  butter, cubed

½ teaspoon sea salt
¼ teaspoon white pepper
6 (8-ounce) boneless skinless
  chicken breasts
1 teaspoon kosher salt
½ teaspoon black pepper
10 large basil leaves, julienned
1 cup goat cheese (chevre)

1. Soak the sun-dried tomatoes in warm water until soft. Drain well and set
   aside.

2. Heat the olive oil in a large saucepan and sauté the garlic and shallot
   until softened. Stir in the white wine and lemon juice, increase the heat,
   and reduce the liquids by more than half; the liquid should be thickened, almost like a syrup.

3. Turn down the heat to its lowest setting and whisk in the cubes of butter,
   one at a time, until all the butter is incorporated. Season with the sea salt
   and white pepper, then set aside and keep warm.

4. Light a charcoal barbecue or heat a gas grill to medium. Clean the grate
   and coat it with vegetable oil.

5. Season the breasts with the salt and pepper. Grill the chicken 5 to 6 minutes per side, turning once, or until cooked through and no longer pink
   in the center. Remove from the grill and keep warm.

6. Add the sun-dried tomatoes and basil to the sauce. Stir until well blended.

7. Place the chicken on warmed plates. Crumble some of the goat cheese on each breast and spoon the butter sauce over each portion of chicken and cheese. Serve any remaining sauce on the side.

Serves 6

Serve the Chicken Bryan with your favorite rice or potatoes and a side of freshly steamed vegetables.

CARRABBA'S ITALIAN GRILL
Marsala Di Carrabba

A CLASSIC CARRABBA COMBO, STEAK AND CHICKEN MARSALA IS A PROTEIN
LOVER'S DREAM. THE CHICKEN AND SAUCE CAN BE STARTED WHILE THE GRILL IS
HEATING. BOTH SHOULD COME TO THE TABLE HOT AND JUICY.

4 (4-ounce) boneless skinless
chicken breasts
4 (4-ounce) sirloin steaks
1½ teaspoons kosher salt
½ teaspoon pepper
3 tablespoons olive oil
1 large clove garlic, minced
1 small shallot, minced

1 cup large, stemmed, and sliced
white mushrooms
¼ cup all-purpose flour
2 ounces thinly sliced prosciutto
½ cup Marsala
4 tablespoons (½ stick) unsalted
butter, cubed
2 tablespoons finely chopped
parsley

1. Put the chicken breasts between 2 sheets of plastic wrap and lightly
   pound with a meat mallet until ¼-inch thick.

2. Season the chicken and steaks with salt and pepper.

3. Light a charcoal barbecue or heat a gas grill to medium. Clean the grate
   and coat it with vegetable oil.

4. Heat the olive oil in a large skillet and stir in the garlic and shallot.
   When they have softened, add the mushrooms and sauté until lightly
   browned. Season with salt and pepper.

5. Dredge the flattened chicken in the flour. Move the mushrooms to the
   side of the skillet and sauté the chicken until browned on each side.

6. Sprinkle the prosciutto into the skillet and combine with the mushrooms
   and chicken. Lower the heat and pour in the Marsala. Bring the mixture
   to a boil, then reduce the heat to a low simmer.

7. Grill the sirloin steaks 3 to 4 minutes per side, or until cooked to your preferred doneness. Set the steaks on warmed plates while you finish the chicken.

8. Increase the temperature to medium low, and when the sauce bubbles, whisk in the cubed butter, one piece at a time.

9. When all the butter has been incorporated, put a breast on the plate with the steak and spoon the mushroom sauce over each piece of chicken. Sprinkle with the chopped parsley and serve hot.

Serves 4

There aren't any really good substitutes for Marsala. In a pinch, you can use sweet sherry or mirin, a sweet Japanese rice wine, but they are not at all close to the real deal. Marsala is inexpensive and won't go bad. You may find a use for it with other chicken dishes, or veal and pork cutlets, so do make an effort to get it.

CARRABBA'S ITALIAN GRILL
Pollo Hilario

BUTTERFLIED CHICKEN BREASTS ARE STUFFED AND GRILLED, THEN SIMMERED IN A BUTTERY MARSALA SAUCE WITH MUSHROOMS AND TOMATOES. THE FIRST PART OF THIS RECIPE CAN BE PREPARED AHEAD OF TIME AND FINISHED JUST BEFORE DINNER. TRY IT ON A BUSY WORK DAY WHEN TAKEOUT JUST WON'T DO.

2 (5-ounce) boneless skinless chicken breasts
½ teaspoon kosher salt
¼ teaspoon pepper
1 large red bell pepper
1 small zucchini
¼ cup goat cheese (chevre)
2 tablespoons olive oil
1 clove garlic, minced
1 small shallot, minced

½ cup large, stemmed, and sliced white mushrooms
½ cup Marsala
½ cup chicken broth
2 tablespoons (¼ stick) unsalted butter, quartered
1 large Roma tomato, diced
1 tablespoon finely chopped parsley

1. Light a charcoal barbecue or heat a gas grill to medium. Clean the grate and coat it with vegetable oil.

2. Butterfly the chicken breast by slicing through the thicker edge and leaving the rib side, or thinner edge, intact. Season the chicken with salt and pepper.

3. Grill the bell pepper until the skin is charred. When cool enough to handle, rub or peel the skin off. Remove the top and bottom ends, seed the pepper, then cut it in half, from top to bottom, into 2 large pieces.

4. Cut 2 long diagonal slices, about ¼-inch thick, from the zucchini and grill them on both sides until cooked but still firm.

5. Lay half a pepper and a slice of zucchini on one side of each breast. Top with a portion of the goat cheese then cover with the other side of the

breast, like a closed book. You may want to secure the open ends of the breast with a toothpick to make grilling easier.

6. Grill the stuffed chicken on both sides, turning once, until cooked through and no longer pink in the center. Set the chicken aside while you prepare the sauce.

7. Heat the olive oil in a medium skillet and stir in the garlic and shallot. When they have softened, add the mushrooms and sauté until lightly browned.

8. Pour in the Marsala and chicken broth. Bring the pan to a boil, then turn the heat down to medium-low and simmer until reduced by half.

9. When the sauce has reduced, turn down the heat and whisk in the pieces of butter, one at a time, until it is all incorporated. Slip the cooked chicken into the mushroom sauce and heat through without letting the sauce boil.

10. Put the chicken on warmed plates and top it with the diced tomatoes. Spoon the mushroom sauce over the top and sprinkle with the chopped parsley.

Serves 2

Once the chicken breasts are stuffed and grilled, you can refrigerate them, even overnight, and heat them through in the sauce when you want to serve them. Make sure the pepper and zucchini are not overcooked so that they will stay firm if you do prepare the chicken ahead of time.

CARRABBA'S ITALIAN GRILL

Sausage and Peppers

NOTHING SAYS ITALIAN HOME COOKING LIKE SAUSAGE AND PEPPERS, SO FILLING AND FLAVORFUL, YET SO EASY TO PULL TOGETHER AT THE LAST MINUTE. KEEP MARINARA SAUCE AND A CAN OF CRUSHED TOMATOES IN THE PANTRY FOR THOSE TIMES WHEN YOU NEED SOMETHING FAST. COUNT ON ONE SAUSAGE PER PERSON, AND SERVE WITH CRUSTY ITALIAN BREAD QUICKLY WARMED IN THE OVEN.

1 (12-ounce) package sweet Italian fennel sausages

Pepper Sauce
2 tablespoons olive oil
1 large green bell pepper, sliced in ½-inch strips
1 large yellow bell pepper, sliced in ½-inch strips

1 large red bell pepper, sliced in ½-inch strips
½ small red onion, sliced in ½-inch-thick strips
3 cloves garlic, minced
1 (14-ounce) can crushed tomatoes
½ cup marinara sauce
2 teaspoons kosher salt
1 teaspoon pepper

1. Light a charcoal barbecue or heat a gas grill to medium. Clean the grate and coat it with vegetable oil.

2. Grill the sausages, turning once, until cooked through and no longer pink in the center, 7 to 8 minutes per side. Set aside.

3. For the Pepper Sauce, heat the olive oil in a large skillet until very hot. Add the peppers, onion, garlic, tomatoes, marinara sauce, salt, and pepper all at once. Cover the pan and lower the heat. Simmer for 30 minutes, stirring occasionally.

4. When the peppers are cooked, spoon a portion of the sauce on each warmed plate and top with a sausage. Serve hot.

Traditional sausages are made with pork and fennel or anise. You can try this recipe with any sausage, just make sure they are about 4 ounces each and that you cook them through. If grilling is not an option, poach them in a skillet with water that covers them only half way. Cook for 7 minutes on one side, then turn them and cook on the other side. Heat the oil in a separate skillet and brown the sausages before serving on top of the peppers.

CARRABBA'S ITALIAN GRILL

T-Bone Steaks with Herbed Garlic Sauce

YOU CAN USE ANY STEAK FOR THIS ENTRÉE, BUT T-BONES HAVE A FANTASTIC FLAVOR. DO AS THE ITALIANS DO, AND SPREAD A LITTLE HERBED OIL OVER A SIZZLING STEAK. WHATEVER IS LEFT OVER CAN BE USED AS A DIP FOR HOT BREAD.

Herbed Garlic Sauce
½ cup chopped fresh basil
¼ cup chopped fresh mint
5 large cloves garlic, minced
3 tablespoons lemon juice
1 tablespoon white wine vinegar
1 teaspoon dried oregano

1½ teaspoons kosher salt
½ teaspoon pepper
1 cup extra virgin olive oil

2 T-bone steaks, at least 1-inch thick
1½ teaspoons kosher salt
½ teaspoon pepper

1. Do ahead: To make the Herbed Garlic Sauce, place the basil, mint, garlic, lemon juice, vinegar, oregano, salt and pepper in the jar of a food processor or blender. Pulse until the mixture is well ground. Pour in the olive oil and pulse just until blended. Set the sauce aside in a covered container until ready to use.

2. Light a charcoal barbecue or heat a gas grill to medium. Clean the grate and coat it with vegetable oil.

3. Season the steaks with the salt and pepper. Cook the meat for 5 to 6 minutes per side, turning once, or until cooked to your preferred doneness.

4. Serve the steaks on warmed plates with the sauce on the side.

Serves 2

This sauce can be refrigerated and will last about a week if tightly covered. Let it come to room temperature and give it a few shakes before using.

CHEESECAKE FACTORY
Baja Chicken Hash

THIS IS A BREAKFAST FAVORITE AT MANY CHEESECAKE FACTORIES, ESPECIALLY IN THE SOUTHWEST. MAKE SURE YOU GET CHORIZO SAUSAGE LINKS, NOT BULK. RANCHERO SAUCE IS A MIXTURE OF CHILIES, SPICES, AND TOMATOES, AND CAN BE FOUND IN THE LATIN SECTIONS OF LARGE MARKETS OR ONLINE. HOLLANDAISE SAUCE CAN BE MADE FROM A QUICK BLENDER RECIPE OR PURCHASED AS A MIX.

1 (4-ounce) boneless skinless chicken breast
½ teaspoon kosher salt
¼ teaspoon pepper
1 small poblano chili
½ pound chicken chorizo sausage
2 tablespoons vegetable oil
½ pound red potatoes, diced
¼ cup frozen corn kernels
2 green onions, chopped

1 small red bell pepper, seeded and diced
1 small yellow bell pepper, seeded and diced
½ cup ranchero sauce
4 eggs
4 corn tortillas, fried crisp
½ cup Hollandaise sauce
1 tablespoon chopped cilantro

1. Light a charcoal barbecue or heat a gas grill to medium. Clean the grate and coat it with vegetable oil.

2. Season the chicken with the salt and pepper. Grill the breast 4 to 5 minutes per side, turning once, or until cooked through and no longer pink in the center. When cool enough to handle, slice into bite-sized pieces.

3. Put the poblano chili on the grill and turn it until charred on all sides. Set off to the side of the grill, then cook the chorizo, turning frequently, until cooked through, about 15 minutes.

4. When the chili is cool, rub off the skin, remove the seeds, and dice. Cut the chorizo into bite-sized pieces.

5. Heat the vegetable oil in a large skillet and sauté the potatoes until lightly browned. Add the corn and green onions. When the onions are soft, stir in the red and yellow peppers. Sauté the vegetables until they are just cooked through.

6. Add the cooked chicken breast and chorizo pieces to the skillet and season with salt and pepper.

7. Stir in the ranchero sauce and grilled poblano pieces. Let the mixture simmer for about 5 minutes.

8. Cook each of the eggs in your preferred way.

9. Place the fried tortillas on warmed plates and top with a portion of the hash. Top each portion of hash with the cooked egg and spoon a little of the Hollandaise over the egg.

10. Sprinkle the chopped cilantro over each of the plates and serve hot.

Serves 4

Make this a dinner entrée. Use two fried corn tortillas per person and overlap them on the plate. Spread the hash over both of the tortillas and add an extra egg on top.

CHEESECAKE FACTORY
Luau Salad

GRILLED CHICKEN GOES TROPICAL WITH FRESH MANGO AND MACADAMIA NUTS.
GREAT FOR A SUMMER BUFFET.

3 (4-ounce) boneless skinless
chicken breasts

2 teaspoons kosher salt

½ teaspoon pepper

6 cups mixed greens

1 large red bell pepper, seeded,
cored, and thinly sliced

1 large yellow bell pepper, seeded,
cored, and thinly sliced

½ pound green beans, trimmed
and halved, blanched

1 medium cucumber, peeled and
sliced

1 small red onion, finely chopped

1 medium mango, peeled and
diced

8 (6-inch) egg roll wrappers, fried
crisp

½ cup sweet and sour sauce,
such as La Choy, Kikkoman,
Panda, or your own

1 large carrot, thinly sliced

1 small green bell pepper, seeded,
cored, and thinly sliced

½ cup chopped and lightly
toasted macadamia nuts

Balsamic Dressing

1 cup balsamic vinaigrette

¼ cup rice wine vinegar

¼ cup golden brown sugar

½ teaspoon sesame oil

1 tablespoon white sesame seeds,
lightly toasted

1. Light a charcoal barbecue or heat a gas grill to medium. Clean the grate and coat it with vegetable oil.

2. Season the chicken with 1 teaspoon salt and ¼ teaspoon pepper. Grill 5 to 6 minutes per side, turning once, or until cooked through and no longer pink in the center. Let rest 10 minutes before slicing into thin strips.

3. To make the Balsamic Dressing, combine the vinaigrette, vinegar, sugar, sesame oil, and sesame seeds in a blender and pulse until well blended and smooth. This may be stored in an airtight container for a week in the refrigerator.

4. In a large bowl, toss the mixed greens with the cooked chicken, red and yellow peppers, green beans, cucumber, onion, and mango. Season the mixture with the remaining 1 teaspoon salt and ¼ teaspoon pepper, then toss with just enough Balsamic Dressing to evenly coat the ingredients.

5. Brush each fried wrapper with the sweet and sour sauce. Build four stacks of alternating salad and coated wrappers on 4 plates. Start with a wrapper, then salad, wrapper, salad, wrapper, and finish with salad.

6. Sprinkle each stack with the carrots and green peppers, then finish with the macadamia nuts.

Serves 4

Since macadamia nuts can be expensive, consider using toasted almond slivers for the crunchy garnish.

CHEESECAKE FACTORY
SkinnyLicious Grilled Chicken

USE A LIGHT VERSION OF YOUR FAVORITE DIJON MUSTARD VINAIGRETTE TO KEEP
THE CALORIE COUNT DOWN.

2 (6-ounce) boneless skinless
chicken breasts
I teaspoon kosher salt
¼ teaspoon pepper
¼ cup Dijon mustard vinaigrette
2 medium Roma tomatoes, cut in
½-inch dice
I cup baby arugula
2 cups cooked white rice

8 jumbo asparagus spears,
trimmed and steamed or
grilled
I tablespoon basil olive oil
I tablespoon grated Parmesan
cheese
Chopped fresh parsley, for
garnish

1. Light a charcoal barbecue or heat a gas grill to medium. Clean the grate
   and coat it with vegetable oil.

2. Cut each breast into 3 pieces and lightly pound them between 2 sheets
   of plastic wrap. Season the chicken with the salt and pepper and grill
   3 to 4 minutes per side, turning once, or until cooked through and no
   longer pink in the center.

3. Combine 2 tablespoons of the Dijon vinaigrette with the tomatoes in a
   small saucepan. Simmer the tomatoes for 30 seconds over low heat, then
   set the pan aside.

4. Toss the arugula with the remaining vinaigrette in a small bowl and keep
   cold.

5. When ready to serve, divide the cooked rice among 4 dinner plates and
   center each portion on the plate.

6. Lay a pair of asparagus spears on each side of the rice and top it with the
   chicken breasts, shingled over the rice in a single, overlapping layer.

7. Spoon equal portions of the warmed tomatoes over the chicken and
   drizzle with the basil oil.

8. Lightly mound the arugula over the chicken and sprinkle the assembled ingredients with the Parmesan cheese and garnish with chopped parsley, if desired.

Serves 4

You can enhance the essence of the basil oil by finishing the dish with fresh julienned basil instead of parsley.

CHEVY'S FRESH MEX
Fuego Spice Mix

KEEP THIS SIGNATURE SPICE BLEND ON HAND TO ADD AUTHENTIC SOUTHWESTERN FLAVOR TO LATIN RECIPES.

¼ cup sweet paprika
2 tablespoons kosher salt
2 tablespoons ground black pepper
2 tablespoons granulated garlic

2 tablespoons chili powder
2 tablespoons dried Mexican oregano
2 teaspoons ground white pepper
2 teaspoons cayenne pepper

1. Whisk together all the ingredients in a large bowl until well blended.
2. For a finer blend, pulse in a food processor until the oregano is well ground.

Makes 1 cup

Keep stored in a dry location in an airtight container.

CHEVY'S FRESH MEX
Salsa

KEEP THIS RECIPE IN MIND FOR SERVING WITH HOT TORTILLA CHIPS FOR A BACK-YARD BARBECUE OR PICNIC.

8 large Roma tomatoes, halved
and seeded
1 medium yellow onion, cut in
quarters
2 medium jalapeños

1 tablespoon olive oil
2 teaspoons kosher salt
1 teaspoon pepper
2 tablespoons chopped cilantro

1. Light a charcoal barbecue or heat a gas grill to medium. Clean the grate and coat it with vegetable oil.

2. Char the tomatoes, onion, and jalapeños, turning frequently, until the skins are blistered. Set the vegetables aside in a medium bowl covered with plastic wrap for a few minutes to let them steam.

3. Peel the skins or rub them off, using a kitchen cloth or paper towels. Remove the stems and seeds from the jalapeños.

4. Combine the vegetables in a food processor with the olive oil and pulse until ground to a medium consistency.

5. Pour the salsa back into the bowl and stir in the salt, pepper, and cilantro. Let cool a bit before storing in an airtight container.

Makes about 4 cups

This salsa can be refrigerated for up to 5 days. It improves in flavor if you let it sit overnight before serving.

CHEVY'S FRESH MEX
Smokin' Hot Habañero Steak Fajitas

UNLESS YOU ARE SERIOUSLY FOND OF HEAT, DON'T PLAY WITH FIRE! THE MARINADE FOR THESE FAJITAS COMBINES BOTH JALAPEÑO AND HABAÑERO PEPPERS, AND THEY ARE ONLY SOMEWHAT TAMED BY THE ADDITION OF PINEAPPLE JUICE AND OTHER INGREDIENTS.

Fajita Marinade
8 habañero peppers, stemmed and seeded
3 large jalapeño peppers, stemmed and seeded
3 large cloves garlic, chopped
1 small yellow onion, chopped
¼ cup red wine vinegar
½ cup canola oil
¾ cup pineapple juice
¼ cup achiote paste, available in specialty markets or online

2 pounds skirt steak
1½ teaspoons kosher salt
½ teaspoon pepper
Flour tortillas, heated

Condiments
Vegetables, such as bell peppers and onions
Cheddar or Jack cheese, shredded
Sour cream
Guacamole
Salsa

Wear disposable gloves while working with the peppers and avoid touching any part of your face, especially the mouth or eyes.

1. To make the Fajita Marinade, combine the peppers, garlic, and onion in a food processor and pulse until well ground. Add the vinegar and canola oil. Pulse until well blended. Whisk together the pineapple juice and achiote paste. When well combined, add to the pepper mixture and pulse until well blended.

2. Lay the pieces of meat in a large baking dish. Spread the marinade over the beef, covering all of its surfaces. Cover the dish with plastic wrap and refrigerate overnight, or at least 8 hours.

3. Light a charcoal barbecue or heat a gas grill to medium. Clean the grate and coat it with vegetable oil.

4. Remove the meat from the marinade and shake off any excess. Season it with the salt and pepper.

5. Grill the steak 2 to 3 minutes per side, turning once or twice, or until cooked to your preferred doneness. Remove it from the grill and let rest for about 10 minutes.

6. Slice the beef into 1-inch-wide strips, cutting against the grain, and serve with the tortillas and desired condiments.

Serves 4

Achiote paste is produced from the annatto seed and other spices. It is fairly neutral in flavor, but adds a rich yellow or dark orange color to the foods it's cooked with.

CHEVY'S FRESH MEX
Veggie Burrito

CHEVYS RECENTLY REVAMPED ITS MENU, DROPPING SOME ITEMS AND BRING-
ING BACK OTHERS. THE VEGGIE BURRITO HAS MADE THE TRANSITION, AND THIS
RECIPE OFFERS ONE OF THE EARLIER VERSIONS.

2 zucchini, quartered lengthwise

2 yellow squash, quartered
lengthwise

2 large red bell peppers, seeded
and quartered

2 tablespoons olive oil

2 large cloves garlic, minced

1 tablespoon minced fresh
oregano

1 teaspoon kosher salt

½ teaspoon pepper

4 (12-inch) flour tortillas, heated

½ cup tomatillo salsa, purchased
or your own

Avocado Corn Relish

4 ears corn, husks and silk
removed

2 tablespoons olive oil

1 teaspoon kosher salt

½ teaspoon pepper

1 red bell pepper, seeded and
diced

2 green onions, thinly sliced

2 Anaheim green chilies, roasted
and diced

2 tablespoons red wine vinegar

¼ teaspoon cumin

¼ teaspoon red pepper flakes

2 avocados, diced

1. Toss the zucchini, squash, and peppers with the olive oil, garlic, oregano, salt, and pepper. Let them marinate at room temperature for about 1 hour.

2. Make the Avocado Corn Relish while the vegetables are marinating.

3. Cut the corn kernels from the cobs and sauté in the olive oil with the salt and pepper. Add the red pepper and green onions. Sauté until the vegetables are just cooked through. Stir in the roasted chilies, vinegar, cumin, and red pepper flakes, then set aside. Fold in the avocado just before making the burritos.

4. Light a charcoal barbecue or heat a gas grill to medium. Clean the grate and coat it with vegetable oil.

5. Grill the marinated vegetables just until cooked through, not charred. Set them aside.

6. Flip the tortillas on the hot grill just long enough to heat through and soften them.

7. Divide the grilled vegetables among the 4 tortillas by putting a strip each of zucchini, squash, and red pepper in the center of each tortilla.

8. Place a few spoonfuls of the Avocado Corn Relish over the vegetables and top with some of the tomatillo salsa. Any remaining relish can be refrigerated in an airtight container for 4 days.

9. Fold the bottom quarter of each tortilla up, then close the left and right sides and roll the tortilla up into a burrito. Serve hot or at room temperature.

Serves 4

Chevy's serves the burrito with pico de gallo, black beans, rice, and a small corn tamale.

CHI CHI'S
Chicken Nachos Grande

SERVE THESE NACHOS WITH PLENTY OF EXTRA TOPPINGS THAT GUESTS CAN PILE ON THEMSELVES.

Marinade
2 tablespoons lime juice
2 teaspoons white wine vinegar
¼ cup water
1 tablespoon olive oil
2 large cloves garlic, minced

1 (8-ounce) boneless skinless
  chicken breast

½ teaspoon kosher salt
¼ teaspoon pepper
12 tortilla chips or scoops
1 cup salsa, purchased or your own
  (see page 97 for DIY recipe)
2 cups shredded Mexican cheese
  blend
2 green onions, chopped
1 jalapeño, seeded and minced

1. Do ahead: Whisk together all the ingredients for the marinade and pour into a resealable plastic bag. Add the chicken breast and refrigerate overnight, or at least 4 hours.

2. Light a charcoal barbecue or heat a gas grill to medium. Clean the grate and coat it with vegetable oil.

3. Remove the chicken from the marinade and shake off any excess. Season it with the salt and pepper and grill 4 to 5 minutes per side, turning once, or until cooked through and no longer pink in the center. Set it aside and let it rest for 10 minutes, then shred it.

4. Preheat the oven to 375°F.

5. Evenly place the tortilla chips in a baking dish. Spoon some salsa onto each chip. Add the shredded chicken, then top with the cheese, green onions, and diced jalapeño.

6. Bake in the hot oven for about 10 minutes, or until the cheese has melted.

7. Serve directly from the baking dish or on a heated platter.

2 to 4

Use sour cream, sliced olives, guacamole, and shredded lettuce for toppings.

CHI CHI'S
Margarita Marinade

USE THIS MARINADE FOR SKIRT STEAK FAJITAS OR FLANK STEAK. THE LIME AND ORANGE JUICES WORK AS TENDERIZERS ON NORMALLY TOUGH CUTS OF MEAT.

¼ cup orange juice
¼ cup lime juice
¼ cup tequila
2 tablespoons extra virgin olive oil

1 large clove garlic, minced
1 tablespoon brown sugar
1 tablespoon lime zest
1 (10-ounce) can diced tomatoes with green chilies, drained

1. Whisk together all the ingredients and refrigerate in an airtight container. Shake the container occasionally to mix the ingredients.
2. Discard the marinade after using for beef, chicken, or pork. Any unused portion may be briefly simmered and used as a sauce or dressing.

Makes about 2 cups

The marinade may be refrigerated for up to 5 days.

CHICK-FIL-A
Honey Roasted BBQ Sauce

MORE OF A SWEET AND SAVORY CONDIMENT THAN A BARBECUE SAUCE, THIS MIXTURE IS A WONDERFUL ADDITION TO BOTH MEATS AND FISH. TRY IT BRUSHED OVER ANY GRILLED ITEM, INCLUDING SHRIMP AND SCALLOPS, TO ENJOY THE COMBINATION OF HONEY AND SPICED MUSTARD.

¼ cup French mustard, such as Grey Poupon
½ teaspoon smoked paprika
½ teaspoon sea salt
½ teaspoon ground white pepper
¼ teaspoon granulated garlic
¼ teaspoon onion powder
¼ cup honey

½ cup olive oil
1 teaspoon ketchup or chili sauce
1 teaspoon brown sugar
2 tablespoons white wine vinegar
1 tablespoon lemon juice
2 tablespoons water
1 tablespoon cornstarch
1 egg yolk, optional

1. Whisk together the mustard with the dry spices. Stir in the honey, olive oil, ketchup, and sugar. Heat the mixture in a small saucepan until boiling.

2. Remove the pan from the heat and stir in the vinegar and lemon juice.

3. Make a paste of the water and corn starch and whisk into the sauce if not using right away. Refrigerate in a covered container until ready to use.

4. If you will be using the sauce immediately, whisk the egg yolk and water together until frothy, about 2 minutes. Slowly whisk the egg mixture into the sauce, stirring constantly, until completely incorporated and creamy.

Makes about 1 cup

Because the egg is uncooked, the shelf life for this sauce is limited. Thickening a sauce with corn starch does not carry the risk of uncooked egg.

CHILI'S
Cajun Chicken Pasta

WHILE SOME CREAM SAUCES CAN BE BLAND, CHILI'S FIRES UP THE SPICE FACTOR WITH THIS RICH AND PEPPERY SAUCE FOR PENNE. THE CAJUN-COATED CHICKEN IS GOOD ENOUGH TO BE ENJOYED ON ITS OWN!

4 tablespoons (½ stick) unsalted butter
2 (6-ounce) boneless skinless chicken breasts
2 tablespoons Cajun seasoning
3 cups whipping cream
1 teaspoon lemon pepper
½ teaspoon ground white pepper

1 teaspoon black pepper
2 teaspoons kosher salt
1 teaspoon granulated garlic
1 (12-ounce) box penne, cooked according to package directions
½ cup shredded Parmesan cheese
2 medium Roma tomatoes, diced

1. Light a charcoal barbecue or heat a gas grill to medium. Clean the grate and coat it with vegetable oil.

2. Melt 2 tablespoons of the butter and brush it over the chicken. Rub the Cajun seasoning into the chicken, covering both sides.

3. Grill the breasts for 5 to 6 minutes per side, turning once, or until cooked through and no longer pink in the center. Set the chicken aside and let it rest for 10 minutes, then cut it into long strips.

4. Melt the remaining butter in a medium saucepan and stir in the whipping cream. Bring the cream to a boil, then reduce the heat and simmer. Whisk in the lemon pepper, white and black pepper, the salt, and garlic. Simmer for 5 minutes.

5. Add the cooked pasta to the cream sauce and let it heat through. Stir the pasta and sauce until thoroughly combined.

6. Spoon the pasta onto warmed plates or shallow serving bowls. Arrange the sliced chicken on top of each portion, then sprinkle with the Parmesan cheese and garnish with the diced tomatoes.

Serves 4

Try a different pasta shape for variety. Bowties, shells, or large elbow macaroni would be good choices.

CHILI'S
Fire-Roasted Corn Guacamole

GRILLED CORN ON THE COB HAS A UNIQUE FLAVOR THAT CAN'T BE DUPLICATED. MAKE SURE THE COBS ARE DRY WHEN YOU SET THEM ON THE GRILL TO AVOID MESSY EXPLOSIONS.

2 ears corn, husks and silk removed
2 medium jalapeños
4 large avocados, split and pitted
2 teaspoons kosher salt
½ teaspoon pepper

2 tablespoons lime juice
1 tablespoon lemon juice
½ cup Pico de Gallo (recipe on next page)
2 tablespoons chopped cilantro

1. Light a charcoal barbecue or heat a gas grill to medium. Clean the grate and coat it with vegetable oil.

2. Grill the corn and jalapeños, turning frequently, until the corn is lightly charred and the jalapeños are blistered.

3. When cool enough to handle, cut the kernels from the cobs. Peel or rub the skins, using paper towels, off the peppers, remove the stems and seeds. Dice the peppers and add to the corn kernels.

4. Scoop the avocados out of their skins and mash with a fork. Stir in the salt, pepper, lime and lemon juices, and the Pico de Gallo.

5. Fold in the cilantro with the peppers and corn. Stir just until blended.

Serves 4 to 8

Serve this not only as a dip with chips, but also as a topping for tacos and grilled meats.

CHILI'S
Grilled Caribbean Chicken Salad

A HALLMARK OF TROPICAL FOOD IS ITS AMAZING CONTRAST IN FLAVORS. IN THIS EASY RECIPE, PINEAPPLE AND HONEY ARE COMBINED WITH JALAPEÑOS AND SESAME. IT MAY SOUND UNUSUAL, BUT IT'S OH SO TASTY!

4 (4-ounce) boneless skinless chicken breasts
½ cup teriyaki marinade
½ cup Honey Lime Dressing
1 cup Pico de Gallo
1 cup tortilla chips, lightly crushed

Salad Mix
6 cups mixed greens
½ cup shredded red cabbage
1 (8-ounce) can pineapple chunks, drained

Honey Lime Dressing
¼ cup Dijon mustard
¼ cup honey

1 tablespoon rice wine vinegar
3 tablespoons lime juice
1 teaspoon sesame oil
1 teaspoon brown sugar
½ teaspoon sea salt

Pico de Gallo
2 large Roma tomatoes, diced
1 small yellow onion, finely diced
1 small jalapeño, seeded and minced
1 tablespoon olive oil
2 teaspoons red wine vinegar
½ teaspoon kosher salt
¼ teaspoon pepper
1 tablespoon chopped cilantro

1. Do ahead: Put the chicken breasts in a resealable plastic bag and pour the teriyaki marinade over them. Push the air out of the bag and seal it, making sure the chicken is well coated. Refrigerate the breasts for at least 2 hours, turning occasionally.

2. Do ahead: For the Salad Mix, toss the mixed greens with the cabbage and pineapple. Refrigerate until ready to serve.

3. Do ahead: To make the Honey Lime Dressing, whisk all the ingredients together in a small bowl, or pulse them a few times in a blender. Reserve it at room temperature. The dressing can be made a day ahead of time

and refrigerated in an airtight container. Let it come to room temperature before using.

4. Light a charcoal barbecue or heat a gas grill to medium. Clean the grate and coat it with vegetable oil.

5. Discard the marinade and shake off any excess. Grill the chicken 5 to 6 minutes per side, turning once, or until cooked through and no longer pink in the center. Let it rest for 10 minutes, then cut the chicken into strips and set them aside.

6. Combine all the ingredients for the Pico de Gallo in a large bowl, stirring them just until blended. It can be made a day ahead of time and refrigerated in an airtight container. Strain out excess liquid before using.

7. Combine the Salad Mix and the Honey Lime Dressing in a large bowl. Add the Pico de Gallo and crushed tortillas. Toss until well mixed. Portion the salad onto 4 chilled plates and top with strips of the cooked chicken.

Serves 4

This Honey Lime Dressing is a great condiment to keep on hand. Quadruple the recipe, and use it as a basting sauce for chicken and seafood on the grill, as well as a salad dressing.

CHILI'S
Low-Fat Fajitas

CHICKEN OR BEEF FAJITAS CAN BE AN EASY DIET-FRIENDLY MENU CHOICE. WITH JUST A FEW ADJUSTMENTS, EVEN MORE CALORIES CAN BE ELIMINATED, BUT THE FLAVOR STAYS THE SAME.

Marinade
¼ cup lime juice
2 tablespoons canola oil
4 large cloves garlic, lightly smashed
1 tablespoon soy sauce
1 teaspoon kosher salt
½ teaspoon black pepper
¼ teaspoon cayenne pepper
½ teaspoon liquid smoke flavoring, optional

4 (4-ounce) boneless skinless chicken breasts

Fajitas
1 tablespoon canola oil

1 large red bell pepper, seeded and thinly sliced
1 large yellow bell pepper, seeded and thinly sliced
1 large green bell pepper, seeded and thinly sliced
1 medium red onion, halved and cut into strips
1 tablespoon lime juice
2 tablespoons water
½ teaspoon kosher salt
¼ teaspoon pepper

2 tablespoons chopped cilantro, for garnish

1. Do ahead: Whisk together the ingredients for the marinade. Pour the mixture into a large resealable plastic bag and add the chicken breasts. Push the air out of the bag and seal it. Make sure the chicken is well coated and refrigerate overnight, or at least 2 hours, turning occasionally.

2. Light a charcoal barbecue or heat a gas grill to medium. Clean the grate and coat it with vegetable oil.

3. Remove the chicken from the marinade and cook it 5 to 6 minutes per side, turning once, or until cooked through and no longer pink in the center. Let it rest 10 minutes, then slice the breasts into long strips.

4. Heat the oil for the fajitas in a large skillet. When hot, add the bell peppers and onion. Sauté until the vegetables are cooked through and have started browning. Remove the pan from the heat and add the lime juice, water, salt, and pepper.

5. Toss the vegetables with the chicken strips and garnish with cilantro, if desired.

Serves 4

Fajitas are traditionally served with warm flour tortillas. To cut calories and fat, grill 8 or 10 corn tortillas until lightly charred and flexible. Serve with low-fat sour cream and salsa to keep the extra pounds away. You might want to skip the frying pan altogether and grill the peppers and onions, requiring no oil at all. The smoky essence of the grill adds wonderful flavor to peppers, and you won't need to add the liquid smoke flavoring.

CHILI'S
Ranchero Chicken Quesadilla

RATHER THAN GRILLED AND CUT INTO WEDGES, THIS QUESADILLA FROM CHILI'S IS MORE LIKE A CALZONE. THE TORTILLAS ARE STUFFED WITH GRILLED CHICKEN CHEESE AND SAUCE, THEN FOLDED OVER AND GRILLED OVER HOT COALS UNTIL LIGHTLY CHARRED ON THE OUTSIDE AND MELTED INSIDE. SERVE THEM SLICED OR WHOLE, TO BE EATEN LIKE A SANDWICH.

Ranchero Sauce
1 tablespoon vegetable oil
2 large cloves garlic, minced
1 small yellow onion, chopped
1 large serrano chili, seeded and chopped
6 large Roma tomatoes, diced
1 teaspoon dried oregano
1 teaspoon chili powder
1 teaspoon kosher salt
½ teaspoon pepper
½ teaspoon cumin

2 (8-ounce) boneless skinless chicken breasts
4 tablespoons (½ stick) unsalted butter, softened
1 teaspoon kosher salt
½ teaspoon pepper
2½ cups Ranchero Sauce
4 (10-inch) flour tortillas
1 cup shredded Cheddar cheese
1 cup sour cream
1 cup Pico de Gallo (see page 143)

1. Do ahead: Make the Ranchero Sauce before grilling the chicken so that it has time to blend. Heat the vegetable oil in a medium skillet and sauté the garlic and onion until softened. Stir in the serrano chili and cook 2 minutes more, stirring occasionally. Add the tomatoes and spices to the skillet and stir until well blended. Simmer for 5 to 8 minutes more, then pulse in a blender or food processor until smooth, or leave it chunky. Set aside.

2. Light a charcoal barbecue or heat a gas grill to medium. Rub the chicken breasts with 1 or 2 tablespoons of the softened butter and season on both sides with the salt and pepper.

3. Grill the chicken 6 to 7 minutes per side, turning once, or until cooked through and no longer pink in the center. Let the chicken rest for 10 minutes, then cut into thin strips.

4. Stir the cooked chicken into the Ranchero Sauce and mix well.

5. Butter 1 side of each tortilla and place, buttered side down, on a piece of waxed paper. Spread a portion of the cheese over one half of the tortilla and top with a portion of the chicken mixture. Leave about an inch around the edge so the mixture doesn't spill out onto the grill.

6. Fold the other side of the tortilla over the filling like a closed book. When the quesadillas are assembled, grill them on both sides until lightly toasted, but not burned.

7. Put each quesadilla on a plate and slice or leave whole. Serve with individual ramekins of sour cream and Pico de Gallo.

Serves 4

This is a great go-to idea when you have all the ingredients on hand. Think about it next time you have leftover chicken that can be sliced or shredded. Ranchero sauce can be purchased, and salsa, cheese, and sour cream are refrigerator staples.

CHILI'S
Southwestern Eggrolls

MORE OF A CHIMICHANGA THAN AN EGG ROLL, CHILI'S USES FLOUR TORTILLAS
TO TIGHTLY WRAP SEASONED CORN, BEANS, AND CHEESE INTO ROLLS THAT ARE
FROZEN, THEN DEEP FRIED UNTIL CRISPY. FOLLOWING STEPS 1–6 WILL GIVE YOU
A PERFECT PREP-AND-HEAT RECIPE WHEN YOU NEED A FAST MEAL AT HOME.

1 (10-ounce) boneless skinless
  chicken breast
½ teaspoon kosher salt
¼ teaspoon pepper
5 (7-inch) flour tortillas
1 cup Mexican shredded blend
  cheese

Eggroll Filling
2 tablespoons olive oil
1 small red bell pepper, seeded
  and diced
1 small green bell pepper, seeded
  and diced
1 large jalapeño, seeded and minced
2 green onions, chopped
1 cup fresh spinach, lightly
  steamed and squeezed dry
½ cup frozen corn kernels, thawed
½ cup cooked canned black
  beans, rinsed and drained
1 teaspoon chili powder
1 teaspoon kosher salt
½ teaspoon black pepper

¼ teaspoon cayenne pepper
1 tablespoon chopped cilantro

**Avocado Ranch Dipping
Sauce**
½ large avocado
¼ cup mayonnaise
¼ cup sour cream
¼ cup buttermilk
1 teaspoon kosher salt
½ teaspoon dried parsley
½ teaspoon onion powder
½ teaspoon dried dill
½ teaspoon granulated garlic
¼ teaspoon ground white pepper
2 teaspoons white wine vinegar

4 to 6 cups canola oil, for frying
¾ cup Avocado Ranch Dipping
  Sauce
1 chopped green onion, for garnish
¼ cup quartered cherry
  tomatoes, for garnish

1. Do ahead: Light a charcoal barbecue or heat a gas grill to medium. Clean
   the grate and coat it with vegetable oil.

2. Season the chicken with the salt and pepper. Grill the breast for 7 to 8 minutes per side, turning once, or until it is cooked through and no longer pink in the center. Let it rest for 10 minutes before cutting into a small dice. Set aside.

3. Do ahead: To make the Eggroll Filling, heat the olive oil in a large skillet and sauté the bell peppers and jalapeño for 2 minutes or until softened. Add the green onions, spinach, corn, and black beans. Simmer for about 4 minutes.

4. Add the chili powder, salt, black pepper, and cayenne. Stir in the cilantro and the diced chicken. Cook until heated through.

5. Grill the tortillas for just a few seconds until flexible. Lay each tortilla flat and put a portion of the cheese in the center. Spoon some of the filling on top of the cheese, then fold in the ends and roll the tortilla tightly over the filling. Secure the seam with a toothpick.

6. Line a plate with plastic wrap and arrange the egg rolls, seam side down, on top. Wrap the plate tightly in more plastic wrap and freeze at least 4 hours, or overnight.

7. Do ahead: To make the Avocado Ranch Dipping Sauce, mash the avocado with a fork, then whisk in the mayonnaise, sour cream, and buttermilk. When the mixture is smooth, add the salt, parsley, onion powder, dill, garlic, pepper, and vinegar. Whisk until well blended, then refrigerate until ready to use.

8. Heat the canola oil in a large, heavy-bottomed saucepan to medium high, or 375°F. Fry the frozen egg rolls, 1 or 2 at a time, until golden brown on each side, 10 to 12 minutes.

9. Remove each roll with a slotted spoon and drain on paper towels or a wire rack.

10. To serve, remove the toothpick from each roll and slice it diagonally lengthwise. Arrange the sliced rolls on a heated platter surrounding a ramekin of the Avocado Ranch Dipping Sauce. Sprinkle with the chopped onion and cherry tomato.

Serves 4 to 8

Keep the dipping sauce in mind for other uses, such as tortilla chips, veggies, or nachos. Because of the avocado, you can't make it too far in advance, but it should be fine if covered and refrigerated 1 to 2 days. Give it a quick whisk before serving if it has darkened on the surface.

CHILI'S
Steak Marinade

THIS MARINADE IS AN ALL-AROUND WINNER FOR FLANK, SKIRT, AND TOP ROUND STEAKS THAT NEED EXTENDED MARINATING TO BECOME TENDER. USE A LITTLE LESS TIME FOR SIRLOIN AND OTHER LEAN CUTS.

⅔ cup honey
3 cups low-sodium soy sauce
¼ cup Worcestershire sauce
3 large cloves garlic, crushed

1-inch piece ginger, peeled and
  chopped
½ cup water

1. Whisk the honey and soy sauce until smooth. Stir in the Worcestershire sauce, garlic, and ginger.
2. Add the water to the other ingredients in the container, then shake to blend thoroughly before using.
3. Refrigerate in a tightly sealed container until ready to use.

Makes about 4 cups

If the honey sweetens the marinade too much, next time you can substitute dark brown sugar and whisk with the liquids until dissolved.

CHIPOTLE MEXICAN GRILL
Ancho Chile Marinated Chicken Breast

AMERICANS ARE ADDICTED TO THE BEEF, CHICKEN, AND PORK THAT GO INTO CHIPOTLE'S TACOS AND BURRITOS. ONCE YOU MASTER MAKING THIS MARINADE, YOU'LL NEVER GO BACK TO THE STORE BOUGHT BRANDS.

1 (2-ounce) package dried ancho chilies
1 teaspoon pepper
2 teaspoons cumin
2 tablespoons chopped fresh oregano, leaves only

6 large cloves garlic, chopped
½ medium red onion, roughly chopped
¼ cup canola oil
4 (4-ounce) boneless skinless chicken breasts

1. Cut the stems off the chilies and butterfly them. Remove the seeds and layer the chilies in a saucepan. Fill the pan with warm water to cover and let soak overnight.

2. When the chilies are soft, discard the soaking water, and combine them with the pepper, cumin, oregano, garlic, onion, and oil in a blender and puree until smooth.

3. Pour the marinade into a large resealable plastic bag and add the chicken. Press the bag to thoroughly cover the chicken with the mixture. Push the air out of the bag and seal it.

4. Marinate the chicken for at least 4 hours, or overnight.

5. Light a charcoal barbecue or heat a gas grill to medium. Clean the grate and coat it with vegetable oil.

6. Grill the chicken for 5 to 6 minutes per side, turning once, or until no longer pink in the center.

7. Let the chicken rest about 10 minutes before chopping or slicing for tacos, burritos, salad, or quesadillas.

* * * * * * * * * *

Serves 4

* * * * * * * * * *

For a larger crowd, double or triple the marinade recipe, and use as a basting sauce for ribs and burgers.

CHIPOTLE MEXICAN GRILL
Burrito Bowls

CHIPOTLE HAS A HIT ON THEIR HANDS WITH THESE BURRITO BOWLS. NEVER AGAIN WORRY ABOUT A SOGGY BURRITO FALLING APART IN YOUR HANDS. IF YOU MISS THE TORTILLA, JUST TOSS 1 OR 2 ON THE GRILL AND ENJOY THEM WITH YOUR BOWL.

1 tablespoon chili powder
1 teaspoon dried minced onion
1 teaspoon granulated garlic
1 teaspoon cumin
½ teaspoon dried Mexican oregano
1 teaspoon kosher salt
½ teaspoon pepper
1 tablespoon olive oil
4 (6-ounce) boneless skinless chicken thighs

Corn Salsa
1½ cups frozen corn kernels, thawed
½ small red onion, diced
2 tablespoons lime juice
1 teaspoon kosher salt
½ teaspoon pepper

Guacamole
2 large avocados
1 jalapeño, seeded and minced
1 medium Roma tomato, diced
½ teaspoon kosher salt
¼ teaspoon pepper
1 tablespoon lime juice

1 cup cooked white rice
2 cups Corn Salsa
2 cups Guacamole

1. Do ahead: Whisk together the chili powder, onion, garlic, cumin, oregano, salt, and pepper. Stir into the olive oil and rub over the chicken thighs. Cover and refrigerate at least 4 hours, or overnight.

2. Do ahead: To make the Corn Salsa, drain any liquid from the corn and toss with the onion, lime juice, salt, and pepper. Cover and refrigerate until ready to use.

3. Light a charcoal barbecue or heat a gas grill to medium. Clean the grate and coat it with vegetable oil.

4. Grill the thighs for 9 to 10 minutes per side, turning once, or until cooked through and no longer pink in the center. Set aside for 10 minutes, then cut into bite-sized cubes. Keep warm.

5. Make the Guacamole while the chicken is grilling. Mash the avocados with a fork, then stir in the jalapeño, tomato, salt, pepper, and lime juice.

6. To assemble the burrito bowl, portion the cooked rice into the bottom of each bowl and fill a third of the surface with the grilled chicken, a third with the corn salsa, and a third with the guacamole. Serve warm.

Serves 4

Vary the toppings according to taste. Try ground beef, salsa, and shredded cheese. You can also serve over brown rice or use your favorite recipe for Spanish rice.

CLAIM JUMPER
Pork or Beef Ribs

NO ONE WILL BELIEVE YOU WHEN YOU DESCRIBE THE INGREDIENTS TO THE "MYS-TERIOUS" MARINADE USED IN THIS DISH. YOU CAN FIND CLAIM JUMPER ORIGINAL BARBECUE SAUCE AT ANY OF THEIR NUMEROUS LOCATIONS OR ON THEIR WEBSITE.

1 (12-ounce) can regular Coca Cola, not diet
1 (12-ounce) bottle zesty Italian salad dressing
1 teaspoon liquid smoke flavoring
3 to 4 pounds pork or beef ribs
1 (20-ounce) bottle Claim Jumper Original Barbecue Sauce

1. Do ahead: Whisk together the soda, salad dressing, and smoke flavoring. Put the meat in a container large enough to hold it and pour the marinade over the ribs. Turn them to make sure all surfaces are covered. Cover the container and refrigerate overnight.
2. Light a charcoal barbecue or heat a gas grill to medium. Clean the grate and coat it with vegetable oil.
3. Grill the ribs, basting with the Claim Jumper Barbecue Sauce, turning often until cooked through and tender.
4. Serve with more barbecue sauce on the side.

Serves 6

If there's not a Claim Jumper restaurant near you, use a barbecue sauce that is tomato based and includes a sweetener such as brown sugar, as well as smoke flavor, garlic, mustard, and a touch of Worcestershire sauce.

CLAIM JUMPER
Yukon Blend Marinade

CLAIM JUMPER'S OWN BRAND OF BARBECUE SAUCE IS THE BOLDEST NOTE IN THIS MARINADE, BUT ANY BRAND WILL DO. GO FOR A SMOKY-SWEET STYLE WITH A THICK TOMATO BASE.

1 (12-ounce) bottle Claim Jumper Original Barbecue Sauce
1 (8-ounce) bottle Italian salad dressing
¾ cup light soy sauce
¾ cup beer
⅓ cup Worcestershire sauce
3 large cloves garlic, minced
1 teaspoon kosher salt
½ teaspoon black pepper

1. Whisk together all the ingredients or pulse them in a blender.
2. Refrigerate in an airtight container for up to 1 week.
3. Use for all types of meats, chicken, and ribs. Marinate the meat for at least 1 hour before grilling.

Makes about 5 cups

Use any type of beer you wish, regular or light, but a lighter lager or pale ale would be more suitable than stout.

COPELAND'S OF NEW ORLEANS
Guitreau

THIS POPULAR NEW ORLEANS SAUCE IS NAMED AFTER THE REPAIRMAN OF A WELL-KNOWN RESTAURANT. CRAYFISH AND SHRIMP ARE POACHED IN BUTTER, THEN SPOONED OVER GRILLED FISH FILLETS. IT IS RICH, DECADENT, AND VERY, VERY GOOD!

1 teaspoon mayonnaise
1 (8-ounce) fillet red snapper
¾ teaspoon kosher salt
¼ teaspoon pepper
½ cup (1 stick) butter
1 small yellow onion, chopped
½ teaspoon granulated garlic
½ teaspoon paprika

¼ teaspoon ground white pepper
¼ pound small shrimp, peel and deveined
¼ pound crayfish tails
½ pound button mushrooms, stemmed
1 green onion, chopped

1. Light a charcoal barbecue or heat a gas grill to medium. Clean the grate and coat it with vegetable oil.

2. Put a thin coat of mayonnaise over the snapper and season with ¼ teaspoon salt and the black pepper. Grill 3 to 4 minutes per side, turning once, until it is no longer translucent in the center. Use a wide, flexible spatula to turn the fish.

3. Melt the butter in a medium saucepan and cook the onion over low heat until soft. Stir in the garlic, paprika, white pepper, and remaining ½ teaspoon salt.

4. Add the shrimp and simmer until cooked.

5. Add the crayfish and mushrooms and simmer until cooked through. Add the green onion just before serving.

6. Put the snapper fillet on a warmed plate and spoon the sauce over the fish. Serve any extra sauce on the side.

Serves 1

Serve this sauce over steaks, chicken, or chopped-beef steaks that are grilled or broiled.

CRACKER BARREL
Applefest Grilled Chicken Salad

THIS SALAD IS ALL ABOUT APPLES, BACON, AND GOOD GRILLED CHICKEN. BLUE CHEESE AND CANDIED PECANS ARE THE FINAL TOUCHES OF SWEET AND SAVORY THAT MAKE THIS SALAD A CLASSIC.

2 (4-ounce) boneless skinless chicken breasts
1 cup raspberry vinaigrette
2 Gala apples, or other crisp, sweet apple
1 tablespoon fresh lemon juice
1 (12-ounce) bag mixed greens

2 tablespoons chopped candied pecans
2 tablespoons crumbled blue cheese
4 strips applewood smoked bacon, cooked crisp

1. Put the chicken breasts and a half cup of the raspberry vinaigrette in a resealable plastic bag and marinate at least 4 hours, or overnight.

2. Light a charcoal barbecue or heat a gas grill to medium. Clean the grate and coat it with vegetable oil.

3. Discard the used vinaigrette and shake off any excess. Grill the chicken 5 to 6 minutes per side, turning once, until cooked through and no longer pink in the center. Let it rest 10 minutes, then cut into thin slices.

4. Core and slice the apples into bite-sized pieces and toss with the lemon juice.

5. Toss the mixed greens with ¼ cup of the remaining vinaigrette and mound them on chilled plates. Surround the greens with the apples, arranged so the skin is facing outward.

6. Sprinkle the candied pecans over the salad, then place the cooked chicken in a pin-wheel arrangement on top. Scatter the blue cheese over the chicken, then crumble the bacon over all.

7. Serve the remaining raspberry vinaigrette on the side.

You can also use apple cider vinaigrette or a raspberry walnut salad dressing. Any fruity, sweet salad dressing would be fine.

CRACKER BARREL
Grilled Chicken Tenders

THIS IS ONE OF THE EASIEST RECIPES FOR GRILLED TENDERS YOU WILL COME ACROSS. PERFECT FOR PARTIES, KIDS' LUNCHES, OR ANYTIME YOU WANT GOOD FOOD WITHOUT MUCH FUSS.

½ cup zesty Italian dressing
1 teaspoon lime juice

2 teaspoons honey
1 pound chicken tenders

1. Whisk together the dressing, lime juice, and honey. Pour the marinade over the tenders in a resealable plastic bag and marinate at least 4 hours, or overnight.
2. Light a charcoal barbecue or heat a gas grill to medium. Clean the grate and coat it with vegetable oil.
3. Shake off any excess marinade and discard it. Grill the tenders, 2 to 3 minutes per side, or until cooked through and no longer pink in the center.
4. Serve hot or room temperature.

Serves 2

You can make a substantial meal by serving these with an entrée-sized salad or steamed rice and mixed vegetables.

DAVE AND BUSTER'S
Cheeseburger Pizza

DAVE AND BUSTER'S HAS THE ANSWER TO A FREQUENT QUESTION: BURGERS OR PIZZA? THE ANSWER IS: BOTH! A UNIQUE BLEND OF GRILLED CHEESEBURGER PIECES BAKED IN FRESH PIZZA DOUGH, FINISHED WITH YOUR FAVORITE TOPPINGS. THE BEST OF BOTH IN ONE BIG PIE!

½ teaspoon kosher salt
¼ teaspoon pepper
¾ cup shredded American and Jack cheese blend
8 ounces ground beef or chuck
2 to 3 tablespoons all-purpose flour
1 (8-ounce) package fresh pizza dough
1 tablespoon cornmeal
¼ cup ketchup

¼ cup yellow mustard
8 pickle slices, julienned
2 slices red onion, separated into rings
½ cup shredded mozzarella cheese
¼ cup spicy ketchup
2 strips bacon, cooked crisp
1 medium tomato, thinly sliced
¼ cup chopped yellow onion
1 cup shredded iceberg lettuce

1. Using your hands, mix the salt, pepper, and ¼ cup cheese blend into the ground beef. Form a large patty, then refrigerate for at least 10 minutes, covered.

2. Light a charcoal barbecue or heat a gas grill to medium. Clean the grate and coat it with vegetable oil.

3. Grill the patty, turning once, until cooked through; the finished temperature won't matter because the burger will be baked into the pizza. Set the patty aside for 10 minutes, then cut into small pieces.

4. Preheat the oven to 450°F.

5. Sprinkle a work surface with the flour and coat the pizza dough. Roll it out to a 10- or 11-inch circle. Lightly dust a sheet pan with the cornmeal and transfer the pizza to the pan.

6. Whisk together the ketchup and mustard and spread it evenly over the pizza, leaving a little room at the edges.

7. Layer the remaining half cup of the shredded cheese over the sauce, then scatter the pieces of grilled burger, pickles, onion rings, and mozzarella on top.

8. Bake the pizza for 12 to 15 minutes, or until the crust is lightly golden on the bottom and the cheese is melted.

9. Take the pizza out of the oven and drizzle with the spicy ketchup. Crumble the bacon and scatter it over the pizza along with the sliced tomato and chopped onion. Return the pizza to the oven for a couple minutes more to let the toppings heat through.

10. Top the finished pizza with the shredded lettuce just before serving. Cut into wedges and serve hot.

Serves 4 to 6

Making your own spicy ketchup is easy. Take 1 cup of your regular brand and whisk in 1 tablespoon prepared horseradish and ½ teaspoon cayenne pepper.

DENNY'S
Bacon Caesar Burger

ANOTHER EXAMPLE OF TWO IDEAS COMING TOGETHER AS ONE. A SIZZLING BEEF BURGER IS FLAVORED WITH CAESAR SALAD DRESSING AND SERVED WITH CRISP ROMAINE LETTUCE. SAVE A LITTLE EXTRA DRESSING ON THE SIDE FOR DIPPING FRENCH FRIES.

6 ounces ground beef or chuck
1 teaspoon Worcestershire sauce
1 small clove garlic, minced
½ teaspoon kosher salt
¼ teaspoon pepper
¼ teaspoon red pepper flakes, optional
1 sesame seed hamburger bun, split in half
¼ cup Caesar salad dressing

1 leaf romaine lettuce, chopped
2 slices tomato, thickly sliced
2 slices kosher dill pickles
1 slice red onion, cut ¼-inch thick
2 slices Cheddar or Monterey Jack cheese
2 slices smoked bacon, cooked crisp

1. Using your hands, mix the ground beef with the Worcestershire sauce, garlic, salt, pepper, and pepper flakes, if desired. Do not overmix the meat, just work it enough to blend the ingredients. Form the beef into a patty and refrigerate at least 10 minutes before grilling.

2. Light a charcoal barbecue or heat a gas grill to medium. Clean the grate and coat it with vegetable oil.

3. Grill the patty 3 to 4 minutes per side, turning once, or until cooked to your preferred doneness. Set the patty aside.

4. Grill the hamburger bun until lightly toasted, taking care to not let it burn.

5. To assemble the burger, toss some of the Caesar dressing with the chopped romaine and pile it on the bottom half of the bun. Top with the sliced tomatoes, pickles, sliced onion, then the patty. Top the patty with the cheese and cooked bacon and finish with the top half of the bun.

Serves 1

Amp up the Caesar in this burger by dressing the bun on the toasted side with some of the dressing and mixing 2 tablespoons of shredded Parmesan cheese into the ground beef.

DENNY'S
Grilled Red Potatoes

DENNY'S OFFERS THE PERFECT ACCOMPANIMENT TO A SIMPLE PIECE OF GRILLED FISH OR CHICKEN. TENDER RED POTATOES ARE SEASONED WITH BUTTER AND HERBS, THEN WRAPPED IN A FOIL PACKET AND SET ON A HOT GRILL. TRY THIS NEXT TIME YOU'VE GOT THE GRILL FIRED UP.

I large red potato, scrubbed
½ teaspoon kosher salt
¼ teaspoon pepper
I tablespoon unsalted butter

¼ teaspoon chicken bouillon powder
¼ teaspoon dried oregano
¼ teaspoon dried basil

1. Light a charcoal barbecue or heat a gas grill to medium. Clean the grate and coat it with vegetable oil.

2. Cut the potato in half lengthwise then slice each half very thin. Season with the salt and pepper.

3. Cut a length of aluminum foil. Shingle the sliced potatoes down the center of the foil and top with the butter, bouillon powder, oregano, and basil.

4. Roll the edges of the foil up tightly to form a packet. Put the packet on the hot grill and cook for about 20 minutes, or until the potatoes are tender.

Makes 1 serving

Add a few hickory chips to the grill and close the lid to give the potatoes a slightly smoky flavor.

DON PABLO'S
Chicken Parilla

MARINATE CHICKEN IN THIS SIMPLE RECIPE AND GRILL OVER MESQUITE CHIPS. PERFECT FOR FAJITAS, BURRITOS, AND TACOS.

I bunch cilantro, leaves only
I tablespoon lime juice
I tablespoon seasoned salt, such
   as Lawry's

4 (4-ounce) boneless skinless
   chicken breasts

1. Chop the cilantro and mix in a bowl with the lime juice and seasoned salt. Add the chicken breasts and toss, then cover and refrigerate at least 1 hour.
2. Light a charcoal barbecue or heat a gas grill to medium. Clean the grate and coat it with vegetable oil.
3. Grill the chicken for 5 to 6 minutes per side, turning once, or until cooked through and no longer pink in the center.
4. Let the chicken rest at least 10 minutes before cutting or slicing.

Serves 2

Refrigerate the marinade in an airtight container for a day if you want to make it ahead of time.

EL POLLO LOCO
Chicken Rice Bowl

THEIR SIGNATURE FLAME-BROILED CHICKEN SERVED IN A BOWL OVER SPANISH RICE, BEANS, AND FRESH GARNISHES.

1 whole chicken, split lengthwise
1 teaspoon kosher salt
½ teaspoon pepper
½ teaspoon cumin
¼ cup vegetable oil
¼ cup unsalted butter, melted
1 teaspoon dried minced onion
1 teaspoon granulated garlic
1 tablespoon fresh lemon or lime juice
¼ cup shredded Mexican blend
1 large Roma tomato, diced
½ small yellow onion, diced
2 tablespoons chopped cilantro

Spanish Rice
1¼ cups white rice
1 tablespoon unsalted butter, melted
2 cups chicken broth

1 (14½-ounce) can diced tomatoes, with liquid
2 teaspoons chili powder
½ teaspoon cumin
½ teaspoon dried Mexican oregano
½ teaspoon granulated garlic
1 teaspoon kosher salt
½ teaspoon pepper

Pinto Beans
1 tablespoon canola oil
1 large serrano or jalapeño pepper, seeded and diced
1 (28-ounce) can pinto beans, rinsed and drained
1 teaspoon New Mexico–style chili powder
¼ cup water
1 green onion, chopped

1. Do ahead: Season the chicken with the salt and pepper and rub it with the cumin. Whisk together the oil and melted butter and stir in the onion, garlic, and lemon juice. Pour the marinade over the chicken, cover, and refrigerate overnight.

2. Light a charcoal barbecue or heat a gas grill to medium. Clean the grate and coat it with vegetable oil.

3. Grill the chicken on both sides until the skin is browned and the chicken is cooked through. Check the meat against the bone to make sure it is no longer pink. Set the chicken aside for about 15 minutes, then cut into pieces.

4. To make the Spanish Rice, sauté the rice in the melted butter in a medium saucepan, stirring frequently to lightly toast it.

5. Pour in the chicken broth and bring it to a boil. Stir in the diced tomatoes, chili powder, cumin, oregano, garlic, salt, and pepper. Cover the pot and reduce the heat to low. Cook for 20 minutes, then set aside, leaving it covered.

6. Heat the oil for the Pinto Beans in a small saucepan and sauté the serrano pepper until soft. Stir in the pinto beans, chili powder, and water. Bring to a boil, then lower the heat and simmer for 15 minutes. Add the green onion and set aside.

7. To make the rice bowls, spoon a portion of the Spanish Rice and Pinto Beans into the bottom of 4 to 6 bowls. Lay a few pieces of chicken in each bowl, then garnish with the cheese, tomatoes, onion, and chopped cilantro. Serve warm.

Serves 4 to 6

To make grilling and eating easier, use boneless skinless chicken breasts or thighs for this recipe. Marinate the pieces at least 4 hours and grill until cooked through. You can serve the pieces whole or cut them into bite-sized pieces.

EL TORITO GRILL
Fire-Roasted Tomato Soup

TOMATOES, CORN, AND PEPPERS ARE CHARRED OVER HOT COALS, LENDING THEIR
SMOKY FLAVOR TO THIS POPULAR SOUP. THE CREAM AND PUREED AVOCADO
BLEND BEAUTIFULLY WITH THE BRIGHT, CLEAN FLAVORS OF FRESH VEGETABLES.
IT MAKES A BIG POT, SO SAVE SOME FOR OTHER MEALS.

3 pounds Roma tomatoes, halved
1 large poblano chile
1 small yellow onion, quartered
1 ear corn, husks and silk
   removed
4 ounces bulk chicken chorizo
1½ cups chicken broth
1 large clove garlic, minced
1 cup whipping cream
1 teaspoon kosher salt
½ teaspoon ground white pepper
¼ teaspoon Mexican oregano
¼ teaspoon cayenne pepper
1 cup Crema Fresca
1 cup Avocado Sauce
2 tablespoons cilantro, chopped

Crema Fresca
⅔ cup sour cream
⅓ cup half-and-half

Avocado Sauce
1 large avocado, seeded and
   chopped
1 serrano or jalapeño pepper,
   seeded and diced
1 green onion, chopped
1 tablespoon cilantro, chopped
1 large clove garlic, minced
1 tablespoon juice from pickled
   jalapeños or adobo sauce
½ teaspoon kosher salt
¼ cup water, or more if needed

1. Light a charcoal barbecue or heat a gas grill to medium. Clean the grate and coat it with vegetable oil.

2. Grill the tomatoes and poblano until the skins blacken and blister, turning frequently. Grill the onion and corn until charred. Peel or rub the skins off the tomatoes and chile and cut the kernels from the ear of corn. Remove the stem and seeds from the poblano and roughly chop the vegetables.

3. Heat a large saucepan over medium heat and cook the chorizo. When it is cooked through, pour in the chicken broth and add the grilled toma-

toes, onions, chile and minced garlic. Simmer for about 10 minutes over low heat. Stir in the cream, salt, white pepper, oregano, and cayenne. Simmer another 5 minutes.

4. Ladle the hot soup into a blender and puree in batches until smooth. Return it to the saucepan and stir in the grilled corn. Keep warm.

5. To make the Crema Fresca, whisk together the sour cream and half-and-half until very smooth and creamy.

6. Combine all the ingredients for the Avocado Sauce in a blender and puree until smooth.

7. To serve, ladle the soup into warmed bowls. Use a teaspoon or squeeze bottle to drizzle each of the sauces in a zigzag pattern over the soup.

8. Garnish with the chopped cilantro.

Serves 6 to 8

You can make the soup 2 days ahead of time and keep it refrigerated in a covered container. It's best to make the sauces just prior to serving the soup.

FAMOUS DAVE'S
BBQ Sauce

FAMOUS DAVE'S BARBECUE SAUCES ARE AVAILABLE AT THE FAMOUS DAVE'S WEB-
SITE, AS WELL AS FROM ONLINE RETAILERS. MAKING YOUR OWN IS NOT ONLY
WELL WORTH THE EFFORT, BUT ALSO MUCH LESS EXPENSIVE. MAKE A FEW LARGE
BATCHES TO HAVE ON HAND OR TO GIVE AS GIFTS.

2 slices hickory smoked bacon
1 small sweet onion, chopped
¼ cup water
¾ cup peach schnapps
½ cup raisins
1 large jalapeño, seeded and
chopped
2 large cloves garlic, minced
⅓ cup balsamic vinegar
½ small apple, cored and
chopped
¼ cup tangerine juice
concentrate
¼ cup pineapple juice
concentrate
2 tablespoons lemon juice
2 tablespoons lime juice

3 tablespoons molasses
2 tablespoons apple cider vinegar
2¼ cups corn syrup
1 (12-ounce) can tomato paste
½ cup brown sugar
½ cup Worcestershire sauce
2 tablespoons yellow mustard
2 teaspoons chili powder
1 teaspoon Maggi seasoning
1 teaspoon cayenne pepper
1 teaspoon kosher salt
½ teaspoon red pepper flakes
¼ teaspoon black pepper
¼ cup Kahlua or other coffee
liqueur
1 teaspoon liquid smoke flavoring

1. Fry the bacon until all the fat is rendered. Save the bacon for some other
   use and reserve 1 tablespoon of the fat.

2. Sauté the onion in the bacon fat, then add the water. Simmer over low
   heat until the onion is well browned.

3. Stir in the schnapps, raisins, jalapeño, and garlic. Simmer until reduced
   to the consistency of syrup.

4. Stir in the balsamic vinegar, apple, the fruit juices, molasses, and cider vinegar. Simmer a few minutes, then transfer the mixture to a blender and process until pureed, working in batches if necessary.

5. Return the puree to the saucepan and add the corn syrup, tomato paste, sugar, Worcestershire sauce, mustard, chili powder, Maggi seasoning, cayenne, salt, pepper flakes, and black pepper. Bring the mixture to a boil, then reduce the heat and simmer 20 minutes, stirring occasionally.

6. Remove the pan from the heat and whisk in the Kahlua and liquid smoke. Let the mixture cool, then refrigerate in a covered container.

Serves 4

Use this sauce for basting ribs, steaks, chicken, and pork chops. The sauce thickens over time, so you may need to add a little water to thin it.

FAMOUS DAVE'S
Citrus Grilled Salmon

THE PREPARATION FOR THIS RECIPE IS FAIRLY SIMPLE, BUT THE RESULTS ARE SPECTACULAR. GRILLED MELON AND ORANGE SEGMENTS ARE AN AMAZING CONTRAST TO THE RICHNESS OF THE SALMON.

4 (6-ounce) salmon fillets
I teaspoon kosher salt
½ teaspoon pepper
2 teaspoons olive oil
2 tablespoons lime juice
½ medium cantaloupe, peeled
　and cut in 1½-inch wedges

2 navel oranges, segments
　separated and white
　membranes removed
I tablespoon chopped cilantro,
　for garnish

1. Light a charcoal barbecue or heat a gas grill to medium. Clean the grate and coat it with vegetable oil.

2. Season the salmon fillets with the salt and pepper, then rub with the olive oil. Grill until no longer translucent, turning once. Use a wide, flexible spatula to help turn the salmon. Baste both sides with some of the lime juice while the fish is cooking.

3. Grill the cantaloupe wedges just long enough to make diamond-shaped grill marks on one side of each piece. Don't cook it all the way through.

4. Put each fillet on a warmed dinner plate and surround with some of the orange segments and grilled cantaloupe.

5. Garnish with the chopped cilantro.

Serves 4

Other melons and citrus can be used in season. Honeydew stands up well to the grill, and tangerines and sweet grapefruit are great with fish.

FAMOUS DAVE'S
Citrus Grilled Shrimp

NOTHING BEATS FRESH SHRIMP RIGHT OFF THE GRILL. JUST A FEW MINUTES IN AN ORANGE AND LIME MARINADE IMPARTS A TANGY FRESHNESS TO BALANCE THE SMOKE OF THE GRILL. IT'S BOUND TO BE ONE OF YOUR FAVORITE GRILL MARINADES FOR SEAFOOD AND FISH.

½ cup fresh orange juice
1 tablespoon fresh lime juice
3 tablespoons chopped orange zest
1 tablespoon chopped lime zest
1 tablespoon light brown sugar

1½ teaspoons red pepper flakes
2 pounds large shrimp, peeled and deveined
1 teaspoon kosher salt
¼ teaspoon pepper

1. Whisk together the orange and lime juices, then add the orange and lime zests, sugar, and red pepper flakes.

2. Put the cleaned shrimp in a large resealable plastic bag and pour the marinade over them. Push the air out of the bag and seal it. Refrigerate for 15 minutes.

3. Light a charcoal barbecue or heat a gas grill to medium. Clean the grate and coat it with vegetable oil.

4. Remove the shrimp from the marinade and shake off any excess. Combine the salt and pepper, then season the shrimp on both sides.

5. Grill the shrimp for 1 or 2 minutes per side, turning once, or just until they have lost their translucency. Serve hot.

Serves 4 to 6

Serve with hot buttered rice and mixed vegetables.

FAMOUS DAVE'S
Grilled Chipotle Caesar

USE YOUR OWN RECIPE FOR CAESAR DRESSING OR A FAVORITE BRAND. THIS
UNUSUAL CAESAR SALAD IS ANOTHER EXAMPLE OF HOW FAMOUS DAVE'S USES
IMAGINATIVE PAIRINGS OF INGREDIENTS TO KEEP YOUR TASTE BUDS HAPPY.

6 heads romaine hearts
2 tablespoons extra virgin olive
 oil
1 tablespoon finely ground sea
 salt

1 tablespoon freshly ground
 pepper
2 cups Caesar dressing
2 chipotle peppers, mashed
¼ cup grated Parmesan

1. Light a charcoal barbecue or heat a gas grill to medium. Clean the grate
   and coat it with vegetable oil.

2. Split each romaine heart lengthwise, leaving the core intact. Brush the
   face of each half with the olive oil and season with the salt and pepper.

3. Grill the romaine, cut side down, for 30 seconds. Turn the heads over
   and grill another 30 seconds.

4. Whisk together the Caesar dressing and chipotle peppers and set aside.

5. Remove the core from the romaine and plate 2 halves per guest on
   chilled plates. Drizzle with the chipotle Caesar and garnish with the
   Parmesan cheese.

Serves 6

Have some garlic bread ready, to serve with the salad.

FAMOUS DAVE'S

Grilled Peaches with Vanilla Bean Ice Cream

PEACHES AND ICE CREAM MAKE FOR A SIMPLE YET ELEGANT DESSERT. MAKE THIS
ONLY DURING PEACH SEASON; ANYTHING LESS THAN PERFECTLY RIPE FRUIT WILL
NOT BE THE SAME.

¼ cup balsamic vinegar
¼ cup Tupelo honey
6 ripe peaches, halved and pitted
6 scoops premium vanilla ice
 cream

Sprig of mint
½ cup warm caramel sauce,
 optional

1. Light a charcoal barbecue or heat a gas grill to medium. Clean the grate
   and coat it with vegetable oil.

2. Stir together the balsamic vinegar and honey until well blended. Coat
   the peach halves with the mixture.

3. Grill the peaches, cut side down, for 4 to 5 minutes, or until soft. Baste
   with the honey mixture as they grill.

4. Place a portion of ice cream in a chilled bowl and top with a grilled
   peach. Garnish with the mint sprig, and drizzle with the caramel sauce,
   if desired.

Serves 6

*Golden amber and heavy-bodied Tupelo is a premium honey
from the north Florida area. Clover or orange blossom honey
works just as well.*

FAMOUS DAVE'S
Marinated Grilled Flank Steak

FAMOUS DAVE'S TEXAS PIT BBQ SAUCE IS THEIR ORIGINAL SAUCE, AND THE ONE THAT MADE THEM FAMOUS, ACCORDING TO COMPANY HISTORY.

1½ cups Famous Dave's Texas Pit BBQ Sauce, or other sweet and tangy sauce
½ cup dark honey

1 tablespoon prepared horseradish
1½ pounds flank steak

1. Whisk together the barbecue sauce, honey, and horseradish. Coat the flank steak with the marinade, cover, and refrigerate for at least 6 hours or overnight.

2. Light a charcoal barbecue or heat a gas grill to medium. Clean the grate and coat it with vegetable oil.

3. Shake any excess sauce from the meat and grill 10 to 12 minutes per side, turning once, or until cooked to your preferred doneness. Let the meat rest for 15 minutes before serving.

4. Slice the meat against the grain in thin pieces and serve warm.

Serves 4 to 6

Leftover pieces of steak can be reheated and served on top of a salad the next day.

FAMOUS DAVE'S
Pit Barbecue Ribs

YOU WILL NEED A GRILL WITH A COVER OR A SMOKER TO PREPARE THESE RIBS AND LOTS OF TIME. THEY NEED 4 HOURS IN A WET MARINADE, OVERNIGHT REFRIGERATION IN DRY SPICES, AND 6 HOURS TO SMOKE.

Rib Rub

2 cups dark brown sugar
1 cup kosher salt
¼ cup granulated sugar
½ cup granulated garlic
¼ cup Mrs. Dash's Seasoning Mix
¼ cup New Mexico chili powder
¼ cup lemon pepper
¼ cup minced dried onion
¼ cup black pepper
1 tablespoon celery salt
1 tablespoon cayenne pepper
1 teaspoon ground cloves

2 racks beef spareribs
½ cup Italian salad dressing
1 cup minced dried onions
1 teaspoon pepper
½ cup dark brown sugar
1 cup Rib Rub
Hickory chips soaked in warm water
1 (20-ounce) bottle Famous Dave's Texas Pit Barbecue Sauce or other barbecue sauce

1. Stir together all the ingredients for the Rib Rub and store it in an airtight container until ready to use.

2. Trim any excess fat from the ribs and put them in a large resealable plastic bag with the Italian dressing. Refrigerate for 4 hours.

3. Remove the ribs from the dressing and dry them with paper towels. Stir together the dried onions with the pepper and brown sugar. Coat each rack with the spices and wrap them individually in plastic wrap and refrigerate overnight.

4. The next day, wipe the coating from the racks and rub each with ½ cup of the Rib Rub, coating both sides of the meat. Refrigerate while you prepare the smoker.

5. Light 15 pieces of hardwood charcoal. When they're red hot, move them to one end of the grill and surround with presoaked hickory chips.

6. Place the ribs, bone side down, away from the hot coals, and smoke for 3 hours. The temperature of the smoker must remain at 200° to 225°F, so add more hot charcoals and hickory chips as needed.

7. Remove the ribs and wrap them tightly in aluminum foil. Lay them on the far end of the grill, away from the hot coals, at a temperature of 180° to 200°F for 1½ to 2 hours, or until fork tender.

8. Build a bed of hot coals along the length of the grill bed. Unwrap the ribs and grill them over the hot coals until sizzling and lightly charred. Lightly brush the ribs with the barbecue sauce and let the heat caramelize them. Serve hot with sauce on the side.

Serves 4 to 6

Keep the remaining Rib Rub in an airtight container for use with other grilled meats.

FUDDRUCKERS
Burger

FUDDRUCKERS LETS YOU BUILD YOUR OWN BURGER BY CHOOSING THE WEIGHT OF THE PATTY AND YOUR FAVORITE TOPPINGS. IT'S THEIR SPECIAL SEASONING SPRINKLED ON THE BEEF THAT MAKES THE FLAVOR STAND OUT.

1 pound ground beef or chuck
1 tablespoon smoked paprika
2 teaspoons dark brown sugar
1 teaspoon kosher salt
½ teaspoon pepper
½ teaspoon granulated garlic

¼ teaspoon onion powder
¼ teaspoon cayenne pepper
4 hamburger buns, split in half
Sliced tomatoes, onions, pickles,
   lettuce, cheese

1. Form the beef into 4 patties and refrigerate, covered, for at least 30 minutes before cooking.

2. Light a charcoal barbecue or heat a gas grill to medium. Clean the grate and coat it with vegetable oil.

3. Stir all the spices together. Sprinkle some of the spice mixture on both sides of each patty.

4. Grill the patties 3 to 4 minutes per side, turning once, or until cooked to your preferred doneness.

5. Build the burger your way—top with any of the suggested favorites—or with none at all, and enjoy it hot off the grill.

Serves 4

The spice ingredients can be easily expanded and used on everything from baked potatoes to zucchini.

HARDEE'S
Mushroom and Swiss Burger

SAUTÉED MUSHROOMS IN CREAMY MUSHROOM SOUP FALL OVER MELTED SWISS CHEESE ON THIS BURGER FROM THE POPULAR HARDEE'S CHAIN. DON'T FORGET THE NAPKINS!

1 pound ground beef or chuck
1 tablespoon unsalted butter
½ pound white mushrooms, stemmed and sliced
1 (14½-ounce) can mushroom soup, undiluted
1 teaspoon Worcestershire sauce
1 teaspoon Lawry's Seasoned Salt
1 teaspoon Accent, optional (see note)
½ teaspoon pepper
4 hamburger buns, split in half
4 slices Swiss cheese

1. Form the beef into 4 patties, cover, and refrigerate at least 30 minutes before cooking.

2. Heat the butter in a small saucepan and sauté the mushrooms until lightly golden. Stir in the mushroom soup and Worcestershire sauce. Simmer over low flame 5 minutes, then set aside and keep warm.

3. Combine the dry seasonings.

4. Light a charcoal barbecue or heat a gas grill to medium. Clean the grate and coat it with vegetable oil.

5. Put the burgers on the grill and sprinkle some of the dry seasoning mixture on the top. Cook for 3 to 4 minutes per side, turning once, or until your desired doneness. Season the burgers once more when you turn them over.

6. Place the buns on the grill until lightly toasted, taking care to not let them burn.

7. Put a slice of Swiss cheese on each patty and let it melt a bit before removing it from the grill.

8. Put a patty on the bottom half of each bun, then spoon a portion of the mushroom sauce over the cheese. Finish with the top half of the bun.

Makes 4

*Accent is a brand name for monosodium glutamate; those with
sensitivities to MSG should eliminate it from the mix.*

HOUSTON'S
Hawaiian Steak Marinade

MOST OF THE HOUSTON'S RESTAURANTS USE THIS MARINADE WITH THEIR RIB-EYE STEAK. FANS WILL WAIT IN LONG LINES ON BUSY NIGHTS JUST TO HAVE A PIECE OF STEAK PARADISE. IT'S JUST AS GOOD AT HOME.

½ cup dark brown sugar
1 cup pineapple juice
¼ cup apple cider vinegar

1 cup light soy sauce
2 teaspoons granulated garlic
1 teaspoon ground ginger

1. Whisk together the brown sugar and pineapple juice until the sugar is dissolved.
2. Stir in the remaining ingredients and bring to a low simmer in a small saucepan, stirring occasionally.
3. Let the marinade cool, then refrigerate it until completely cold.
4. When you're ready to marinate your choice of steak, put the steak in a large resealable plastic bag and pour in the marinade. Push out the air and seal the bag.
5. Refrigerate at least 2 days, turning the bag over regularly so the meat is evenly marinated.
6. Shake any excess marinade off the steak and pat it dry before grilling to your preferred doneness.

Makes about 2½ cups

Using dried spices lengthens the shelf life of this marinade. If you choose, you may use 2 cloves of minced garlic and 1 teaspoon of grated ginger, but be sure to use the marinade within 3 days of preparation.

HOUSTON'S
Veggie Burger

NOT EVERYTHING THAT'S GOOD FOR YOU TASTES BORING OR BLAND. THE VEGGIE BURGERS FROM HOUSTON'S ARE KNOWN FOR THEIR SPICY KICK AND SATISFYING TEXTURE. TRY THEM WITH MELTED CHEESE; THEY MIGHT BECOME YOUR BURGER OF CHOICE.

Veggie Burger Patty Mix
¼ cup barbecue sauce
1 tablespoons molasses
1 (15-ounce) can black beans, rinsed and drained
2 cups cooked brown rice
¼ cup very finely chopped yellow onion
¼ cup finely chopped canned beets
1 tablespoon instant oatmeal
1 small pickled pepper, seeded and finely chopped
1 teaspoon beet juice
1 teaspoon chili powder

1 teaspoon kosher salt
½ teaspoon cumin
½ teaspoon pepper
2 egg whites

2 teaspoons olive oil
4 slices Monterey Jack cheese
2 tablespoons unsalted butter, melted
4 hamburger buns, split in half
4 slices tomato, thickly sliced
4 slices red onion, cut ¼-inch thick
4 leaves green leaf lettuce
2 tablespoons yellow mustard

1. To make the Veggie Burger Patty mix, whisk together the barbecue sauce and molasses. Set aside.

2. Combine the remaining ingredients plus half the barbecue sauce mixture in a food processor. Pulse until well ground but not pureed. The mixture should be similar to the consistency of ground beef.

3. Form the mix into 4 patties and refrigerate for at least 30 minutes.

4. Light a charcoal barbecue or heat a gas grill to medium. Clean the grate and coat it with vegetable oil.

5. Brush the patties with the olive oil and grill about 2 minutes per side. Brush with the remaining barbecue sauce mixture before turning them

over, then brush again. Use a wide, flexible spatula to turn the veggie patties.

6. Place a slice of cheese on each patty and let it melt slightly.

7. Heat the melted butter in a large skillet and toast the hamburger buns. Place a patty on the bottom half of each bun, then top with tomato, onion, and lettuce. Spread the top half of each bun with the mustard and finish the burgers. Serve hot.

Serves 4

You can save a step and toast the hamburger buns directly on the hot grill, taking care to not let them burn.

IN-N-OUT BURGER
The Double-Double Burger

ALMOST EVERYONE HAS A FAVORITE BURGER, BUT THIS IS THE HANDS-DOWN WINNER IN THE DOUBLE-DOUBLE CATEGORY.

Special Sauce

½ cup mayonnaise

2 tablespoons ketchup

1 tablespoon white wine vinegar

2 teaspoons sweet pickle relish

2 teaspoons grated yellow onion

½ teaspoon sugar

¼ teaspoon kosher salt

¼ teaspoon pepper

2 (6-ounce) ground beef patties

½ teaspoon kosher salt

¼ teaspoon pepper

2 slices American cheese

1 hamburger bun, split in half

2 tablespoons Special Sauce

1 slice tomato, thickly sliced

1 leaf iceberg lettuce

1 slice yellow onion, cut ¼-inch thick

1. Do ahead: Whisk together the ingredients for the Special Sauce and refrigerate in a covered container. The sauce may be made 2 days ahead of time.

2. Light a charcoal barbecue or heat a gas grill to medium. Clean the grate and coat it with vegetable oil.

3. Season the beef patties with the salt and pepper. Spread a teaspoon of the Special Sauce on top of each patty and grill 3 to 4 minutes per side, turning once, or until cooked to your preferred doneness. Top the patties with the cheese and set them aside to let the cheese melt slightly.

4. Put the buns on the grill and lightly toast them, taking care to not let them burn.

5. To build your burger, spread a spoonful of Special Sauce on the bottom half of the bun. Place the tomato on the bun, then the lettuce. Place the first patty and cheese on the lettuce, then add the onion. Top the onion with the second patty and cheese.

6. Spread a spoonful of the Secret Sauce on the top half of the bun and finish the burger. Serve hot.

Serves 1

For the complete In-N-Out experience, devour your burger with a soda and fries.

JACK IN THE BOX
Mini Sirloin Burgers

SLIDER-SIZED BURGERS BUNS ARE NOW CROPPING UP EVERYWHERE. THESE BABY
BURGERS WILL DISAPPEAR FASTER THAN YOU CAN GET THEM ON A PLATE.

1 pound ground sirloin
1 tablespoon Lawry's Seasoned
  Salt
1 teaspoon pepper
1 small yellow onion, thinly sliced

8 mini hamburger buns, split in
  half
8 slices dill pickle
2 slices American cheese,
  quartered
¼ cup ketchup or chili sauce

1. Combine the ground sirloin with the seasoned salt and pepper. Use your
   hands to blend the ingredients, but do not overmix. Form the mixture
   into 8 patties about ½-inch thick and refrigerate at least 30 minutes
   before grilling.
2. Light a charcoal barbecue or heat a gas grill to medium. Clean the grate
   and coat it with vegetable oil.
3. Grill the patties 3 to 4 minutes per side, turning once, or until cooked to
   your preferred doneness.
4. Put the sliced onion on the grill and cook until lightly charred.
5. Assemble the burgers with the pickles on the bottom half of the bun,
   then the cooked patty, cheese, grilled onion, ketchup, and the top of the
   bun. Serve hot.

Serves 4

Make a double batch of these burgers for a party or game day.

JOE'S CRAB SHACK
Barbecued Alaskan King Crab

EVEN THOUGH JOE'S IS THE HOME OF FLORIDA STONE CRAB, THEY JUST CAN'T RESIST OFFERING THE DELECTABLE ALASKAN KING CRAB WHEN IT'S IN SEASON.

Barbecue Sauce
1 large yellow onion, quartered
2 small cloves garlic, minced
1½ cups apple cider vinegar
1 cup chili sauce or ketchup
¼ cup dark brown sugar
¼ cup canola oil
¼ cup Grey Poupon or other Dijon mustard

2 tablespoons Worcestershire sauce
1 tablespoon celery seeds
2 teaspoons Tabasco sauce
¼ teaspoon cayenne pepper
½ teaspoon turmeric

3½ pounds King crab legs, shells split

1. Do ahead: To make the Barbecue Sauce, puree the onion, garlic, and vinegar in a blender until smooth and transfer the mixture to a medium saucepan.

2. Add the remaining ingredients and mix well. Bring the mixture to a boil, then reduce the heat and simmer for 20 minutes, or until the sauce has thickened.

3. Let the sauce cool, then transfer to an airtight container and refrigerate, covered, until ready to use.

4. Light a charcoal barbecue or heat a gas grill to medium. Clean the grate and coat it with vegetable oil.

5. Keep the crabs in the shells and grill them, turning frequently, until hot. Crack the shells open and brush with the barbecue sauce.

6. Return the crab to the grill until the sauce is heated through. Serve hot with extra sauce on the side.

Serves 2 to 3

This recipe makes more sauce than is needed for the crab. The sauce will keep for up to 2 weeks in the refrigerator, so use it for shrimp and other seafood.

KENNY ROGERS
B-B-Q Sauce

KENNY ROGERS MAKES AN ALL-AROUND BARBECUE SAUCE THAT CAN BE USED FOR MULTIPLE TASKS, INCLUDING BASTING MEATS ON THE GRILL, GLAZING BROILED CHOPS, AND SERVING ALONGSIDE PULLED PORK AND CHICKEN.

1 cup unsweetened applesauce
1¼ cups dark brown sugar
½ cup ketchup or chili sauce
¼ cup fresh lemon juice
2 tablespoons white wine vinegar

1 tablespoon smoked paprika
1 tablespoon kosher salt
1 teaspoon pepper
½ teaspoon cinnamon

1. Combine all the ingredients in a medium saucepan. Whisk constantly as the mixture comes to a boil.

2. Reduce the heat to low and simmer the sauce for 15 minutes, stirring frequently. Make sure the brown sugar is dissolved and not sticking to the bottom of the pan.

3. Set the sauce aside if using right away and keep warm. If making the sauce for future use, let it cool, then store it in an airtight container in the refrigerator for up to 3 weeks.

Makes about 3 cups

This sauce freezes well. Put a piece of plastic wrap on the surface of the sauce to keep ice crystals from forming, then seal tightly.

KFC
Honey BBQ Sauce

THIS SAUCE HAS BEEN SERVED BY KFC FRANCHISES FOR YEARS, AND THE FLAVOR
NEVER CHANGES. IT'S A TRUE AMERICAN CLASSIC!

1¼ cups ketchup
¼ cup dark molasses
¼ cup clover honey
¼ cup white wine vinegar

1 teaspoon liquid smoke flavoring
1 teaspoon kosher salt
1 teaspoon onion powder
½ teaspoon chili powder

1. Combine the ingredients in a small saucepan and whisk until well blended.
2. Bring the sauce to a boil, then lower the heat and simmer for 20 minutes. If using right away, set it aside to keep warm. If making the sauce for a future use, let cool, then store in an airtight container for up to 3 weeks in the refrigerator.

Makes about 2 cups

The sauce goes well with any grilled meat, but it's best with fried chicken and French fries!

KRYSTAL
Bar-B-Q Bacon Big Angus Burger

KRYSTAL IS A LEGEND IN TENNESSEE AND THE SOUTH. IT STARTED IN THE MIDST OF THE DEPRESSION AND, RECENTLY, WAS THE FIRST OF THE MAJOR CHAINS TO OFFER FREE WI-FI. THEY MAKE A WIDE RANGE OF BURGERS AND BREAKFASTS, AND HOT DOGS AND WINGS ARE ON THE MENU AS WELL.

½ pound ground Angus beef
½ teaspoon kosher salt
¼ teaspoon pepper
2 slices American cheese
4 slices Smithfield bacon, cooked crisp
2 hamburger buns, split in half

4 tablespoons sweet-and-spicy barbecue sauce
6 dill pickle chips
I large leaf iceberg lettuce, halved
I romaine leaf, halved
6 grape or cherry tomatoes, diced

1. Combine the ground beef with the salt and pepper. Use your hands to gently mix the ingredients. Mix until just blended, then form 2 patties and refrigerate them for at least 30 minutes.

2. Light a charcoal barbecue or heat a gas grill to medium. Clean the grate and coat it with vegetable oil.

3. Grill the patties 3 to 4 minutes per side, turning once, or until cooked to your preferred doneness. Place a slice of cheese and 2 strips of the bacon on each patty and set them aside to keep warm.

4. Place the buns on the grill and let them lightly toast, taking care to not let them burn.

5. To assemble the burgers, spread the bottom half of each bun with barbecue sauce, followed by the cooked patty with the cheese and bacon.

6. Top the bacon with the pickles, lettuces, and diced tomatoes.

7. Spoon more barbecue sauce on top of the tomatoes and finish with the top half of the bun. Serve hot.

Serves 2

LONE STAR STEAKHOUSE
Mesquite-Grilled Shrimp

LONE STAR OFFERS SHRIMP COCONUT FRIED OR MESQUITE GRILLED. TRY THIS SPICE RUB FOR GRILLED SHRIMP WITH A FEW MESQUITE CHIPS THROWN OVER THE HOT COALS.

1½ teaspoons granulated garlic
1½ teaspoons ground white pepper
1½ teaspoons kosher salt
1½ teaspoons onion powder
½ teaspoon poultry seasoning
¼ teaspoon cayenne pepper

1 pound medium shrimp, peeled and deveined
¼ cup dry white wine or lemon juice, plus more for serving, optional
Melted butter, optional

1. Stir together the dry spices and toss in a large bowl with the shrimp. Sprinkle with 2 tablespoons of the wine or juice and refrigerate for 30 minutes.
2. Light a charcoal barbecue or heat a gas grill to medium. Clean the grate and coat it with vegetable oil.
3. Grill the seasoned shrimp 1 to 2 minutes per side, taking care to not overcook them. They should not be translucent, but just barely cooked through. Baste with the remaining wine or juice.
4. Serve hot off the grill with extra wine or melted butter, if desired.

Serves 2

The shrimp can be sautéed in a little unsalted butter if a grill is not available. Broiling is another option, but be careful not to dry them out.

LONE STAR STEAKHOUSE
Steak Sauce

EVERY STEAKHOUSE NEEDS A SIGNATURE SAUCE TO SERVE WITH STEAKS AND CHOPS. THIS SAUCE GOES WITH BURGERS AND SANDWICHES, AS WELL AS GRILLED BEEF AND PORK.

½ cup clarified butter
1 clove garlic, minced
½ cup fresh lemon juice
2 tablespoons Worcestershire sauce

½ teaspoon Tabasco sauce
1 teaspoon dry mustard
½ teaspoon pepper

1. Melt the butter in a small saucepan and skim off the solids as they rise to the top.
2. Whisk together the clarified butter and the rest of the ingredients, then simmer over very low heat for 15 minutes.
3. Strain and store in an airtight container.

Makes about 1 cup

The sauce will keep in the refrigerator about 1 week. Let it come to room temperature before using.

LONGHORN STEAKHOUSE

Grilled Lime Shrimp with Guacamole Ranch Dip

LARGE SHRIMP ARE MARINATED THEN SKEWERED FOR A QUICK TURN ON THE GRILL. SERVE THEM WITH THE TANGY GUACAMOLE AS AN APPETIZER, OR WITH RICE AND SALAD FOR AN ENTRÉE.

Shrimp Marinade
¼ cup olive oil
2 tablespoons lime juice
1 tablespoon chopped cilantro
½ teaspoon cumin
½ teaspoon kosher salt
¼ teaspoon chili powder
¼ teaspoon pepper

Guacamole Ranch Dipping Sauce
1 large avocado, halved and pitted
½ cup bottled ranch dressing
2 tablespoons lime juice
2 tablespoons chopped cilantro
½ teaspoon cumin
½ teaspoon kosher salt

1 lime, quartered
4 bamboo skewers, soaked in water for an hour
20 large shrimp, peeled and deveined, leaving tails intact
3 tablespoons lime juice
¼ cup Shrimp Marinade
1 cup Guacamole Ranch Dipping Sauce

1. Whisk together the ingredients for the Shrimp Marinade and set aside.

2. Put 1 wedge of lime on each skewer, follow with 5 shrimp, threaded through the head and tail. Lay the skewers in a baking dish and pour half the marinade over them. Turn the skewers to coat both sides.

3. Do ahead: To make the Guacamole Ranch Dipping Sauce, scoop the avocado out of the skin and combine it with the ranch dressing in a blender. Pulse until well blended. Add the remaining ingredients and pulse again to make a smooth sauce. Refrigerate in a covered container until ready to use.

4. Light a charcoal barbecue or heat a gas grill to medium. Clean the grate and coat it with vegetable oil.

5. Remove the shrimp from the marinade and shake off any excess. Grill the skewers, 1 to 2 minutes per side, just until the shrimp lose their translucency. Baste frequently with the remaining marinade.

6. Remove the lime wedge and squeeze the juice over the shrimp. Serve hot with the dipping sauce.

Serves 2 to 4

For a fantastic entrée, take the shrimp off the bamboo skewers after grilling and place them around hot cooked rice or a tropical salad.

LONGHORN STEAKHOUSE
Outlaw Ribeye

TAKE THIS MOUTH-WATERING COPYCAT DISH EVEN FURTHER AND SERVE THIS BONE-IN RIB EYE STEAK WITH MASHED POTATOES AND BROCCOLI, JUST AS LONGHORN STEAKHOUSE DOES.

Prairie Dust Steak Seasoning
1 tablespoon kosher salt
1 ½ teaspoons black pepper
1 ½ teaspoons sweet paprika
1 teaspoon granulated garlic
1 teaspoon onion powder

½ teaspoon turmeric
½ teaspoon ground coriander
¼ teaspoon cayenne pepper

2 (18-ounce) bone-in rib eye steaks

1. Whisk together the Prairie Dust spices and put them in a medium-hole shaker.
2. Light a charcoal barbecue or heat a gas grill to medium. Clean the grate and coat it with vegetable oil.
3. Shake the spices over one side of the steaks and lay them on the grill, spice side down. Cook 9 to 10 minutes per side, turning once, or until cooked to your preferred doneness. Shake the spices over the top side before turning the steak over.
4. Let the steaks rest a few minutes before serving with the vegetables of your choice.

Serves 2

Bone-in steaks take a little longer to cook. To check for doneness, cut a small slit near the bone to check the meat. Bright red means it's still rare at the thickest part of the steak.

LUBY'S CAFETERIA
Luau Sauce

CREATE YOUR OWN OUTDOOR LUAU WITH CHICKEN, SHRIMP, SCALLOPS, OR RIBS,
ALL COATED WITH THIS TROPICAL SAUCE FROM LUBY'S.

12 ounces frozen peaches, thawed

2 teaspoons ground ginger

½ cup apple cider vinegar

¼ cup light soy sauce

¾ cup golden brown sugar

½ cup ketchup or chili sauce

1 teaspoon granulated garlic

½ teaspoon kosher salt

1. Combine the thawed peaches and ginger in a food processor. Pulse until the peaches are well ground.

2. Add the vinegar, soy sauce, and brown sugar to the processor. Pulse until the mixture is smooth and transfer it to a medium saucepan. Stir in the ketchup, garlic, and salt.

3. Bring the pan to a boil, then reduce the heat and simmer 3 minutes, stirring frequently.

4. Let the mixture cool, then refrigerate it in an airtight container.

Makes about 4 cups

Use this recipe as a dipping sauce as well as a basting sauce.
Keep it in mind for egg rolls and fried chicken tenders.

OLIVE GARDEN
Chicken and Sausage Mixed Grill

MARINATED CHUNKS OF TENDER CHICKEN BREAST ARE GRILLED ALONGSIDE PIECES OF JUICY ITALIAN SAUSAGE AND CHERRY TOMATOES IN THIS RUSTIC ITALIAN FAVORITE. THE SKEWERS ARE EASY TO PREPARE AND KEEP REFRIGERATED UNTIL THE GRILL IS HOT AND READY TO GO.

Chicken Marinade

¼ cup lemon juice

¼ cup olive oil

¼ cup dry white wine

1 tablespoon chili oil

2 large cloves garlic, crushed

1 teaspoon kosher salt

2 tablespoons chopped fresh rosemary leaves

½ teaspoon pepper

3 medium fresh bay leaves, halved

1 cup Chicken Marinade

4 (8-ounce) boneless skinless chicken breasts

1 pound mild Italian link sausages

32 bamboo skewers, soaked in water 30 minutes

2 cups large cherry tomatoes

2 lemons, quartered, for garnish

4 sprigs fresh rosemary, for garnish

1. Whisk together the ingredients for the Chicken Marinade. Put the chicken breasts in a large resealable plastic bag and pour the marinade over them. Push the air out of the bag and seal.

2. Refrigerate the chicken for at least 3 hours.

3. Cut the sausage links into 1-inch pieces.

4. Remove the chicken and cut each breast into 1-inch pieces. Thread the skewers with the sausage and chicken with a cherry tomato in between the meats. Refrigerate until ready to use.

5. Light a charcoal barbecue or heat a gas grill to medium. Clean the grate and coat it with vegetable oil.

6. Grill the skewers until the chicken and sausage are cooked through and no longer pink in the center, turning frequently.

7. Plate the grilled meats on a warmed platter and garnish with lemon wedges and rosemary sprigs.

Serves 4 to 8

To cut the grilling time down, you can bake the sausages whole at 350°F for about 20 minutes, then cut them into pieces and thread them onto the skewers with the chicken. They should be cooked all the way through and still get hot and juicy on the grill.

OLIVE GARDEN
Chicken Spiedini

COLORFUL VEGETABLES ARE QUICKLY GRILLED WITH PIECES OF CHICKEN BREAST MARINATED IN GARLICKY OLIVE OIL WITH MUSTARD AND HERBS. SERVED WITH A CREAMY DIPPING SAUCE THAT CAN ALSO BE USED WITH COOKED SHRIMP OR RAW VEGGIES.

Spiedini Dipping Sauce
1 cup mayonnaise, regular or
   reduced calorie
½ cup pineapple concentrate
2 large cloves garlic, minced
2 teaspoons dried tarragon
2 teaspoons Grey Poupon
   mustard
½ teaspoon kosher salt

Chicken Marinade
1 teaspoon brown sugar
1 teaspoon kosher salt
¼ cup balsamic vinegar
¼ cup olive oil
2 large cloves garlic, crushed

1 tablespoon Grey Poupon
   mustard
½ teaspoon pepper
½ teaspoon dried oregano
½ teaspoon dried tarragon

4 (6-ounce) boneless skinless
   chicken breasts
3 large red bell peppers, seeded
2 large green bell peppers,
   seeded
1 large sweet onion
2 dozen bamboo skewers, soaked
   in water
1 teaspoon kosher salt
½ teaspoon pepper
1½ cups Spiedini Dipping Sauce

1. Do ahead: To make the Spiedini Dipping Sauce, whisk together the mayonnaise with the pineapple concentrate. When well blended, whisk in the minced garlic, tarragon, mustard, and salt. Transfer to a ramekin and refrigerate, covered, until ready to use.

2. Prepare the Chicken Marinade by combining the sugar and salt with the balsamic vinegar. Whisk until they are dissolved. Whisk in the remaining marinade ingredients and set aside.

3. Pound the chicken breasts between 2 sheets of plastic wrap until less than ¼-inch thick. Cut the chicken into 1-inch pieces and add to the marinade, stirring until well coated. Cover the bowl and refrigerate for at least 2 hours.

4. Cut the red and green bell peppers into 1-inch square pieces. Separate the onion into layers and cut them into 1-inch pieces.

5. Remove the chicken from the marinade and drain. Assemble the spiedini, starting with a red pepper, then onion, then chicken. Repeat until each skewer has 4 pieces of chicken and end with a piece of red bell pepper. Refrigerate the spiedini until ready to cook.

6. Light a charcoal barbecue or heat a gas grill to medium. Clean the grate and coat it with vegetable oil.

7. Season the spiedini with the salt and pepper and grill them, turning frequently until the chicken is cooked through and the vegetables are tender.

8. Put the ramekin of Spiedini Dipping Sauce in the center of a large platter and surround it with the skewers of chicken and vegetables.

9. Serve the spiedini hot off the grill, or at room temperature.

Serves 6 to 8

Other vegetables can be used on the spiedini. Try red onion, sliced mushroom, thin pieces of fennel, and zucchini.

OLIVE GARDEN
Grilled Chicken Flatbread

GRILLED CHICKEN AND PEPPERS ARE SMOTHERED IN MOZZARELLA AND ALFREDO SAUCE ON FOCACCIA IN THIS OLIVE GARDEN FAVORITE. SHOWERED WITH FRESH BASIL AND LACED WITH GARLIC, THIS CREAMY, CHEWY OPEN-FACE SANDWICH MAKES A SATISFYING DINNER WITH A MIXED GREEN SALAD AND A GLASS OF CRISP WHITE WINE.

1 (8-ounce) boneless skinless chicken breast
½ teaspoon kosher salt
¼ teaspoon pepper
1 large red bell pepper
1 large clove garlic, lightly smashed

1 (15-inch) focaccia bread
1 cup Alfredo sauce (see page 110)
½ cup shredded mozzarella cheese
¼ cup shredded fresh basil

1. Light a charcoal barbecue or heat a gas grill to medium. Clean the grate and coat it with vegetable oil.

2. Season the chicken breast with the salt and pepper. Grill about 6 to 7 minutes per side, turning once, or until cooked through and no longer pink in the center. Set it aside to rest at least 10 minutes, then slice the chicken into 1-inch pieces.

3. Grill the red bell pepper until charred on all sides. Peel or rub off the skin. Remove the stem and seeds, then dice the pepper.

4. Preheat the oven to 350°F.

5. Rub the garlic over the focaccia and layer the bread with the sliced chicken. Spoon the Alfredo sauce over the chicken and top with half the diced red bell pepper.

6. Sprinkle the shredded mozzarella over the focaccia and bake until the cheese is melted, 6 to 8 minutes.

7. Remove the focaccia from the oven and top with the remaining diced pepper and fresh basil. Cut into slices and serve hot.

Serves 2 to 4

Cut into bite-sized squares, this is a fantastic party appetizer.

OLIVE GARDEN
Shrimp Caprese

CAPRESE IS A TRADITIONAL ITALIAN COMBINATION OF FRESH TOMATOES MIXED
WITH CHUNKS OF MOZZARELLA, OLIVE OIL, AND BASIL. OLIVE GARDEN OFFERS
IT IN A PASTA DISH WITH CAPELLINI AND A WHITE WINE CREAM SAUCE, TOPPED
WITH GRILLED SHRIMP.

1½ pounds Roma tomatoes, cut in large dice
½ cup shredded fresh basil
2 tablespoons extra virgin olive oil
2 large cloves garlic, minced
1 teaspoon Italian seasoning
1 teaspoon kosher salt
¼ cup unsalted butter
½ cup dry white wine

1½ cups whipping cream
1 cup grated Parmesan cheese
1½ pounds small shrimp, peeled and deveined
1 pound angel hair pasta, cooked according to package directions
2 cups shredded mozzarella cheese

1. In a medium bowl, combine the chopped tomatoes, basil, olive oil, garlic, Italian seasoning, and salt. Toss well to blend.

2. In a medium saucepan, melt the butter and add the white wine. Bring the mixture to a boil, then add the cream and Parmesan cheese. Simmer until reduced and thickened, stirring frequently to keep the cheese from sticking.

3. Light a charcoal barbecue or heat a gas grill to medium. Clean the grate and coat it with vegetable oil.

4. Grill the shrimp only a minute or two—since they are small, they will cook rapidly. Set aside.

5. Heat the broiler and toss the cooked pasta with the tomato mixture and the cream sauce. When well combined, put the pasta in an ovenproof baking dish and sprinkle with the mozzarella. Broil until the cheese is melted and bubbly, 2 to 3 minutes.

6. Top the pasta with the grilled shrimp and serve hot.

Serves 4

This is a fairly rich pasta dish. Serve it with a crisp green salad and dry white wine, leaving the garlic bread for another time.

OLIVE GARDEN
Steak Toscano

STEAKS IN ITALY ARE GENERALLY BRUSHED AND GRILLED WITH AN HERB-INFUSED OLIVE OIL OR AN HERBAL SEASONING MIX. THE STEAK TOSCANO AT OLIVE GARDEN HAS A LITTLE BIT OF BOTH.

Italian Herb Seasoning
1 teaspoon dried thyme
1 teaspoon dried rosemary
1 teaspoon dried basil
½ teaspoon dried oregano
½ teaspoon dried marjoram

¼ cup olive oil

4 (8-ounce) sirloin steaks
2 teaspoons kosher salt
1 teaspoon pepper

1. Add all the Italian Herb Seasoning ingredients and the olive oil in a small saucepan. Heat through about 5 minutes, then set aside to cool.

2. Light a charcoal barbecue or heat a gas grill to medium high. Clean the grate and coat it with vegetable oil.

3. Season the steaks with the salt and pepper and brush on one side with the Italian herb oil. Cook 4 to 5 minutes per side, turning once, or until cooked to your preferred doneness. Brush the top sides of the steaks with the herb oil before turning them over.

4. Let the meat rest at least 10 minutes before carving. Brush with more herb oil and carve into thin slices, if desired, or serve the steaks whole.

5. Put the remaining herb oil in a ramekin and let guests add more oil if they choose.

Serves 4

The Italian herb oil can be made ahead of time and stored in an airtight container. Warm it slightly before using on steaks or any other meat, chicken, or seafood you are grilling.

OLIVE GARDEN

Venetian Apricot Chicken

THIS IS AN UNUSUAL COMBINATION OF FLAVORS THAT WORK VERY WELL TO-
GETHER. THE FRESH TOMATO AND BASIL MIXTURE IS A MAINSTAY OF ITALIAN
CUISINE. IN THIS CASE, IT'S PAIRED WITH GRILLED VEGETABLES AND CHICKEN
COATED IN A SAVORY APRICOT SAUCE.

Tomato Mixture
6 large Roma tomatoes, cut in
   1-inch dice
¼ cup shredded fresh basil
½ teaspoon kosher salt

Apricot Sauce
½ cup chicken broth
½ cup apricot jam
½ teaspoon kosher salt
¼ teaspoon pepper

Garlic Herb Seasoning
3 teaspoons garlic pepper

1 teaspoon Italian seasoning
2 large cloves garlic, minced

4 (4-ounce) boneless skinless
   chicken breasts
12 jumbo asparagus, trimmed and
   blanched
½ teaspoon kosher salt
¼ teaspoon pepper
1 tablespoon olive oil
2 cups blanched broccoli florets
Chopped parsley, for garnish

1. Do ahead: For the Tomato Mixture, combine all the ingredients and toss well. Set aside.

2. Do ahead: To prepare the Apricot Sauce, heat the chicken broth in a small saucepan and whisk in the apricot jam, salt, and pepper. Bring to a boil, then remove from the heat and set aside.

3. Do ahead: Combine the ingredients of the Garlic Herb Seasoning and set aside.

4. Season the chicken breasts and asparagus with salt and pepper. Toss the asparagus with ½ tablespoon olive oil.

5. Light a charcoal barbecue or heat a gas grill to medium. Clean the grate and coat it with vegetable oil.

6. Grill the seasoned asparagus a few minutes on all sides, just until lightly charred, and set aside.

7. Grill the seasoned chicken breasts 6 to 7 minutes per side, turning once, or until the chicken is cooked through and no longer pink in the center. Let the chicken rest for at least 10 minutes before serving.

8. Heat the remaining ½ tablespoon olive oil in a medium skillet and lightly sauté the broccoli florets. Season with the Garlic Herb Seasoning and keep warm.

9. To serve, place the asparagus and broccoli florets on a warmed plate with a chicken breast between them. Pour the Tomato Mixtures over the vegetables and coat the chicken with the Apricot Sauce. Sprinkle with the chopped parsley. Serve hot.

Serves 4

A mix of grilled vegetables, such as zucchini, bell peppers, and onion would all go well with the tomato basil mixture in this dish.

OUTBACK STEAKHOUSE

Grilled Shrimp on the Barbie

OUTBACK MADE ITS NAME WITH AN AUSTRALIAN THEME, BUT REMOULADE SAUCE
AND CHILI-PEPPER SHRIMP ARE VERY NEW ORLEANS.

Shrimp Seasoning

2 teaspoons kosher salt
1 teaspoon granulated garlic
1 teaspoon onion powder
1 teaspoon black pepper
1 teaspoon chili powder
1 teaspoon sugar
½ teaspoon cayenne pepper
¼ teaspoon allspice

Remoulade Sauce

1 cup mayonnaise
2 tablespoons Dijon mustard
1½ tablespoons milk
2½ teaspoons prepared
  horseradish
½ small stalk celery, minced
1 small shallot, minced

¼ small green bell pepper, minced
½ teaspoon minced parsley
½ teaspoon white wine vinegar
½ teaspoon paprika
¼ teaspoon black pepper
¼ teaspoon cayenne pepper
¼ teaspoon kosher salt

12 jumbo shrimp, peeled and
  deveined
2 metal or bamboo skewers
  (if bamboo, soak in water
  before use)
1 tablespoon lemon juice
1 tablespoon unsalted butter,
  melted
1 tablespoon minced parsley
1 cup Remoulade Sauce

1. Do ahead: Make the Remoulade Sauce a day ahead of time, if possible, to let the flavors combine. Whisk the mayonnaise with the remaining remoulade ingredients and refrigerate in a covered container.

2. Do ahead: Whisk together the spices for the Shrimp Seasoning and set aside.

3. Light a charcoal barbecue or heat a gas grill to medium. Clean the grate and coat it with vegetable oil.

4. Thread the shrimp onto skewers. Sprinkle each side with some of the lemon juice and brush with the melted butter.

5. Sprinkle the Shrimp Seasoning on 1 side of the shrimp, then lay them on the grill, seasoned side down. Cook until the spices are lightly charred, 1 to 2 minutes, then season the top side of the shrimp, and turn the skewers over. Stop cooking the shrimp when they have just lost their translucency to avoid overcooking.

6. Slide the cooked shrimp onto warmed plates and garnish with the chopped parsley.

7. Serve with a ramekin of Remoulade Sauce.

Serves 2

Leaving the tail and the last section of shell on the shrimp makes them easier to pick up, but it is not absolutely necessary. With spice-crusted shrimp like this, a fork might be your best bet.

OUTBACK STEAKHOUSE
Steakhouse Style Dry Rub

EVER WONDER WHY STEAKHOUSE MEAT TASTES SO DIFFERENT FROM WHAT YOU GRILL AT HOME? DRY RUB SEASONING IS ONE ANSWER. TRY THIS BLEND FROM OUTBACK THE NEXT TIME YOU PLAN ON GRILLING STEAKS.

3 tablespoons kosher salt
2 tablespoons smoked paprika
1 teaspoon black pepper
1 teaspoon onion powder

1 teaspoon granulated garlic
1 teaspoon cayenne pepper
½ teaspoon ground coriander
½ teaspoon turmeric

Whisk the seasonings together and store in an airtight container.

Seasons 4 steaks

It's easy to expand this recipe. If you like it, make a large batch to keep on hand for chicken and chops, as well as steak.

OUTBACK STEAKHOUSE
Teriyaki Filet Medallions

OUTBACK SERVES THESE TENDER MEDALLIONS OVER SEASONED RICE WITH A CHOICE OF SIDES. THE MEAT AND VEGETABLES ARE SEARED OVER AN OAK-FIRED GRILL. YOU CAN PREPARE THE SAME DINNER WITH YOUR CHOICE OF SEASONED RICE AND OAK CHIPS SCATTERED OVER HOT COALS.

1 pound beef tenderloin
1 large red bell pepper
1 large green bell pepper
1 large red onion
4 metal skewers
Oak wood chips, soaked in water

Teriyaki Marinade
1½ cups apple cider vinegar
½ cup dark brown sugar
½ cup pineapple concentrate
1 cup light soy sauce
1 teaspoon granulated garlic
1 teaspoon kosher salt
1 teaspoon pepper

1. Cut the beef into 16 equal pieces. There will be 4 pieces of filet per skewer.

2. Do ahead: To make the Teriyaki Marinade, whisk the vinegar and brown sugar in a medium bowl until the sugar is dissolved. Stir in the remaining ingredients and add the pieces of beef. Cover the bowl and refrigerate for 4 hours.

3. Cut the bell peppers and onion into squares approximately the same size as the meat. Drain the beef and thread the skewers.

4. Start with the vegetables. Put a slice of onion between a red and green pepper like a sandwich. Put a veggie sandwich first on the skewer, then a piece of beef, then another sandwich, then beef, and so on, until you have 4 pieces of filet on a skewer, ending in a veggie sandwich.

5. When all the skewers are assembled, lay them in a flat baking dish and pour the Teriyaki Marinade over them. Cover and refrigerate for 1 hour.

6. Light a charcoal barbecue or heat a gas grill to medium. Clean the grate and coat it with vegetable oil. Scatter the soaked wood chips over the charcoal when they are hot.

7. Shake the excess marinade from the skewers and grill over the hot coals. Turn them over regularly to cook evenly, 2 to 3 minutes per side, or until the beef is cooked to your preferred doneness.

8. Serve the meat and vegetables hot off the grill, either still on the skewer, or carefully slide the meat and vegetables onto a warmed plate.

Serves 4

Use different vegetables if you wish; just make sure that they can stand up to the grill for as long as it takes to cook the beef. Mushrooms, fennel, and carrots are all hardy choices.

OUTBACK STEAKHOUSE
Wood-Fire Grilled Salmon

THICK SALMON FILLETS ARE COATED WITH OUTBACK'S SPECIAL BLEND OF FLA-VORFUL INGREDIENTS. GRILLING THE SALMON OVER AN OAK WOOD FIRE GIVES IT THE SMOKY FLAVOR CUSTOMERS LOVE, AND OUTBACK'S VERSION OF TARTAR SAUCE GETS MANY REQUESTS FOR EXTRA TO TAKE HOME.

Tartar Sauce
¾ cup sour cream
¼ cup mayonnaise
2 tablespoons prepared
  horseradish
2 tablespoons finely chopped
  fresh basil
1 tablespoon lemon juice
1 teaspoon soy sauce
½ teaspoon kosher salt
¼ teaspoon ground white pepper

3 tablespoons mayonnaise
1 tablespoon prepared
  horseradish
1 tablespoon soy sauce
1 clove garlic, minced
½ teaspoon kosher salt
¼ teaspoon pepper
Oak wood chips, soaked in water
6 center-cut salmon fillets

1. Do ahead: Make the Tartar Sauce a day ahead to give the flavors a chance to combine. Whisk the sour cream and mayonnaise until creamy, then whisk in the remaining ingredients. Refrigerate in a covered container until ready to use.

2. Light a charcoal barbecue or heat a gas grill to medium. Clean the grate and coat it with vegetable oil.

3. Whisk together the mayonnaise, horseradish, soy sauce, garlic, salt, and pepper.

4. Sprinkle the wood chips around the red hot coals. Brush each salmon fillet with the seasoned coating and place them, seasoned side down, on the grill. Cook the fillets 4 to 5 minutes per side, turning once, or until

the center of the fillet has just lost its translucency. Overcooking salmon will make it dry. Use a wide, flexible spatula to turn the fish over.

5.   Serve the salmon with the Tartar Sauce on the side.

Serves 6

A fresh vegetable medley and a crisp glass of wine provide a perfect contrast to the richness of the salmon and the spice of the tartar sauce.

PANDA EXPRESS
Mandarin Chicken

THIS RESTAURANT CHAIN HAS ALL THE TRADITIONAL CHINESE RESTAURANT FAVORITES IN A SPEEDY TO-GO OPERATION. MANDARIN CHICKEN IS OFTEN AT THE TOP OF LOYAL CUSTOMERS' LISTS.

Mandarin Sauce
¼ cup light soy sauce
1 cup dark brown sugar
2 tablespoons orange juice
   concentrate
4 cloves garlic, minced
1-inch piece ginger, peeled and
   minced

¼ cup water
2 tablespoons cornstarch

1 pound boneless skinless
   chicken thighs
Rice or vegetables, for serving,
   optional

1. Do ahead: To prepare the Mandarin Sauce, whisk together the soy sauce and brown sugar in a small saucepan, until the sugar is dissolved. Stir in the orange juice, garlic, and ginger and bring the sauce to a boil. Lower the heat and simmer 2 minutes. In a separate bowl, combine the water and cornstarch to make a paste. Raise the heat under the saucepan and whisk in the paste. Stir until the sauce thickens, then let it cool completely before marinating the chicken.

2. Do ahead: Pour half the cooled sauce over the chicken thighs. Cover and refrigerate at least 1 hour.

3. Light a charcoal barbecue or heat a gas grill to medium. Clean the grate and coat it with vegetable oil.

4. Shake the excess sauce off the thighs and grill them 7 to 8 minutes per side, turning once, or until cooked through and no longer pink in the center. Thighs are more dense than breasts and will take longer to cook.

5. Set the cooked thighs aside and let them rest for 10 minutes. Once rested, cut them into long strips.

6. Reheat the remaining Mandarin Sauce over a low flame. Arrange the cooked thighs over a bowl of rice or vegetables, if desired, and cover with the warmed Mandarin Sauce. Serve hot.

Serves 4

A simple sprinkling of sesame seeds and thinly sliced green onion would take this dish up a notch.

PANERA BREAD
Asian Sesame Chicken Salad

NOT EVERYTHING AT PANERA COMES IN A SANDWICH. THEY ALSO ARE WELL KNOWN FOR THE CRISP INGREDIENTS AND TEMPTING FLAVORS OF THEIR ASIAN CHICKEN SALAD.

Salad Dressing
½ cup rice wine vinegar
¼ cup light brown sugar
2 tablespoons olive oil
½ teaspoon toasted sesame oil
½ teaspoon kosher salt
¼ teaspoon pepper
½ teaspoon white sesame seeds

Chicken Marinade
3 tablespoons light soy sauce
2 teaspoons light brown sugar
½ teaspoon toasted sesame oil
1 teaspoon powdered ginger
1 teaspoon granulated garlic

4 (4-ounce) boneless skinless
　chicken breasts
1 (12-ounce) bag baby spinach
　leaves
1 (12-ounce) bag romaine,
　chopped
¼ cup Chicken Marinade
1 cup Salad Dressing
Salad Toppings, optional

Salad Toppings
1 tablespoon chopped cilantro
¼ cup Mandarin orange segments
¼ cup slivered almonds
½ cup fried wonton strips
½ cup crispy fried rice noodles
1 tablespoon white sesame seeds

1. Do ahead: To make the Salad Dressing, combine the vinegar and brown sugar in a small saucepan and stir over low heat until the sugar is dissolved. When it has cooled, stir in the remaining ingredients. Refrigerate in a covered container until ready to use.

2. Do ahead: Whisk together the ingredients for the Chicken Marinade, making sure the sugar is dissolved. Add the chicken breasts, cover, and refrigerate until ready to use, not longer than an hour.

3. Light a charcoal barbecue or heat a gas grill to medium. Clean the grate and coat it with vegetable oil.

4. Shake the excess marinade from the chicken and grill 5 to 6 minutes per side, turning once, or until cooked through and no longer pink in the center. Let the chicken rest 10 minutes, then slice into thin strips.

5. To assemble the salad, combine the spinach and romaine and place a portion of the greens on chilled plates.

6. Arrange the cooked chicken slices over each portion of greens and drizzle with the Salad Dressing.

7. Finish each salad with your choice of toppings from the list suggested or your own favorites.

Serves 4

Toasted sesame oil can be found in the Asian food aisle of larger markets and at specialty food stores.

PANERA BREAD
Bistro Steak Salad

GRILL THE STEAK OF YOUR CHOICE—SIRLOIN OR A NEW YORK STRIP WOULD BE
A WINNER.

1 (10-ounce) beef steak
1 teaspoon kosher salt
½ teaspoon pepper
2 cups baby mixed greens
2 cups romaine, torn into
   bite-sized pieces

¼ cup balsamic vinaigrette
¼ cup chopped walnuts
2 tablespoons crumbled
   Gorgonzola cheese

1. Light a charcoal barbecue or heat a gas grill to medium. Clean the grate and coat it with vegetable oil.

2. Season both sides of the steak with the salt and pepper. Grill 4 to 5 minutes per side, turning once, or until cooked to your preferred doneness. Let the steak rest 10 minutes, then slice against the grain into thin strips.

3. Combine the baby mixed greens with the romaine and toss with the balsamic dressing. Portion the greens onto chilled plates, then arrange the strips of steak around each mound of greens.

4. Sprinkle the walnuts and the Gorgonzola into the salad. Serve with extra dressing on the side.

Serves 2

This is a great way to use leftover steak. Heat it up gently so that it just warms through.

PANERA BREAD

Coffee Steak Sandwich on Texas Toast

DEEP, RICH COFFEE IS A SURPRISING COMPLIMENT TO CHILIES AND PEPPERS. CHOOSE THE DARKEST ESPRESSO OR FRENCH ROAST FOR THIS RECIPE.

2 tablespoons finely ground espresso instant coffee granules
1 teaspoon New Mexico chili powder
½ teaspoon cumin
½ teaspoon brown sugar
1 ½ teaspoon kosher salt
½ teaspoon pepper

1 pound flank steak
1 large avocado, pitted
¼ cup sour cream
8 thick slices whole grain bread, toasted
4 thick slices tomato
4 leaves romaine lettuce, torn into bite-sized pieces

1. Whisk together the coffee granules, chili powder, cumin, sugar, ½ teaspoon salt, and ¼ teaspoon pepper. Season both sides of the flank steak, wrap in plastic, and refrigerate for at least 1 hour.

2. Light a charcoal barbecue or heat a gas grill to medium. Clean the grate and coat it with vegetable oil.

3. Unwrap the flank steak and grill for 5 to 6 minutes per side, turning once, or until cooked to your preferred doneness. Let the meat rest 10 to 15 minutes, then slice it against the grain in very thin strips.

4. In a small bowl, mash the avocado with a fork and combine it with the sour cream. Whisk in the remaining salt and pepper and set aside.

5. Clean the grill with a wire brush and toast the slices of bread on both sides, taking care to not let them burn.

6. Spread the creamy avocado mixture on each slice of toast, then top with slices of flank steak. Place a slice of tomato on top of the meat and cover with romaine pieces.

7. Finish the sandwich with the remaining piece of toasted bread and slice in half diagonally.

Serves 4

Make a larger batch of the coffee spice rub and store in an airtight container. Use it on ribs and burgers as well as steak.

PANERA BREAD
Frontega Chicken Panini

PANERA USES A PANINI PRESS TO MAKE THESE GRILLED CHICKEN AND CHIPOTLE MAYONNAISE SANDWICHES. ACHIEVE SIMILAR RESULTS ON YOUR GRILL BY PRESSING THE ASSEMBLED SANDWICH DOWN UNTIL MARKS FROM THE HOT GRILL CHAR THEIR WAY INTO THE FOCACCIA.

Chipotle Mayonnaise
½ cup mayonnaise, regular or
   reduced calorie
2 chipotle peppers, mashed
1 tablespoon adobo sauce, from
   canned chipotle pepper
½ teaspoon dried basil
½ teaspoon dried rosemary

2 (8-ounce) boneless skinless
   chicken breasts
½ teaspoon kosher salt
¼ teaspoon pepper
1 (8-inch) round focaccia
1 small red onion, thinly sliced
4 slices mozzarella cheese,
   regular or part skim

1. Do ahead: Make the Chipotle Mayonnaise a day ahead of time, so the flavors have time to combine. In a food processor, mix the mayonnaise, chipotles, and adobo sauce. Pulse until the mixture is completely blended and smooth. Add the dried herbs and pulse until blended. Refrigerate in a covered container until ready to use.

2. Light a charcoal barbecue or heat a gas grill to medium. Clean the grate and coat it with vegetable oil.

3. Season the chicken breast with the salt and pepper and grill 6 to 7 minutes per side, turning once, until the chicken is cooked through and no longer pink in the center. Let the chicken rest 10 minutes, then cut it into thin slices.

4. Cut the focaccia in half, so that there is a top and bottom for the sandwich. Spread the bottom half liberally with the Chipotle Mayonnaise and layer it with the sliced chicken. Arrange the sliced onions on top of the chicken, then shingle the slices of mozzarella over the onions. Finish the sandwich by spreading the top half of the focaccia with the Chipotle Mayonnaise and laying it on top.

5. Carefully move the assembled sandwich to the grill and grill the bottom side. Press down evenly with your hands or with the bottom of a clean frying pan. When the bottom is toasted, carefully turn the sandwich over and repeat the process.

6. Move the grilled sandwich to a clean surface and cut into quarters. Serve warm.

Serves 4

A crisp salad is all that's needed to make this the perfect lunch. Focaccia are available at bakeries and larger markets. They usually come seasoned and often have tomatoes or olives baked in.

PANERA BREAD
Greek Grilled Chicken Salad

FETA CHEESE MAKES IT GREEK. FRESH VEGETABLES AND HERBS MAKE IT DELI-CIOUS.

3 tablespoons red wine vinegar
¼ cup olive oil
1 teaspoon chopped fresh oregano
1 large clove garlic, minced
2 (8-ounce) boneless skinless chicken breasts
1 teaspoon kosher salt
¼ teaspoon pepper

Salad Mixture
1 (10-ounce) bag romaine, torn in bite-sized pieces
1 cup halved cherry tomatoes
1 small cucumber, peeled, quartered, and sliced
½ small red onion, thinly sliced
¼ cup sliced, pitted Kalamata olives

½ cup crumbled Feta cheese
1 lemon, quartered

1. Light a charcoal barbecue or heat a gas grill to medium. Clean the grate and coat it with vegetable oil.

2. Whisk together the vinegar, olive oil, oregano, and garlic in a medium bowl and set aside.

3. Season the chicken with the salt and pepper and grill 6 to 7 minutes per side, turning once, until it is cooked through and no longer pink in the center.

4. Immediately place the grilled chicken in the vinaigrette and turn a few times to evenly coat. Let the chicken rest the vinaigrette for about 5 minutes, then slice it in thin pieces. Return the pieces to the bowl for a few minutes, then remove to a plate.

5. For the Salad Mixture, combine the lettuce, tomatoes, cucumber, onion, and olives in the bowl with the vinaigrette. Toss well and portion the mixture onto chilled plates.

6. Arrange the sliced chicken over the salads and scatter the crumbled Feta cheese over the top. Garnish each salad with a lemon wedge.

Serves 4

Make a little extra of the vinaigrette if you would like to serve more dressing on the side.

PANERA BREAD
Grilled Flank Steak with Pickled Onion

PICKLED ONIONS SOUND LIKE AN UNUSUAL CHOICE FOR THIS SANDWICH, BUT
THEY DEVELOP A BIT OF DEPTH WHEN FIRST SAUTÉED IN OLIVE OIL.

1 pound flank steak
1 teaspoon kosher salt
½ teaspoon pepper
2 tablespoons extra virgin olive oil

Pickled Onions
1 large red onion, sliced thin
2 tablespoons olive oil
½ teaspoon kosher salt
¼ teaspoon pepper
½ cup apple cider vinegar

2 tablespoons sugar

Horseradish Aioli
½ cup mayonnaise
1 tablespoon smoked paprika
1 teaspoon prepared horseradish
½ teaspoon kosher salt
¼ teaspoon pepper

8 slices Italian bread
2 cups arugula

1. Do ahead: Season the flank steak with the salt and pepper. Rub both sides with olive oil, then wrap in plastic wrap and refrigerate overnight.

2. Do ahead: To make the Pickled Onions, sauté the red onion in the olive oil until limp and lightly brown. Season them with the salt and pepper, then add the vinegar and sugar. Bring the pot to a boil, then take it off the heat and let cool. Drain them and set aside once cooled.

3. Do ahead: Make the Horseradish Aioli 30 minutes ahead of time to let the flavors meld. Whisk together the mayonnaise with the paprika, horseradish, salt, and pepper. Refrigerate, covered, until ready to use.

4. Light a charcoal barbecue or heat a gas grill to medium. Clean the grate and coat it with vegetable oil.

5. Grill the flank steak 5 to 6 minutes per side, turning once, or until cooked to your preferred doneness. Let the meat rest 10 to 15 minutes before carving against the grain into thin slices.

6. Grill the slices of Italian bread on both sides until toasted, taking care to not let it burn.

7. To assemble the sandwiches, spread the Horseradish Aioli on 4 pieces of bread. Arrange the sliced steak on top, then cover with the pickled onions and arugula. Finish the sandwich with the remaining toast and slice in half. Serve warm.

Serves 4

Arugula can have a bitter taste. Replace it with green leaf lettuce or shredded iceberg, if you wish.

PANERA BREAD
Grilled Muffuletta Sandwich

THE MUFFULETTA SANDWICH AT PANERA IS A CONTEMPORARY VERSION OF THE NEW ORLEANS CLASSIC. BUY A FOCACCIA AND LAYER ON THE ITALIAN MEATS AND CHEESE. TOAST IT OVER HOT COALS UNTIL THE CHEESE MELTS AND SERVE IT HOT.

1 (8-inch) round focaccia
½ cup oil-packed sun-dried tomatoes
4 slices smoked provolone cheese, halved

2½ cups Muffuletta or olive salad
¼ pound mortadella, sliced thin
¼ pound Genoa salami, sliced thin
¼ pound baked ham, sliced thin

1. Slice the focaccia in half to make a sandwich. Drain the oil from the sun-dried tomatoes and brush both cut sides of the bread with the oil. Slice the tomatoes into thin pieces.

2. Layer the bottom piece of bread with half the provolone slices. Spread with half the Muffuletta salad, then place all of the mortadella, salami, and ham over the salad. Sprinkle with the sun-dried tomatoes, and finish with the remaining Muffuletta salad and a final layer of cheese. Cover with the top piece of bread.

3. Wrap the sandwich in foil and compress it with a frying pan filled with some heavy canned goods. Let the sandwich set for 30 minutes.

4. Light a charcoal barbecue or heat a gas grill to medium low. Clean the grate and coat it with vegetable oil.

5. Move the foil wrapped sandwich to the grill and weight it down as before, turning once, until the cheese is melted and the sandwich is heated through.

6. Cut the sandwich in halves or quarters and serve hot.

Serves 2 to 4

A foil wrapped brick makes an excellent sandwich press. Just make sure it is as long as the sandwich.

PANERA BREAD
Grilled Vegetable Panini

PANERA USES THEIR OWN THREE CHEESE BREAD FOR THIS SANDWICH OF GRILLED
VEGETABLES, PESTO, AND CHEESE. YOU CAN FIND A SIMILAR BREAD IN THE DELI
SECTION OF LARGE MARKETS OR AT SPECIALTY FOOD STORES. A LOAF OF FRENCH
OR ITALIAN BREAD WOULD ALSO WORK WELL.

1 loaf cheese bread or other
  bread
½ cup pesto
1 cup shredded mozzarella
1 Japanese eggplant, sliced
  diagonally ¼-inch thick
2 small red bell peppers, seeded
  and quartered lengthwise

2 medium zucchini, sliced
  lengthwise in ¼-inch strips
½ small red onion, sliced thin
1 teaspoon kosher salt
½ teaspoon pepper
2 tablespoons julienned oil-
  packed sun-dried tomatoes

1. Light a charcoal barbecue or heat a gas grill to medium. Clean the grate
   and coat it with vegetable oil.

2. Cut 6 ½-inch oval slices from the center of the bread. Spread 3 slices
   with the pesto, and top the other 3 with the mozzarella.

3. Season the vegetables with salt and pepper. Grill the eggplant, bell peppers, zucchini, and onion until just tender and lightly charred.

4. Arrange the vegetables over the cheese, trimming them to fit, if necessary,
   and top with the sun-dried tomatoes. Top with the bread with pesto.

5. Put the sandwiches on the grill and toast both sides, turning carefully
   and pressing down with a weight, such as a fry pan.

6. Cut sandwiches in half and serve hot.

Serves 3 to 6

*Use a panini press for making these sandwiches individually. If
using a grill or barbecue, it might be easier to use slices of
mozzarella rather than shredded for a neater sandwich.*

PANERA BREAD
Lemon Rosemary Lamb Steaks

LAMB WITH ROSEMARY AND GARLIC IS A CLASSIC PAIRING. THE LEMON JUICE AND ZEST IN THE MARINADE BRIGHTENS THE HERBS AND GIVES THE LAMB A HINT OF CITRUS TO GO WITH THE FRESH MINT.

2 (2-inch) sprigs rosemary
4 (8-ounce) bone-in lamb steaks
1½ teaspoons kosher salt
½ teaspoon pepper
2 tablespoons lemon juice

¼ teaspoon smoked paprika
1 tablespoon lemon zest
½ cup olive oil
4 thick slices Italian bread
1 tablespoon chopped fresh mint

1. Chop 1 sprig of rosemary, leaving the other whole. Season the lamb steaks with salt and pepper and rub the chopped rosemary into both sides of each steak.

2. Put the lamb into a large resealable plastic bag with the whole piece of rosemary.

3. Whisk the lemon juice with the paprika, lemon zest, and olive oil. Pour the marinade over the lamb and refrigerate, 2 to 8 hours.

4. Light a charcoal barbecue or heat a gas grill to medium. Clean the grate and coat it with vegetable oil.

5. Grill the lamb steaks 3 to 4 minutes per side, turning once, or until cooked to your preferred doneness. Let the lamb rest for 10 minutes.

6. Drizzle a little of the marinade over the slices of bread and add them to the grill. Toast the bread lightly, taking care to not let it burn.

7. Drizzle a little marinade over the lamb and scatter with the mint. Serve the lamb steaks with the grilled bread on the side.

Serves 4

Lamb should be served medium rare in most cases. It gets tough and dry when cooked beyond medium.

PANERA BREAD

Mojito Pork Tenderloin with Mojo Sauce

THE ZESTY MARINADE GIVES THESE PORK TENDERLOINS A CRUSTY CHAR WHEN
GRILLED OVER HOT COALS. LIME JUICE AND MINT COMPLETE THE MOJITO MIX,
AND THE GARLIC AND SPICES BALANCE IT ALL.

2 pork tenderloins, membrane
and silverskin trimmed

6 slices French bread, sliced
½-inch thick

Mojito Marinade

1 tablespoon kosher salt

2 tablespoons dark brown sugar

1 cup hot water

2 tablespoons spiced rum, such
as Captain Morgan's

2 tablespoons lime juice

1 tablespoon lime zest

½ tablespoon chopped fresh
mint

2 cloves garlic, minced

Pork Seasoning

1 tablespoon lime zest

1 tablespoon smoked paprika

½ teaspoon cumin

½ teaspoon pepper

Pork Sauce

¼ cup olive oil

1 clove garlic, minced

2 tablespoons lime juice

1 tablespoon lime zest

2 tablespoons orange juice
concentrate

½ teaspoon dried oregano

½ teaspoon cumin

1 teaspoon kosher salt

¼ teaspoon pepper

½ tablespoon chopped fresh
mint

1. Prepare the Pork Seasoning by combining all the ingredients in one
   bowl.

2. Do ahead: To prepare the Mojito Marinade, whisk the salt and brown
   sugar with the hot water until dissolved. Combine the mixture with the
   rum, lime juice, lime zest, mint, and garlic. Pour the marinade into a
   large resealable plastic bag and let cool.

3. Do ahead: Put the tenderloins into the marinade, push the air out of the bag, and seal. Refrigerate for 3 to 4 hours.

4. Light a charcoal barbecue or heat a gas grill to medium. Clean the grate and coat it with vegetable oil.

5. Shake the excess marinade off the tenderloins and pat them dry. Season the meat with the Pork Seasoning, rubbing it in well.

6. Grill the tenderloins 4 to 5 minutes per side, turning once, until cooked through and no longer pink in the center. Let the meat rest 10 minutes, while making the Pork Sauce.

7. To prepare the Pork Sauce, heat the olive oil in a small saucepan and add the garlic. Let the garlic simmer for about 5 minutes, then take the pan off the heat.

8. Whisk in the lime juice, lime zest, orange juice concentrate, oregano, cumin, salt, pepper, and mint.

9. Slice the pork into medallions and spoon the sauce over the top. Serve with the French bread.

Serves 6

You may want to spread a little of the sauce over the bread and toast the slices while the grill is still hot.

PANERA BREAD
Pesto Chicken Sandwich with Arugula

THIS IS A BASIC GRILLED CHICKEN SANDWICH THAT GOES FROM PLAIN TO ELEGANT WITH SOME SIMPLE INGREDIENTS. FRESH BAKERY BREAD, BASIL PESTO, AND BABY ARUGULA ARE COMBINED FOR A RICHLY SATISFYING SANDWICH THAT'S AS INVITING IN PRESENTATION AS IT IS DELICIOUS.

2 (8-ounce) boneless skinless chicken breasts
1 teaspoon kosher salt
½ teaspoon pepper
½ cup pesto, purchased or your own
1 large ciabatta or French bread loaf

2 ounces domestic goat cheese (chevre), crumbled
2 green onions, minced green part only
¾ cup roasted red peppers
1 cup baby arugula leaves

1. Light a charcoal barbecue or heat a gas grill to medium. Clean the grate and coat it with vegetable oil.

2. Pound the chicken between 2 pieces of plastic wrap until about ¼-inch thick. Season the chicken with the salt and pepper and grill, 4 to 5 minutes per side, turning once, or until cooked through and no longer pink in the center. Set it aside to rest for 10 minutes, then spread some of the pesto over each piece.

3. Slice the ciabatta in half lengthwise evenly through the middle. Grill the bread cut side down, until lightly charred and toasted, taking care to not let it burn.

4. Spread the remaining pesto on the toasted sides of the bread. Sprinkle the goat cheese on the bottom piece and layer with the green onion, roasted red peppers, and arugula leaves.

5. Arrange the cooked chicken over the arugula, cutting the breasts, if necessary, to make them fit.

6. Finish with the top half of the bread and cut into even quarters. Serve hot.

Serves 2

Roasted red peppers can be found in most markets. Look for a jar with whole peppers rather than chopped pieces. They will have retained a better texture during the packing process.

PANERA BREAD
Scallop Stuffed Tomatoes

THIS IS A BEAUTIFUL DISH, SURE TO IMPRESS SPECIAL GUESTS. SELECT EVENLY SIZED DRY-PACKED JUMBO SEA SCALLOPS. BRINED SCALLOPS SHRINK RAPIDLY WHEN COOKED.

8 jumbo sea scallops
¼ cup pesto
¼ cup (½ stick) unsalted butter, divided
2 tablespoons lemon juice
1 teaspoon kosher salt
¼ teaspoon pepper

1 green onion, minced
8 vine-ripened tomatoes, hollowed out
½ cup fresh bread crumbs
2 tablespoons Parmesan cheese
4 leaves green leaf lettuce

1. Toss the scallops with the pesto and refrigerate.

2. Melt half the butter in a medium skillet and swirl over high heat, until it just starts to turn brown. Stir in the lemon juice, salt, pepper, and green onion. Heat the mixture through, then brush it on the insides of the tomatoes, coating them well.

3. Return the skillet to the heat and melt the remaining butter. Add the bread crumbs and stir until they are golden brown. Remove the pan from the heat and stir in the cheese. Set the pan aside.

4. Light a charcoal barbecue or heat a gas grill to medium. Clean the grate and coat it with vegetable oil.

5. Grill the scallops for 3 to 4 minutes per side, turning once, just until they lose their translucency. Put 1 scallop in each of the prepared tomatoes and pack it with the sautéed bread crumb and cheese mixture.

6. Put the tomatoes on the grill and heat through, closing the lid. Grill the tomatoes 1 to 2 minutes, then place 2 tomatoes per person on the leaves of lettuce.

7. Serve warm.

Serves 4 as an entrée, or 8 as an appetizer.

PANERA BREAD
Swordfish with Saffron Garlic Sauce

SAFFRON IS AN EXCEPTIONAL INGREDIENT THAT IS TOO COSTLY FOR EVERYDAY USE BUT, WITHOUT ITS UNIQUE ESSENCE, THE CREAMY AIOLI MADE TO GO WITH THE SWORDFISH WOULD BE UNREMARKABLE. IT'S TIME TO SPLURGE—YOU'LL HAVE ENOUGH TO USE IN OTHER RECIPES.

Saffron Aioli
1 (.07 ounce) package saffron threads
1 tablespoon hot water
½ cup fresh white bread crumbs
1 tablespoon chopped fresh parsley
2 large cloves garlic, minced
1 teaspoon smoked paprika
½ teaspoon fine sea salt
¼ teaspoon cayenne pepper, optional
1 tablespoon roasted red pepper paste
1 large egg yolk
¾ cup extra virgin olive oil

4 (8-ounce) swordfish steaks
1 teaspoon kosher salt
¼ teaspoon pepper
1 large lemon, quartered

1. Do ahead: To make the Saffron Aioli, soak the saffron threads in water until dissolved. In the bowl of a food processor, combine the bread crumbs, parsley, garlic, paprika, salt, and cayenne, if desired. Process until the crumbs are finely ground and the mixture is well blended. In a small cup, blend the pepper paste with the saffron water and add to the mixture. Process until it is absorbed. Add the egg yolk and process; then, with the motor running, add the olive oil in a thin stream until the mixture is the consistency of mayonnaise. Store the aioli in a covered container and refrigerate for up to 2 days before using it.

2. Light a charcoal barbecue or heat a gas grill to medium. Clean the grate and coat it with vegetable oil.

3. Season the swordfish with the salt and pepper. Grill the fish 4 to 5 minutes per side, turning once, or until it is just barely cooked through. You

can pull it off the grill while still a little translucent in the center and the fish will continue to cook. Let the fish rest for 5 minutes before serving.

4. Place the fish on warmed plates and serve with a wedge of lemon and a dollop of the Saffron Aioli. Serve the remaining sauce on the side.

Serves 4

If swordfish is unavailable at your local market, salmon is a great alternative.

PANERA BREAD
Turkey and Smoked Provolone Panini

SMOKED CHEESES ARE MORE POPULAR TODAY THAN EVER BEFORE. DELI CASES FEATURE SELECTIONS OF MOZZARELLA, GOUDA, HAVARTI, CHEDDAR, AND EMMANTALER IN REGULAR AND SMOKED STYLES. TRY SMOKED PROVOLONE AND SMOKED TURKEY IN THIS SANDWICH WITH TOASTED FOCACCIA AND RIPE TOMATOES.

1 (8-inch) focaccia, plain or with cheese

2 tablespoons olive oil

4 tablespoons mayonnaise, regular or reduced calorie

2 tablespoons Gray Poupon, or other Dijon mustard

½ pound smoked turkey breast, sliced thin

¼ pound smoked provolone, sliced thin

1 large tomato, sliced thin

1 cup baby spinach leaves

1. Light a charcoal barbecue or heat a gas grill to medium. Clean the grate and coat it with vegetable oil.

2. Slice the focaccia through the center crosswise, so you have 2 large rounds. Spread each half with a tablespoon of olive oil and grill until lightly charred and toasted, taking care not to let the bread burn.

3. Whisk together the mayonnaise and mustard. Spread the mixture over the grilled side of the top piece of bread. On the bottom half, layer the sliced turkey, cheese, tomato slices, and spinach.

4. Close the sandwich with the top half of the focaccia and place the whole sandwich on the grill. Press down with your hands or with the bottom of a clean frying pan.

5. When the bottom of the bread is grilled, turn the panini over and grill the top half, again weighted.

6. Move the finished panini to a work surface and cut into quarters. Serve hot.

Serves 4

If you can't find a large round focaccia, try a large ciabatta or French bread.

PANERA BREAD
Turkey Apple Burgers

A FEW SPOONS OF APPLE BUTTER GIVE THESE TURKEY BURGERS A HINT OF SWEET-
NESS. APPLES HAVE LONG BEEN USED IN SAUSAGES AND WITH CHICKEN; TURKEY
BURGERS ARE A LOGICAL NEXT STEP. TOP THEM WITH YOUR FAVORITE CONDI-
MENTS AND A SLICE OF SHARP CHEDDAR.

1½ pounds ground turkey
½ cup fresh bread crumbs
¼ cup apple butter
2 tablespoons ketchup or chili sauce
½ small yellow onion, very finely minced
1 tablespoon finely minced fresh parsley

1½ teaspoons kosher salt
½ teaspoon ground white pepper
8 thick slices cheese bread

Toppings
Thick tomato slices
Red onion, sliced ¼-inch thick
Dill pickle chips
Iceberg lettuce
Cheddar or pepper Jack cheese

1. Combine the ground turkey with the remaining burger ingredients, except the cheese bread, and work with your hands until well blended. Shape the mixture into 4 equal balls.

2. Cut 4 small pieces of waxed paper and put a ball on each piece. Gently press the ball into a burger about the same size as a hamburger bun.

3. Put all the patties on a plate and refrigerate at least 30 minutes before grilling.

4. Light a charcoal barbecue or heat a gas grill to medium. Clean the grate and coat it with vegetable oil.

5. Grill the turkey burgers 5 to 6 minutes per side, turning once, or until cooked through and no longer pink in the center. Set them aside.

6. Grill the slices of cheese bread and serve the turkey burgers between 2 pieces of toasted bread, or build a sandwich with the toppings suggested or your own favorites.

Panera uses their Three Cheese Bread for these turkey burgers. You can use any other bread, or hamburger buns, with these burgers. Toast the buns as you would the cheese bread and spread them with a sauce, if you prefer.

Despite its name, there is no butter in apple butter. If you don't want to buy a whole jar just for this recipe, you can make a quick version on your own. Peel, core, and slice a small apple. Simmer it for 20 minutes with ½ cup applesauce. Season with cinnamon and nutmeg, if you like. Mash the sliced apples with a fork and blend with the applesauce. When the mixture is cool, mix it with the ground turkey.

PANERA BREAD
Turkey Artichoke Panini

MAKE GOOD USE OF PURCHASED ITEMS FOR THIS GRILLED SANDWICH. GET FRESH ROASTED TURKEY FROM THE DELI, AS WELL AS A ROUND FOCACCIA.

1 (8-inch) focaccia, plain or with pesto	1 tablespoon red wine vinegar
	½ cup spinach artichoke spread
1 small red onion, sliced ¼-inch thick	½ pound turkey, sliced thin
	4 slices Asiago cheese
1 tablespoon extra virgin olive oil	1 large tomato, sliced thin

1. Light a charcoal barbecue or heat a gas grill to medium. Clean the grate and coat it with vegetable oil.

2. Slice the focaccia in half lengthwise through the center, so that you have a top and bottom half.

3. Heat a medium skillet and sauté the red onion with the olive oil and vinegar until the onion is soft. Set the skillet aside.

4. Grill the cut side of the top and bottom of the focaccia, then coat each piece with half the spinach artichoke spread.

5. Layer the sliced turkey on the bottom half and cover with the remaining spinach artichoke mixture. Arrange the sautéed onion on top, then follow with the Asiago cheese and the sliced tomato. Finish with the focaccia top.

6. Move the sandwich to the grill and weight it with the bottom of a clean frying pan. When the bottom is toasted and the cheese begins to melt, carefully turn the sandwich over and grill the top side. Bring the panini to a work surface and cut it into quarters. Serve hot.

Serves 4

Save the oil and vinegar from the sautéed onions to drizzle over the turkey for a little extra flavor.

PANERA BREAD
Turkey Cranberry Panini

A NEW ANSWER TO AN OLD QUESTION: WHAT TO DO WITH THANKSGIVING LEFT-OVERS? A HOT GRILLED PANINI WITH ROASTED TURKEY, CRANBERRY SAUCE, AND PECANS. THIN SLICES OF BRIE ADD A CREAMY TOUCH.

4 thick slices of bread, such as sourdough

½ cup cranberry sauce, whole or jellied style

¼ cup chopped pecans

¼ pound brie, cut into long pieces, with rind left on

1½ cups roasted turkey meat, light or dark, or combined

2 green onions, green part only, chopped

1 tablespoon Gray Poupon, or other Dijon mustard

1. Light a charcoal barbecue or heat a gas grill to medium. Clean the grate and coat it with vegetable oil.

2. Grill the bread on one side only, until lightly toasted.

3. Mix the cranberry sauce and pecans.

4. Place 2 pieces of the bread, grilled side up on a work surface. Layer the brie over the toasted side, then arrange the cranberry and nut sauce, turkey, and chopped green onion on top.

5. Spread the mustard on the grilled side of the remaining bread and top off the sandwich.

6. Move the sandwiches to the grill and weight them with the bottom of a clean frying pan. When the bottom is grilled, carefully turn the sandwiches over and grill the other side.

7. Return to the work surface and cut in half diagonally. Serve hot.

Serves 2

Other bread choices might be focaccia, or the Three Cheese Loaf available from your local Panera Bread restaurant.

P.F. CHANG'S
BBQ Sauce

THIS LUSCIOUS SAUCE IS A STARTLING COMBINATION OF THE SWEET AND SPICY
FLAVORS SO OFTEN FOUND IN ASIAN CUISINES. HOISIN SAUCE AND SAKE ARE THE
ONLY COMPONENTS YOU MAY NEED TO SEARCH FOR. LARGER SUPERMARKETS OR
SPECIALTY FOOD SHOPS SHOULD HAVE A NUMBER OF CHOICES AVAILABLE.

1 ½ cups golden brown sugar
¼ cup water
¼ cup sake or dry vermouth
3 cups ketchup or chili sauce
¼ cup hoisin sauce

1-inch piece fresh ginger, peeled
and minced
2 large cloves garlic, minced
2 teaspoons Chinese five spice
powder
1 teaspoon ground star anise

1. Whisk together the sugar, water, and sake until the sugar is dissolved.
2. Whisk in the ketchup, hoisin sauce, ginger, garlic, five spice powder, and anise.
3. When thoroughly blended, refrigerate in an airtight container until ready to use.

Makes about 5 cups

Use this on ribs and chops, or on short ribs, as P.F. Chang's does.

P.F. CHANG'S
Shanghai Noodles with Grilled Rib Eye and Broccoli

SHANGHAI NOODLES ARE AVAILABLE EITHER FRESH OR DRIED—YOU CAN USE EITHER IN THIS RECIPE. IF YOU CAN'T FIND THESE CHEWY NOODLES, TRY FRESH OR FROZEN UDON NOODLES, WHICH ARE GENERALLY USED IN JAPANESE CUISINE.

Noodle Sauce
1 cup hoisin sauce
¼ cup orange juice concentrate
¼ cup light soy sauce

Rib Eye Marinade
2 large cloves garlic, minced
1-inch piece fresh ginger, peeled and minced
½ teaspoon red pepper flakes

1 pound Shanghai noodles, cooked according to package directions

2 tablespoons sesame oil
4 (8-ounce) boneless rib eye steaks
2 teaspoons kosher salt
1 teaspoon pepper
1 large sweet onion, sliced
2 large cloves garlic, minced
1-inch piece fresh ginger, peeled and minced
½ teaspoon red pepper flakes
¼ cup mirin or sweet sherry
2 cups broccoli florets, blanched
¼ cup (½ stick) unsalted butter

1. Do ahead: Prepare the Noodle Sauce by combining all the ingredients in a small bowl. Set aside.

2. Do ahead: Whisk together the ingredients for the Rib Eye Marinade. Rub the mixture over the steaks, then refrigerate for at least 2 hours.

3. Heat through the Shanghai noodles, then drain. Lay them out on a sheet pan and coat them with 1 tablespoon of the sesame oil. Set aside.

4. Light a charcoal barbecue or heat a gas grill to medium. Clean the grate and coat it with vegetable oil.

5. Season the steaks with the salt and pepper and grill them 4 to 5 minutes per side, turning once, or until cooked to your preferred doneness. Let the meat rest for 10 to 15 minutes, then cut into thin strips. Set aside.

6. Heat the remaining tablespoon of sesame oil in a large skillet and sauté the sliced onion. When soft, add the garlic, ginger, and red pepper flakes. Stir in the mirin and reduce by half.

7. Stir in the Noodle Sauce and heat through, about 3 minutes. Add the cooked noodles and simmer for 4 minutes.

8. Add the broccoli, then whisk in the butter.

9. When the butter has melted, portion the noodles onto heated plates. Top with the strips of grilled rib eye and serve hot.

Serves 4

Other steaks, such as New York Strip or top sirloin, would also work well with this recipe. Mirin is a sweet cooking wine that does have some alcohol. Cook the alcohol out after adding the mirin to the noodles to eliminate the alcohol but maintain the flavor.

PLANET HOLLYWOOD
Texas Tostadas

NACHO TORTILLA CHIPS ARE SMOTHERED WITH CHEESE, CHICKEN, SALSA, AND
GUACAMOLE IN THIS TRULY TEXAS-SIZED DISH.

2 (8-ounce) boneless skinless
chicken breasts
1 (1-ounce) packet fajita
seasoning mix
1 large yellow onion, diced
1 tablespoon canola oil
½ cup barbecue sauce
2 dozen nacho tortilla chips
1 cup shredded Mexican blend
cheese
½ cup sour cream
1 cup Pico de Gallo
1 cup Guacamole
Cilantro, chopped, for garnish

Pico de Gallo
8 large Roma tomatoes, diced
1 large yellow onion, diced
1 large jalapeño, seeded and
minced

2 tablespoons lime juice
1 tablespoon chopped cilantro
¼ teaspoon granulated garlic
1 teaspoon kosher salt
¼ teaspoon pepper

Guacamole
4 large avocados, pitted
½ small red onion, diced
2 Roma tomatoes, diced
2 teaspoons chopped cilantro
1 teaspoon lemon juice
1½ teaspoons kosher salt
¼ teaspoon pepper
¼ teaspoon granulated garlic
¼ teaspoon cumin
¼ teaspoon cayenne pepper, or
to taste

1. Do ahead: Rub the chicken breasts with the fajita mix. Let rest at least 4
   hours, or overnight.

2. Do ahead: To make the Pico de Gallo, combine all the ingredients in a
   medium bowl and refrigerate, covered, until needed.

3. Do ahead: To make the Guacamole, in a medium bowl mash the avocado pulp with a fork, then mix in the remaining ingredients. Cover

with a piece of plastic wrap on the surface of the guacamole and refrigerate until needed.

4. Light a charcoal barbecue or heat a gas grill to medium. Clean the grate and coat it with vegetable oil.

5. Grill the chicken for 5 to 6 minutes per side, turning once, or until cooked through and no longer pink in the center. Let rest for 10 minutes, then cut into small chunks.

6. Sauté the yellow onion in the oil until softened. Drain the oil and stir the onion in with the barbecue sauce. Fold the diced chicken into the onion mixture and set aside.

7. Preheat the oven to 375°F.

8. Spread the tortilla chips in a single layer on a baking sheet. Heat them in the oven just until warm.

9. Spread the chicken mixture on each chip, then sprinkle with the cheese. Bake until the cheese is melted, then serve with ramekins of sour cream, Pico de Gallo, and Guacamole. Garnish with cilantro.

Serves 4 to 8

Save some time by purchasing fresh pico de gallo and guacamole, found in the refrigerated section of most markets.

PONDEROSA STEAK HOUSE
Steak Sauce

THIS IS A GOOD ALL-AROUND SAUCE THAT WILL GO WITH CHOPS AND RIBS AS WELL AS YOUR FAVORITE STEAK.

½ cup Heinz 57 sauce
½ cup Worcestershire sauce
½ cup A-1 steak sauce

2 tablespoons light corn syrup or maple syrup

Whisk together all the ingredients. When well blended, refrigerate in an airtight container. The sauce should last up to 2 months.

Makes about 1½ cups

A heavier corn syrup will make the sauce a little thicker. Shake the container vigorously before using.

QDOBA MEXICAN GRILL
3-Cheese Burrito

THIS IS THE ULTIMATE BIG BURRITO: CHICKEN, CHEESE, BEANS, AND RICE ARE THE BASICS. YOU CHOOSE FROM A TASTY LIST OF TOPPINGS. IT'S NOT HARD TO PREPARE AT HOME, AND SEVERAL OF THE COMPONENTS CAN BE PREPARED AHEAD OF TIME.

Chicken Marinade
1 (4-ounce) can chipotles in adobo
1 (1-ounce) package fajita seasoning mix
1 tablespoon red wine vinegar
½ cup warm water
½ cup canola oil

4 (6-ounce) boneless skinless chicken breasts

Cilantro-Lime Rice
1 tablespoon canola oil
1 cup white rice
1 teaspoon kosher salt
½ teaspoon pepper
2 cups hot chicken broth
2 tablespoons lime juice
1 tablespoon lime zest
3 tablespoons chopped cilantro

Black Beans
1 (14-ounce) can black beans, rinsed and drained
½ teaspoon kosher salt
½ teaspoon cumin
½ teaspoon chili powder

3-Cheese Sauce
2 medium poblano peppers, roasted, peeled, and seeded
3 large Roma tomatoes, seeded and cut into small dice
½ teaspoon granulated garlic
½ teaspoon minced dried onion
1 teaspoon kosher salt
¼ teaspoon paprika
¼ teaspoon cayenne pepper
¼ cup warm water
1 cup shredded Mexican blend cheese
1 cup shredded Cheddar cheese
1 (10-ounce) container cooking creme, such as Philadelphia

6 (12-inch) flour tortillas

Toppings
Guacamole
Pico de Gallo
Sour cream
Shredded lettuce
Shredded cheese
Grilled vegetables

1. Do ahead: Combine all the ingredients in the Chicken Marinade, including the adobo sauce from the can of chipotles, in a blender and pulse until completely smooth. Pour the mixture into a glass baking dish and add the chicken in a single layer. Turn the breasts over to coat them, then cover the dish and refrigerate at least 4 hours, or overnight.

2. Do ahead: To make the Cilantro-Lime Rice, heat the canola oil in a medium saucepan and sauté the rice until lightly browned. Season with the salt and pepper, then pour in the hot broth, lime juice, and lime zest. Bring the pan to a boil, then cover it and reduce the heat to the lowest setting. Cook for 20 minutes. Stir the rice to fluff it with a fork, then set it aside. Blend in the cilantro just before serving.

3. Light a charcoal barbecue or heat a gas grill to medium. Clean the grate and coat it with vegetable oil.

4. Shake the excess marinade from the breasts and grill them for 5 to 6 minutes per side, turning once, or until cooked through and no longer pink in the center. Let the chicken rest for 10 minutes before cutting into thin strips or slices.

5. Heat the Black Beans with the spices. Set aside and keep warm until ready to use, or refrigerate, covered, and reheat before making the burritos.

6. For the 3-Cheese Sauce, dice the poblanos and add them to a large saucepan with the tomatoes, garlic, onion, salt, paprika, cayenne, and water. Simmer the mixture for 3 to 5 minutes.

7. Whisk together the shredded cheeses and the cooking creme. When thoroughly blended, stir the mixture into the saucepan. Continue to stir until the cheese is melted and the sauce is smooth and creamy. Keep the heat low, so that the sauce doesn't break.

8. To assemble the burritos, heat the tortillas in the microwave or toss them on the grill for a few seconds per side; they should be flexible, not crispy.

9. Lay each tortilla on a work surface and spoon a portion of the Cilantro-Lime Rice in the center and top it with a portion of the Black Beans.

10. Follow the beans with about ½ cup of the 3-Cheese Sauce, more or less to your taste, then arrange the sliced chicken on top.

11. Add some of the suggested toppings or your own favorites to the fillings. Fold in the 2 sides opposite each other, then fold the bottom flap up and roll into a burrito. Serve warm.

Serves 6

You may want to serve the toppings as condiments, rather than as part of the filling. Serve them in ramekins so guests can choose their favorites.

QDOBA MEXICAN GRILL
Grilled Pineapple with Rum Caramel Sauce

GRILLING CARAMELIZES THE SUGAR IN FRUIT BUT DOESN'T OVERWHELM THE NATURAL SWEETNESS. THIS DESSERT IS SURE TO BE A BIG HIT AFTER A SPICY DINNER.

½ cup (1 stick) unsalted butter at room temperature
1 cup light brown sugar
1 cup whipping cream
1 teaspoon vanilla extract
1 cup dark rum
8 pineapple rings, canned or fresh

Toppings
Chopped walnuts
Toasted pecan halves
Slivered almonds
Pumpkin seeds
Crumbled cheese

1. Light a charcoal barbecue or heat a gas grill to medium. Clean the grate and coat it with vegetable oil.

2. While the grill is heating, combine the butter and brown sugar in a medium saucepan and stir over medium-low heat until the butter has melted and the sugar is dissolved.

3. Stir in the whipping cream and bring it to a boil, then lower the heat and simmer for 5 to 10 minutes, or until the sauce has thickened and slightly reduced. Stir in the vanilla extract.

4. Stir in the rum, then carefully tip the pan toward the flame and ignite the rum. This will burn off the alcohol but not eliminate the flavor. Shake the pan a little to distribute the rum and let the flames die out.

5. Place the pineapple slices on the hot grill and give them a quarter turn when marks appear on the bottom. Turn the fruit over and repeat on the second side.

6. Overlap 2 rings per warmed plate and drizzle with the rum sauce. Scatter your choice of toppings over the sauce and serve warm.

Serves 4

Crumbled cheeses might include Gorgonzola or sharp Cheddar, which both go well with fruit. Leftover rum sauce can be refrigerated and gently reheated over low heat.

QDOBA MEXICAN GRILL
Naked Chicken Burrito

THE ONLY THING MISSING FROM THIS FILLING BURRITO IS THE TORTILLA, HENCE THE NAME OF THE DISH. IF YOUR MEAL JUST ISN'T COMPLETE WITHOUT IT, BY ALL MEANS ENCLOSE ALL THE INGREDIENTS FOR THIS POPULAR FAVORITE IN A FLOUR TORTILLA AND ENJOY!

Chicken Marinade
- 1 (1-ounce) package fajita seasoning mix
- 1 tablespoon red wine vinegar
- ¼ cup warm water
- ¼ cup canola oil

- 1 (8-ounce) boneless skinless chicken breast

Black Beans
- 1 (14-ounce) can black beans, rinsed and drained
- 1 teaspoon kosher salt
- ½ teaspoon cumin
- ½ teaspoon chili powder

Guacamole
- 1 large avocado, pitted
- 1 small jalapeño, seeded and minced
- 1 Roma tomato, diced
- ½ small red onion, diced
- 1 tablespoon lime juice
- 1 tablespoon chopped cilantro
- 1 teaspoon kosher salt
- ½ teaspoon pepper

- 1 cup cooked rice

Toppings
Pico de Gallo
Sour cream
Picante salsa

1. Do ahead: Whisk together the ingredients for the Chicken Marinade. Put the chicken breast in a resealable plastic bag and pour the marinade over it. Push the air out of the bag and seal it. Refrigerate the chicken at least 4 hours, or overnight.

2. Do ahead: Heat the Black Beans with the spices. Set aside and keep warm until ready to use, or refrigerate, covered. Reheat before making the burritos.

3. Do ahead: To make the Guacamole, mash the avocado pulp with a fork, then mix in the remaining ingredients. Refrigerate, covered, until ready to use.

4. Light a charcoal barbecue or heat a gas grill to medium. Clean the grate and coat it with vegetable oil.

5. Shake off the excess marinade and grill the chicken 5 to 6 minutes per side, turning once, or until it is cooked through and no longer pink in the center. Let it rest for 10 minutes, then cut it into thin slices or strips.

6. To assemble the Naked Chicken Burrito, spoon some of the cooked rice into the center of a warmed plate. Top it with the black beans and grilled chicken. Layer the burrito with your choice of toppings, then finish it with a spoonful of guacamole.

Serves 2

Dress up your naked plate with a bed of shredded lettuce and diced tomatoes.

RED LOBSTER
Asian Garlic Grilled Salmon

THE RICH FLAVOR OF GRILLED SALMON IS PERFECTLY COMPLEMENTED WITH THIS ASIAN-INSPIRED SAUCE CONTAINING FIG PRESERVES AND SWEET CHILI SAUCE. LOOK FOR THE PRESERVES IN THE JAMS AND JELLIES SECTION, AND THE SWEET CHILI SAUCE AND CHILI GARLIC PASTE IN THE ASIAN PRODUCTS AISLE.

Garlic Sauce
½ cup sweet chili sauce
2 tablespoons fig preserves
1 tablespoon light soy sauce
2 large cloves garlic, minced
½-inch piece fresh ginger, peeled and minced

¼ teaspoon chili garlic paste

4 (6-ounce) salmon fillets
1 teaspoon kosher salt
½ teaspoon pepper

1. Do ahead: Whisk together the ingredients for the Garlic Sauce and microwave it, covered, for a minute. Stir and set aside.

2. Light a charcoal barbecue or heat a gas grill to medium. Clean the grate and coat it with vegetable oil.

3. Season the salmon with the salt and pepper and grill 3 to 4 minutes per side, turning once, or until it just loses its translucency. Do not overcook the salmon unless you prefer it well done.

4. Brush the fish with the Garlic Sauce and serve the remaining sauce on the side.

Serves 4

Serve this salmon with steamed white rice or stir-fried vegetables.

RED LOBSTER
Barbecue Sauce

THIS TOMATO-BASED SAUCE GOES SURPRISINGLY WELL WITH GRILLED-IN-THE-SHELL SHRIMP AND MAKES A WELCOME CHANGE FROM COCKTAIL SAUCE.

½ cup chunky-style marinara sauce, purchased or your own
½ cup chili sauce
1 tablespoon Grey Poupon, or other Dijon mustard

1 tablespoon white wine vinegar
1 teaspoon chili powder
¼ teaspoon dry mustard

Vigorously whisk the ingredients together. Use immediately or refrigerate in an airtight container for up to 1 month.

Makes about 1 cup

This condiment freezes well. Put a piece of plastic wrap directly onto the surface of the sauce to prevent ice crystals from forming.

RED LOBSTER
Cajun Mushroom Sauce

MUSHROOM SAUCES ARE TRADITIONALLY BASED ON WHITE WINE AND BUTTER. THE RED LOBSTER VERSION IS CERTAINLY CREAMY, BUT SPICED UP WITH NOTICEABLE AMOUNTS OF HOT SALSA AND CAJUN SEASONING. ENJOY OVER GRILLED FISH, BURGERS, AND CHICKEN.

2 tablespoons olive oil
1 pound large white mushrooms, stemmed and sliced
½ cup whipping cream
½ cup hot chicken broth
2 tablespoons Wondra flour

½ cup picante or medium-hot salsa
2 tablespoons Cajun seasoning mix
1 teaspoon garlic salt
¼ teaspoon ground white pepper

1. Heat the oil in a large skillet and sauté the mushrooms until lightly browned. Stir in the whipping cream and simmer 2 minutes.

2. Whisk together the hot chicken broth and Wondra flour until smooth. Stir this mixture into the mushrooms and bring the skillet to a boil. Turn down the heat and simmer until the sauce is slightly reduced and thickened.

3. Stir in the salsa, Cajun mix, garlic salt, and white pepper. Let the mixture simmer for another 2 or 3 minutes.

4. Use the sauce immediately, or let cool, then refrigerate in a covered container.

Makes about 5 cups

For variety, substitute your favorite barbecue sauce for the salsa. A smoky-sweet style would be amazing.

RED LOBSTER
Cod Grilled in Foil

THE DELICATE FLESH OF FRESH ATLANTIC COD IS MOIST AND TENDER. ALTHOUGH DIFFICULT TO COOK DIRECTLY ON THE GRILL, IT WILL ABSORB THE SMOKY ESSENCE OF A CHARCOAL FIRE AS IT STEAMS IN FOIL PACKED WITH LEMON AND PARSLEY.

2 tablespoons unsalted butter, melted
¼ cup fresh lemon juice
1 tablespoon chopped fresh parsley
1 teaspoon sea salt
¼ teaspoon ground white pepper
¼ teaspoon sweet paprika
1 medium sweet onion, sliced thin
4 (6-ounce) cod fillets
1 lemon, quartered

1. Light a charcoal barbecue or heat a gas grill to medium. Clean the grate and coat it with vegetable oil to keep the foil packets from sticking.

2. Cut 4 squares of heavy-duty foil large enough to surround the pieces of fish.

3. Whisk the melted butter with the lemon juice, parsley, salt, pepper, and paprika.

4. Arrange the onion slices in the center of each piece of foil. Top with a piece of cod and spoon some of the butter sauce over each piece.

5. Wrap the fish tightly in the foil and grill for 8 to 10 minutes, or until the fish flakes easily when lightly pressed.

6. Serve guests a packet to open themselves and add a wedge of lemon to each plate.

Makes 4 servings

Any other thick, white-fleshed fish can be used, such as halibut, white sea bass, or flounder. Salmon and snapper are also excellent choices.

RED LOBSTER
Grilled Rack of Shrimp

WHERE IS A KABOB A RACK? AT RED LOBSTER, WHERE SEVEN LARGE SHRIMP ARE SKEWERED AND GRILLED. SERVE WITH YOUR FAVORITE BARBECUE SAUCE.

28 large shrimp, peeled and deveined
1 tablespoon olive oil

4 metal skewers
Barbecue sauce, for dipping

1. Light a charcoal barbecue or heat a gas grill to medium. Clean the grate and coat it with vegetable oil.
2. Make racks of 7 shrimp per skewer and brush them with the olive oil.
3. Grill each rack 2 to 3 minutes per side, turning once, or just until the shrimp is pink through the center.
4. Serve with barbecue sauce.

Makes 4 servings

Leave the last knuckle of shell and the tails intact on each shrimp, making it easier to slide off the skewer and dip into the barbecue sauce.

RED LOBSTER
Grilled Rock Lobster

ROCK LOBSTERS ARE ALSO KNOWN AS SPINY LOBSTERS AND CAN BE FOUND FROM NEW ZEALAND TO THE PACIFIC COAST OF MEXICO. THEY ARE ALL TAIL, SO NO FUSSING WITH CLAWS AND KNUCKLES. COOK GENTLY TO KEEP THEM FROM BECOMING TOUGH.

2 (10-ounce) rock lobster tails, fresh or frozen and thawed
¼ cup olive oil
1 tablespoon fresh lemon juice
1 teaspoon sea salt
1 teaspoon sweet paprika
¼ teaspoon granulated garlic
¼ teaspoon ground white pepper
Melted butter and lemon juice, optional

1. Butterfly the lobster tails down the center lengthwise; do not cut all the way through, just deep enough to open each tail like a book.
2. Whisk together the oil, lemon juice, salt, paprika, garlic, and white pepper.
3. Coat each tail thoroughly with the mixture and refrigerate for at least 15 minutes.
4. Light a charcoal barbecue or heat a gas grill to medium low. Clean the grate and coat it with vegetable oil.
5. Grill the tails, cut side down, for 3 to 4 minutes per side, turning once, or until they just lose their translucency in the center.
6. Serve with melted butter and lemon juice, if desired.

Serves 2

Clarified unsalted butter is a good substitute for the olive oil, if you prefer.

RED LOBSTER

Grilled Salmon with Sun-Dried Tomato Vinaigrette

THE FRAGRANCE OF FRESH BASIL AND SUN-DRENCHED TOMATOES COMBINE EAS-
ILY WITH EXTRA VIRGIN OLIVE OIL IN A VINAIGRETTE MADE FOR GRILLED SALMON
AND ASPARAGUS. STIR UP AN EXTRA BATCH FOR SHRIMP, CHICKEN, OR AS A DIP-
PING SAUCE FOR CRUSTY BREAD.

Sun-Dried Tomato Vinaigrette
¼ cup sun-dried tomatoes in oil, chopped
¼ cup balsamic vinegar
½ cup extra virgin olive oil
I large shallot, minced
I large clove garlic, minced
I teaspoon kosher salt
½ teaspoon pepper
½ cup julienned fresh basil

4 (8-ounce) salmon fillets
2 teaspoons seasoning mix, such as Season All or Lawry's Seasoned Salt
I bunch large asparagus, trimmed
I lemon, quartered
I tablespoon chopped parsley

1. Do ahead: Whisk together the ingredients for the Sun-Dried Tomato Vinaigrette and set aside.
2. Light a charcoal barbecue or heat a gas grill to medium. Clean the grate and coat it with vegetable oil.
3. Season all sides of the salmon with the seasoning mix and grill 4 to 5 minutes per side, turning once, or until it just loses its translucency in the center.
4. Toss the asparagus with a tablespoon of the Sun-Dried Tomato Vinaigrette and grill, turning on all sides, until cooked through but still crisp.
5. Serve the salmon and asparagus with some of the vinaigrette spooned over each of them. Divide the asparagus in even numbers for each guest.
6. Dip the lemon quarters into the chopped parsley and add 1 to each plate.

7. Put the remaining vinaigrette in a ramekin and serve on the side.

Serves 4

Serve with your favorite rice dish, perhaps a wild rice blend. Add slivered almonds and herbs to make this restaurant favorite your own.

RED LOBSTER
Hawaiian Skewers

PERFECT FOR A BEACH OR BACKYARD BARBECUE, SHRIMP AND SCALLOPS ARE GRILLED BETWEEN PIECES OF PINEAPPLE, BACON, AND PEPPERS. BRUSHED WITH A DOUBLE-DUTY BASTING AND DIPPING SAUCE, THE SKEWERS CAN BE ASSEMBLED AHEAD OF TIME AND READY TO SLIP ON THE GRILL.

Basting/Dipping Sauce
¾ cup sweet and tangy barbecue sauce
2 cups medium salsa
¼ cup pineapple juice
1 tablespoon white wine vinegar

3 slices smoked bacon
6 large sea scallops

16 chunks pineapple, fresh or canned
1 large green bell pepper, seeded and cut in 1-inch pieces
6 jumbo shrimp, peeled and deveined
2 long metal or bamboo skewers (if bamboo, soak in water before use)

1. Do ahead: Whisk together the ingredients for the Basting/Dipping Sauce and set aside.

2. Cut the bacon strips in half through the middle crosswise and wrap each half around a scallop. Secure it with a toothpick.

3. Start the skewers with a piece of pineapple, then bell pepper, then shrimp, then bacon-wrapped scallop. Repeat twice more and end with pineapple.

4. Light a charcoal barbecue or heat a gas grill to medium. Clean the grate and coat it with vegetable oil.

5. Lightly baste the skewers with the basting sauce and grill, turning once or twice, until the scallops and shrimp are just cooked through. Do not overcook the shrimp or scallops. You can pull them off the grill a few moments before they are cooked through and let the heat from the skewers finish cooking them.

6. Serve hot with the sauce in a ramekin on the side.

Serves 2

Alternate the skewer ingredients if you choose; mushrooms, red onion, and zucchini are excellent choices.

RED LOBSTER
Maple-Glazed Salmon and Shrimp

REAL MAPLE SYRUP AND TART DRIED CHERRIES ARE SIMMERED WITH LEMON
JUICE AND SOY SAUCE TO MAKE A DELIGHTFUL GLAZE FOR COATING SALMON AND
SHRIMP. SAVE THE EXTRA SAUCE FOR BASTING PORK CHOPS AND CHICKEN WINGS,
OR SERVE AS A DIPPING SAUCE FOR SPRING ROLLS AND MEATBALLS.

Maple Cherry Glaze
2 cups maple syrup
½ cup dried tart cherries
¼ cup light soy sauce
¼ cup fresh lemon juice
Sugar, if needed
Water, if needed

4 metal or bamboo skewers
(if bamboo, soak in water
before use)
24 medium shrimp, peeled and
deveined
4 (6-ounce) salmon fillets
1 teaspoon kosher salt
½ teaspoon pepper

1. To make the Maple Cherry Glaze, combine the syrup, cherries, soy sauce, and lemon juice in a small saucepan. Bring the mixture to a boil, then lower the heat and simmer until the cherries are completely soft.

2. Taste the mixture for sweetness, then add equal amounts of sugar and water, if needed, to sweeten the glaze. Dissolve the sugar in the water before adding it to the simmering sauce.

3. Light a charcoal barbecue or heat a gas grill to medium. Clean the grate and coat it with vegetable oil.

4. Thread 6 shrimp onto each of the skewers and brush with the glaze.

5. Season the salmon with the salt and pepper and brush it lightly with the glaze. Grill 4 to 5 minutes per side, turning once, or until just cooked through. Use a wide, flexible spatula to help turn the fish over.

6. Set the salmon aside and grill the shrimp, 2 to 3 minutes per side just until they are pink in the center.

7. Brush the salmon with more glaze and place on a warmed plate. Brush the shrimp with a little more glaze and slide off the skewers onto and around the salmon.

8. Serve hot with extra glaze on the side.

Serves 4

Drizzle the glaze over steamed rice for a delicious side dish.

RED LOBSTER

Peach Bourbon BBQ Shrimp and Bacon-Wrapped Scallops

THE SUGAR IN THE PEACH BOURBON BARBECUE SAUCE CARAMELIZES QUICKLY ON A HOT GRILL, ADDING JUST ENOUGH SWEETNESS TO GO UP AGAINST THE SALT OF THE BACON AROUND THE SCALLOPS AND THE SMOKY ESSENCE OF THE HOT COALS. BE READY TO EAT AS SOON AS THEY COME OFF THE HOT GRILL.

Peach Bourbon Barbecue Sauce

2 cups sweet and smoky barbecue sauce

½ cup peach jam or frozen peaches, chopped and thawed

¼ cup bourbon or American whiskey

24 sea scallops

12 pieces smoked bacon, halved crosswise

6 metal or bamboo skewers (if bamboo, soak in water before use)

24 large shrimp, peeled and deveined

2 teaspoons kosher salt

1 teaspoon pepper

1. Do ahead: For the Peach Bourbon Barbecue Sauce, combine the barbecue sauce and jam or chopped peaches in a small saucepan. Bring the mixture to a boil, then lower the heat and simmer for 2 minutes.

2. Add the bourbon to the pan and raise the heat. Tip the pan to the side to let the bourbon catch the flame. Shake the pan until the flames die out. Flaming the sauce will burn out the alcohol but leave the flavor of the bourbon. Set the sauce aside.

3. Light a charcoal barbecue or heat a gas grill to medium. Clean the grate and coat it with vegetable oil.

4. Wrap each scallop in a piece of bacon.

5. Run a skewer through the shellfish, starting with a shrimp and alternating with the scallops. Each skewer should have 4 scallops and 4 shrimp. Season the shellfish with the salt and pepper.

6. Grill the skewers 2 to 3 minutes per side, turning once or twice. Make sure the shrimp are cooked just until they are pink in the center. Brush the scallops and shrimp lightly with the glaze while they are grilling and add a little more when you pull them off the grill.

7. Serve the grilled shellfish on warmed plates with your favorite rice or vegetables. Serve the remaining barbecue sauce in a ramekin on the side.

Serves 6

RED LOBSTER

Salmon with Lobster Mashed Potatoes

LOBSTER SAUCE MAY NOT BE ON YOUR WEEKLY MENU, BUT DON'T PASS UP THE CHANCE TO IMPRESS FRIENDS AND FAMILY WITH THIS OUTSTANDING PRESENTATION OF WHIPPED POTATOES AND FRESH SALMON SMOTHERED IN CREAMY SAUCE WITH LARGE CHUNKS OF FRESH LOBSTER HERE!

1 teaspoon kosher salt

½ teaspoon pepper

1 teaspoon seasoning, such as Season All or Lawry's Seasoned Salt

4 (8-ounce) center-cut salmon fillets

2 tablespoons chopped parsley

4 green onions, green part only, chopped

1 lemon, quartered

Mashed Potatoes

2½ pounds Russet potatoes peeled and cut into 1-inch chunks

¼ cup (1 stick) unsalted butter, softened

⅓ cup milk

1 teaspoon kosher salt

¼ teaspoon pepper

Lobster Sauce

1½ pounds Maine lobster, live or very fresh

2 tablespoons canola oil

1 large yellow onion, chopped

2 stalks celery, chopped

2 medium carrots, peeled and chopped

¼ cup tomato paste

½ cup dry sherry or dry vermouth

1 large bay leaf

1 teaspoon whole black peppercorns

1 quart whipping cream

¼ cup (1 stick) unsalted butter, softened

¼ cup flour

1 teaspoon fresh thyme, leaves only

1½ teaspoons kosher salt

½ teaspoon ground white pepper

To prepare a live lobster, have a large stock pot of rapidly boiling salted water ready, as well as a large bowl of ice water. Use the point of a very sharp chef's knife to cut straight down the lobster's head and cut quickly between the eyes. Plunge the lobster into the boiling water and cook until the shell is bright red, about 7 minutes. Cool immediately in a large bowl of ice water to stop the cooking.

If you would rather not deal with a live lobster, buy one that has been cooked but not frozen from the fishmonger.

Remove the cooked lobster meat from the tail, claws, and knuckles. Remove the cartilage in the claws and cut the meat into half-inch-sized pieces. Set aside and reserve the shells for the sauce.

1. To make the Mashed Potatoes, place the potato chunks in a large saucepan and cover with cold water. Bring to a medium boil and cook until tender, about 20 minutes. Drain the cooked potatoes and let them dry in the colander for about 30 minutes.

2. Melt the butter with the milk, salt, and pepper over low heat. Put the potatoes in the bowl of an electric mixer and add the butter mixture at low speed. When all the liquid has been added, raise the speed of the mixer until the potatoes are whipped and creamy. Set aside and keep warm.

3. For the Lobster Sauce, heat the canola oil in a large saucepan. Sauté the onion, celery, and carrots until softened and only very lightly browned.

4. Cut up the lobster shells and add them to the sauté, stirring frequently for about 5 minutes.

5. Clear a space in the center of the saucepan and add the tomato paste. Stir rapidly with the shells and vegetables, keeping the flame low enough so that the paste doesn't burn. Cook the tomato paste for 2 minutes. Carefully pour in the sherry and let it reduce by half, stirring frequently.

6. Add the bay leaf and black peppercorns, then stir in the whipping cream. Bring the mixture to a boil, then lower the heat and simmer for 30 minutes.

7. Make a paste of the butter and flour by mixing it together with your hands.

8. Strain the sauce through a large china cap (chinoise) or strainer into a clean saucepan, pushing down on the vegetables and shells with enough pressure to extract all the liquid from the solids. Discard the solids and bring the sauce back to a simmer. Whisk in the butter and flour mixture piece by piece, until it is all incorporated and the sauce is thickened.

9. Stir in the thyme leaves and season with the salt and pepper. Simmer 5 minutes more, then check the seasonings and adjust if necessary.

10. Stir in the lobster meat and keep the sauce warm.

11. Light a charcoal barbecue or heat a gas grill to medium. Clean the grate and coat it with vegetable oil.

12. Combine the salt, pepper, and seasoning in a small bowl and season both sides of the salmon.

13. Grill the fish 5 to 6 minutes per side, turning once, or until the salmon is just cooked through. You can pull it off the grill when there is just a spot of translucency left and let the heat in the fillets finish the cooking.

14. To serve, spoon a portion of the heated mashed potatoes in the center of a warmed plate. Ladle some of the lobster sauce over the potatoes, then center the cooked salmon on top.

15. Spoon more lobster sauce over the salmon and garnish the top of the salmon with the chopped parsley. Scatter the chopped green onions on the plate around the mashed potatoes.

16. Garnish each plate with a quartered lemon.

Serves 4

Serve extra sauce on the side. Any sauce left over can be refrigerated and stored, covered, for up to 4 days.

RED LOBSTER
Summer Seafood Grilling Sauces

THESE FIVE SAUCES ARE PERFECT FOR THE GRILLED FISH AND SEAFOOD OF SUMMER. MOST ARE A SIMPLE MIXTURE OF CONDIMENTS AND SPICES. MAKE A LARGE BATCH OF YOUR FAVORITE TO KEEP ON HAND FOR ALL SORTS OF OCCASIONS, FROM A BACKYARD BARBECUE TO A GAME-DAY BUFFET. EACH ONE WILL ENHANCE ALL YOUR GRILLING OPTIONS.

- Chili-Spiked Mayonnaise
- Sweet Mustard Glaze
- Pico de Gallo
- Cilantro Sour Cream
- Blackberry BBQ Sauce

Chili-Spiked Mayonnaise

1 cup mayonnaise, regular or reduced fat	½ teaspoon kosher salt
¼ cup chili sauce	½ teaspoon Tabasco Chipotle Pepper sauce

1. Whisk all the ingredients together until smooth and creamy. Refrigerate in an airtight container.

2. Serve with grilled salmon.

Makes about 1¼ cups

Sweet Mustard Glaze

1 cup Gray Poupon or other Dijon mustard	2 tablespoons light soy sauce
½ cup honey	1 teaspoon pepper

1. Whisk all the ingredients together until smooth and creamy. Refrigerate in an airtight container.

2. Serve with grilled shrimp.

Makes about 1½ cups

Pico de Gallo

2 Roma tomatoes, diced

1 small jalapeño, seeded and diced

½ small red onion, diced

1 tablespoon chopped cilantro

1 tablespoon lime juice

½ teaspoon kosher salt

¼ teaspoon pepper

1. Stir all the ingredients together. Refrigerate in an airtight container for up to 3 days.
2. Serve with grilled swordfish.

Makes about 1 cup

Cilantro Sour Cream

1 cup sour cream, regular or reduced calorie

2 tablespoons chopped cilantro

½ teaspoon kosher salt

¼ teaspoon pepper

1 teaspoon lime juice

1. Whisk all the ingredients together until smooth and creamy. Refrigerate in an airtight container.
2. Serve with grilled sea bass.

Makes about 1 cup

Blackberry BBQ Sauce

2 cups plain barbecue sauce, purchased or your own

½ cup blackberry jelly, seedless

½ cup sweet chili sauce

¼ cup soy sauce

¼ cup water

1. Combine all the ingredients in a medium saucepan. Whisk over high heat until the mixture comes to a boil. Turn down the heat and simmer for 2 minutes. Cool the sauce down, then refrigerate in an airtight container.
2. Serve with grilled tuna.

Makes about 3½ cups

RED LOBSTER

Wood-Grilled Tilapia in a Spicy Soy Broth

YOU CAN DUPLICATE THE GRILLED FLAVOR OF TOP RESTAURANTS LIKE RED LOB-STER BY USING HARDWOOD CHARCOAL, WOOD, AND WOOD CHIPS FOR THAT SMOKY ESSENCE. A WOOD FIRE BURNS EXTREMELY HOT, SO MOST ARE MADE FROM HARDWOODS AND LOGS SUCH AS OAK, HICKORY, AND MESQUITE. MANY SPECIALTY FOOD STORES WILL CARRY SOME OF THESE HARDWOOD CHARCOALS FOR YOU TO TRY.

Spicy Soy Broth
1 teaspoon sesame oil
1 tablespoon canola oil
8 small or medium shrimp in the
  shell, chopped
4 ounces bay scallops, chopped
4 large shallots, minced
4 large cloves garlic, minced
½ cup mirin or sweet vermouth
¼ cup light soy sauce
¼ cup rice wine vinegar
2 cups chicken broth
1 cup chopped cilantro

1 bunch green onions, green part
  only, chopped
1 medium carrot, julienned
4 (6-ounce) tilapia fillets
1 teaspoon kosher salt
¼ teaspoon pepper
1 teaspoon sesame oil
1 tablespoon canola oil
4 jumbo shrimp, peeled and
  deveined
1 tablespoon wasabi powder
4 large sea scallops
2 teaspoons hot chili sauce, such
  as Thai sriracha
½ cup julienned basil

1. Do ahead: To make the Spicy Soy Broth, heat the sesame and canola oils in a large saucepan and sauté the shrimp, in the shell, and scallops over medium heat until lightly browned.

2. Stir in the shallots and garlic and cook until softened.

3. Add the mirin, soy sauce, and vinegar. Stir in the chicken broth and cilantro and bring the broth to a boil. Reduce the heat and simmer for about 20 minutes, or until the broth is reduced by about a third.

4. Strain the liquid through a china cap (chinoise) or strainer into a clean saucepan. Put enough pressure on the solids to extract all the remaining liquid, then discard the solids.

5. Bring the broth to a simmer and add the green onions and carrot. Take the pan off the heat and set it aside. When the vegetables are tender, remove them with a slotted spoon and set aside.

6. Light a charcoal barbecue with the hardwood charcoal. Clean the grate and coat it with vegetable oil.

7. Season the tilapia with half the salt and pepper. Grill the fish 3 to 4 minutes per side, turning once, or until it is cooked through. Use a wide, flexible spatula to help turn the fish over.

8. Heat the sesame and canola oils in a medium skillet. Toss the shrimp in the wasabi powder. Dry the scallops with paper towels and season with the remaining salt and pepper.

9. Sauté the shrimp and scallops until cooked through, turning once. Cook the shrimp until they are pink in the center and the scallops until lightly golden on both sides.

10. To serve the fish, heat large shallow soup bowls in the oven and bring the broth to a simmer.

11. Spoon a portion of the hot chili sauce in the bottom of each bowl. Scatter the blanched carrots and green onions over the bottom of the bowl. Ladle in half of the hot broth and gently stir with the chili sauce.

12. Lay a tilapia fillet and some shrimp and scallops in the center of each serving bowl and ladle the remaining hot broth over the top. Scatter the basil over the seafood and serve immediately.

Serves 4

You may wish to grill the shrimp and scallops instead of sautéing them. If so, season them with salt and pepper and moisten with a mixture of the sesame and canola oils. Grill quickly, turning once, until the shellfish are cooked through. Proceed with the rest of the recipe as directed.

Mirin and sriracha may be found in the Asian product section of large markets or specialty food stores. For a spicier broth, add more sriracha to each bowl.

RED ROBIN
Bacon Cheeseburger

RED ROBIN MAKES A TASTY TRADITIONAL CHEESEBURGER. THERE IS NO SPECIAL
SAUCE TO GET IN THE WAY OF THE HICKORY SMOKED BACON AND JUICY GROUND
BEEF. THE SESAME SEED BUN IS SIMPLY COATED WITH MAYONNAISE.

¼ teaspoon kosher salt
¼ teaspoon seasoned salt, such
   as Lawry's
¼ teaspoon pepper
5½ ounces ground beef or chuck
2 slices Cheddar cheese
1 sesame seed hamburger bun,
   split in half

2 teaspoons mayonnaise, regular
   or reduced fat
2 thick slices tomato
3 slices hickory smoked bacon,
   cooked crisp
¼ cup shredded green leaf
   lettuce

1. Light a charcoal barbecue or heat a gas grill to medium. Clean the grate
   and coat it with vegetable oil.

2. Combine the salts and pepper. Form the beef into a patty and season
   both sides with the mixture.

3. Grill 3 to 4 minutes per side, turning once, or until cooked to your
   preferred doneness. Place the cheese slices on the burger just moments
   before pulling it off the grill.

4. Grill the top and bottom halves of the bun on the grill until lightly
   toasted, taking care to not let the bread burn.

5. Spread the mayonnaise on the bottom half of the bun. Add the grilled
   burger with the cheese and top with the tomato slices, and then the
   bacon on top of the tomatoes in a triple-X pattern.

6. Arrange the shredded lettuce over the bacon and finish with the top half
   of the bun. Serve hot.

Makes 1 hamburger

You can get the bacon sizzling hot by placing the cooked strips on the hot grill and turning them over once, just before adding them to the burger.

RED ROBIN
Bleu Ribbon Burger

RED ROBIN GOES ALL OUT FOR THIS PREMIUM BURGER. DUPLICATING IT AT HOME
WILL TAKE BLUE CHEESE, HEINZ 57 SAUCE, CHIPOTLES, AND FRIED ONIONS. ALL
GOOD THINGS THAT MAKE A BURGER GREAT.

Chipotle Mayonnaise
¼ cup mayonnaise, regular or
  reduced fat
1 chipotle pepper, minced

5½ ounces lean ground beef or
  chuck
½ teaspoon kosher salt
¼ teaspoon pepper

1 tablespoon Heinz 57 sauce
1 tablespoon crumbled domestic
  blue cheese
1 onion hamburger bun, split in
  half
¼ cup onion straws
2 thick tomato slices
¼ cup shredded green leaf
  lettuce

1. Do ahead: To make the Chipotle Mayonnaise, whisk together the mayonnaise and the chipotle pepper until very well blended, and set aside.

2. Light a charcoal barbecue or heat a gas grill to medium. Clean the grate
   and coat it with vegetable oil.

3. Form a patty from the ground beef and season with the salt and pepper.
   Grill the patty for 3 to 4 minutes per side, turning once, or until cooked
   to your preferred doneness.

4. Coat the top of the patty with the Heinz 57 sauce, then top it with the
   blue cheese. Set it off to the side of the grill a few moments to melt the
   cheese.

5. Grill the hamburger bun until lightly toasted, taking care to not let it
   burn. Spread a tablespoon of the Chipotle Mayonnaise on both toasted
   sides of the bun.

6. Pile the onion straws on the bottom bun and lay the patty and cheese
   on top. Arrange the tomato slices over the cheese and pack the shredded
   lettuce on top. Finish the burger with the top half of the bun. Serve hot.

If planning on making several burgers, save some time by mixing the salt, pepper, and Heinz 57 sauce in the ground beef before forming the patties. Refrigerate the patties at least 30 minutes before grilling.

RED ROBIN
Mexican Rub

KEEP A BATCH OF THIS LATIN-INSPIRED SEASONING MIX HANDY IN THE PANTRY. USE IT TO GIVE A SPICY KICK TO DRESSINGS, VEGETABLES, AND BREAKFASTS, AS WELL AS MEATS AND CHICKEN.

⅓ cup New Mexico chili powder
⅓ cup smoked paprika
2 tablespoons cumin
2 tablespoons crumbled Mexican oregano

2 tablespoons onion powder
2 tablespoons garlic powder
2 teaspoons kosher salt
¼ teaspoon chipotle chili powder
¼ teaspoon cayenne pepper

1. Whisk all the spices together until very well blended. Quickly pulse the mixture in a small food processor to grind the oregano, if desired.
2. Store the mix in an airtight container and keep dry.

Makes about 1 cup

You can vary the amount of spice used in this blend. Use a milder chili powder and decrease or omit the cayenne, if desired.

RED ROBIN
Southwest Chicken Salad

THIS IS AN EASY SALAD FOR TWO, BOTH SPICY AND COOL. THE RANCH-SALSA DRESSING BALANCES THE FIERY KICK FROM DEEP-FRIED JALAPEÑOS. A REAL TREAT IF YOU'VE NOT HAD FRIED PICKLES BEFORE.

Chicken Marinade

1 (1.12-ounce) packet ancho chili marinade
¼ cup water
¼ cup canola oil

2 (4-ounce) boneless skinless chicken breasts
¼ cup ranch dressing
¼ cup medium or hot salsa
4 cups mixed greens
½ small red bell pepper, seeded and diced
½ small green bell pepper, seeded and diced
½ small red onion, diced
½ cup cooked black beans, rinsed and drained
¼ cup frozen corn kernels thawed
½ cup shredded Monterey Jack cheese
1 cup tortilla strips, flavored or plain
½ avocado, pitted, shelled, and diced

Fried Pickled Peppers

1½ cups canola oil
½ cup all-purpose flour
½ teaspoon paprika
½ teaspoon kosher salt
1½ teaspoons baking powder
¼ cup cold water
½ (12-ounce) jar pickled jalapeño slices, drained

1. Do ahead: Whisk together the ingredients for the Chicken Marinade. Place the chicken breasts in a large resealable plastic bag and pour the marinade over them. Push the air out of the bag and seal it. Refrigerate the chicken at least 4 hours, or overnight.

2. Light a charcoal barbecue or heat a gas grill to medium. Clean the grate and coat it with vegetable oil.

3. Remove the chicken from the marinade and shake off any excess. Grill the chicken 5 to 6 minutes per side, turning once, or until cooked

through and no longer pink in the center. Let the chicken rest for 10 minutes before cutting into bite-sized cubes.

4. To make the Fried Pickled Peppers, heat the canola oil in a small, heavy-bottomed saucepan over medium-high heat.

5. Whisk together the flour, paprika, salt, and baking powder. Add the cold water and whisk until smooth.

6. Coat the jalapeño slices in the batter and fry them until golden on both sides. Drain on paper towels and keep warm.

7. Mix the ranch dressing with the salsa. Whisk until well blended.

8. In a large bowl, toss the mixed greens, bell peppers, red onion, beans, corn, and cheese. Add the mixed dressing and toss once more, adding the tortilla strips.

9. Place equal portions of salad on chilled plates. Top each salad with the diced avocado and cooked chicken. Surround each salad with the Fried Pickled Peppers. Serve immediately.

Serves 2

If timing is an issue, make the salads ahead of time and refrigerate them. Keep the fried pickles warm separately. When ready to serve, arrange the fried peppers around the salads. They can also be served as a separate garnish. Red Robin serves the chicken breast whole on top of the salad, which makes a nice presentation. They also use roasted corn, which you can do by grilling a cleaned ear of corn on the hot grill, then slicing the kernels off the cob.

RED ROBIN
Teriyaki Chicken Sandwich

RED ROBIN SERVES THIS GRILLED CHICKEN SANDWICH WITH OPTIONS. KEEP IN MIND THAT YOU CAN CHANGE THE CHEESE, BUN, OR MAYONNAISE AND STILL HAVE A GREAT SANDWICH.

Teriyaki Marinade
½ cup light soy sauce
½ cup dark brown sugar
½ cup rice wine vinegar
I teaspoon sesame oil
½ teaspoon onion powder
½ teaspoon granulated garlic

4 (4-ounce) boneless skinless chicken breasts

8 slices Swiss cheese
4 sesame seed hamburger buns, split in half
8 pineapple rings, fresh or canned
4 tablespoons mayonnaise, regular or reduced fat
8 thick tomato slices
1½ cups shredded green leaf lettuce

1. Do ahead: To make the Teriyaki Marinade, whisk together the soy sauce and brown sugar in a small saucepan. Bring to a simmer and stir until the sugar is dissolved. Whisk in the rice wine vinegar, sesame oil, onion powder, and garlic. Bring to a boil, then reduce the heat and simmer for 5 to 10 minutes. Let the marinade cool completely before using. It can be made a day ahead of time and refrigerated, covered, until ready to use.

2. Put the chicken breasts in a large resealable plastic bag and pour half the marinade over them. Reserve the remaining half for the pineapple. Push the air out the bag and refrigerate at least four hours.

3. Light a charcoal barbecue or heat a gas grill to medium. Clean the grate and coat it with vegetable oil.

4. Shake the excess marinade from the chicken and grill it 5 to 6 minutes per side, turning once, or until cooked through and no longer pink in the center. Top each breast with 2 slices of cheese and set them on a

cooler side of the grill to let the cheese melt a little. Drizzle with some of the reserved marinade.

5. Grill the hamburger buns until lightly toasted, taking care to not burn them.

6. Coat the pineapple rings with the remaining marinade. Grill the rings, making a quarter turn after grill marks appear on the bottom. Flip the rings over and repeat.

7. Spread the toasted side of each bun with some of the mayonnaise. Lay a cooked breast with the cheese on the bottom bun and follow with the sliced tomatoes, grilled pineapple, and shredded lettuce. Finish the sandwich with the top half of the bun. Serve warm.

Serves 4

For quicker cooking, the chicken breasts can be lightly pounded between 2 pieces of plastic before marinating. Grill 3 to 4 minutes per side, or until cooked through as described.

ROMANO'S MACARONI GRILL

Grilled Chicken with Portobello Mushrooms

CUSTOMERS MISS THIS ITEM ON THE MENU AT ROMANO'S MACARONI GRILL. TO PREPARE IT AT HOME TAKES TIME, SO MAKE SURE YOU HAVE A FEW HOURS FREE FOR THE PREPARATION. OR, DO WHAT RESTAURANTS DO AND MAKE THE DEMI-GLACE A DAY AHEAD OF TIME. IT WILL ONLY INCREASE IN FLAVOR AS THE INGREDIENTS MELD.

Demi-Glace

1 tablespoon olive oil
6 cloves garlic, lightly smashed
3 cups beef broth
2 cups chicken broth
2 portobello mushroom stems
1 teaspoon whole black peppercorns
1 large bay leaf
1 sprig fresh rosemary
4 sprigs fresh thyme
1 tablespoon cornstarch
2 tablespoons cold water

4 (8-ounce) boneless skinless chicken breasts
¼ cup stone ground mustard
2 extra-large portobello mushrooms, stems reserved
1 tablespoon olive oil
½ teaspoon kosher salt
¼ teaspoon pepper

8 slices smoked mozzarella cheese
4 cups Orzo, cooked halfway
2 cups Demi-Glace

Orzo

1 (1-pound) package orzo, cooked halfway and drained
1 tablespoon olive oil
4 large cloves garlic, minced
1 large red bell pepper, seeded and diced
1 cup hot chicken broth
¼ cup (½ stick) unsalted butter, cubed
1 teaspoon kosher salt
½ teaspoon pepper
12 ounces baby spinach leaves, chopped

1. Do ahead: Start the Demi-Glace first so that it has a chance to reduce. Heat the oil in a large saucepan or soup pot. Sauté the garlic until soft, then add the beef broth, chicken broth, mushroom stems, peppercorns, bay leaf, rosemary, and thyme. Bring the pot to a boil, then lower the heat to medium and cook until the liquid is reduced to 2 cups.

2. Strain the liquid through a fine strainer into a clean saucepan and discard the solids.

3. Make a paste of the cornstarch and water. Bring the liquid to a high simmer and whisk in the paste. Stir until the Demi-Glace is thickened. Let the sauce cool completely, then refrigerate until ready to use. This is best done very early in the day or, preferably, the day before.

4. Split the chicken breasts and pound each piece between 2 pieces of plastic wrap until they are of uniform thickness. Spread each piece with some of the mustard, cover, and refrigerate for at least 30 minutes.

5. Light a charcoal barbecue or heat a gas grill to medium. Clean the grate and coat it with vegetable oil.

6. Coat the portobello mushrooms with the olive oil and season both sides with the salt and pepper.

7. Grill the mushrooms about 3 minutes per side, turning once. Set them aside to rest for about 5 minutes, then slice them thinly at a very wide angle and set aside.

8. Grill the chicken breasts 4 to 5 minutes per side, turning once, or until cooked through and no longer pink in the center. Move the chicken to a cooler part of the grill and stack each piece with some slices of the mushrooms and 1 slice of the smoked mozzarella. Keep the stacks warm.

9. To finish the orzo pasta, heat the oil in a large saucepan and sauté the minced garlic and diced peppers until soft. Add the strained orzo pasta and the hot chicken broth. Simmer the pasta until it is cooked through but still *al dente*; most of the broth should be absorbed.

10. Whisk in the butter a piece at a time, season with the salt and pepper, and finish with the chopped spinach. The pasta should still be hot enough to just wilt the spinach; it doesn't need to be sautéed.

11. To assemble the dish, heat the Demi-Glace while whisking. Place the finished orzo pasta in the center of warmed plates. Top the pasta with the stacked chicken and drizzle the Demi-Glace over the chicken and onto the pasta, making a zigzag pattern over the whole assembly. Serve hot.

Serves 8

Extra Demi-Glace can be refrigerated up to a month and frozen for at least 3 months.

RUBY TUESDAY
Memphis Dry Rub Ribs

THIS IS A CLASSIC DRY RUB THAT CAN BE USED ON CHOPS AND CHICKEN AS WELL AS RIBS. YOU CAN USE THE BARBECUE SAUCE AS A LIGHT GLAZE OR SERVE ON THE SIDE.

Dry Rub
¼ cup sweet paprika
2 tablespoons dark brown sugar
1 tablespoon black pepper
1 tablespoon kosher salt
1½ teaspoons celery salt
1 teaspoon granulated garlic

1 teaspoon dry mustard
1 teaspoon cumin
1 teaspoon minced dried onion
¼ teaspoon cayenne pepper

1 rack baby back ribs
1 cup barbecue sauce

1. Whisk all the Dry Rub ingredients in a bowl until well blended.
2. Rub the Dry Rub over the ribs and coat both sides with some of the barbecue sauce. Wrap the rack in plastic and marinate overnight.
3. Light a charcoal barbecue or heat a gas grill to medium or medium-low. Clean the grate and coat it with vegetable oil.
4. Unwrap the ribs and set the rack bone side down on the grill. Close the lid and grill the ribs until tender, turning occasionally, and baste with the remaining sauce.

Serves 1 to 2

If your grill or barbecue doesn't have a lid, use a large roasting pan or an aluminum turkey roaster to cover the ribs while they are cooking.

RUBY TUESDAY
Turkey Burger

A PERFECT OPTION FOR NONBEEF EATERS. RUBY TUESDAY BLENDS RED PEPPER
AND CHEESE CRACKERS INTO THEIR PATTIES. GIVE THIS ONE A TRY.

1 pound ground turkey
1 tablespoon granulated garlic
1 tablespoon red pepper flakes
1 teaspoon minced dried onion
1 large egg, well beaten
½ teaspoon kosher salt
¼ teaspoon pepper
½ cup cheese crackers, such as
   Keebler or Goldfish Cheddar
4 hamburger buns, split in half

4 leaves iceberg lettuce
4 thick slices tomato
4 ¼-inch-thick slices red onion
8 pieces dill pickle chips

Garlic Mayo
¼ cup mayonnaise, regular or
   reduced fat
1 teaspoon granulated garlic
1 teaspoon lemon juice

1. Do ahead: Combine the ground turkey, garlic, pepper flakes, dried onion, egg, salt, pepper, and crushed crackers in a medium bowl. Blend the
   mixture with your hands and form 4 equal-sized patties. Put the patties
   on a sheet of waxed paper and refrigerate them, covered, until ready to
   use.

2. Do ahead: To make the Garlic Mayo, whisk together the mayonnaise
   with the garlic and lemon juice and refrigerate, covered, until ready to
   use.

3. Light a charcoal barbecue or heat a gas grill to medium. Clean the grate
   and coat it with vegetable oil.

4. Grill the turkey patties 5 to 6 minutes per side, turning once, or until
   cooked through and no longer pink in the center.

5. Grill the hamburger buns until lightly toasted, taking care to not burn
   the bread.

6. Spread some of the Garlic Mayo on the toasted side of each bun. Place a
   lettuce leaf, trimmed if necessary, on the bottom half of each bun.

7. Follow the lettuce with a slice of tomato, then the red onion, 2 pickle chips, and the cooked turkey patty. Finish the burger with the top half of the bun. Serve hot.

Serves 4

Ruby Tuesday uses different buns for their burgers. Try sesame seed, onion, or a pretzel roll.

SCHLOTZKY'S
Asian Chicken Wrap

SCHLOTZKY'S IS KNOWN FOR THE FRESHNESS AND QUALITY OF THEIR INGREDI-ENTS. THEY OFFER THIS CHICKEN WRAP WITH A SLIGHTLY DIFFERENT TWIST, USING A SAVORY *TONKATSU* SAUCE.

Tonkatsu Sauce
½ cup ketchup or chili sauce
¼ cup Worcestershire sauce
¼ cup sake or dry vermouth
3 large cloves garlic, minced
1-inch piece ginger, peeled and minced
2 tablespoons dark brown sugar
2 tablespoons mirin or sherry

2 (8-ounce) boneless skinless chicken breasts

1 teaspoon kosher salt
½ teaspoon pepper
4 (10-inch) flour tortillas

Sandwich Fillers
2 cups shredded mixed greens
1 small carrot, julienned
2 tablespoons chopped cilantro
¼ cup slivered almonds, toasted
1 small red bell pepper, seeded and diced
1 teaspoon kosher salt
¼ teaspoon pepper

1. Do ahead: Combine the ingredients for the Tonkatsu Sauce in a small saucepan. Whisk vigorously and bring the pan to a boil. Reduce the heat and simmer for 20 minutes. Let the sauce cool completely, then refrigerate in a tightly covered container until ready to use.

2. Pour ½ cup Tonkatsu Sauce into a resealable plastic bag. Add the chicken breasts and massage the sauce all around each one. Seal the bag and refrigerate at least 1 hour. Reserve the remaining sauce.

3. Light a charcoal barbecue or heat a gas grill to medium. Clean the grate and coat it with vegetable oil.

4. Shake the excess marinade from the chicken and season it with the salt and pepper. Grill the breasts 6 to 7 minutes per side, turning once, or until cooked through and no longer pink in the center. Set aside to rest for 10 minutes, then cut into small cubes.

5. To build the wraps, heat the tortillas on the hot grill just until flexible, not crispy.

6. Lay them flat on a work surface and spoon the diced chicken into the center of each one. Drizzle with some of the reserved Tonkatsu Sauce. Layer the mixed greens, carrot, cilantro, almonds, and bell pepper over the chicken and season with salt and pepper. Drizzle with a little more sauce.

7. Fold the 2 opposite flaps in toward the center and fold the bottom flap up. Roll the wrap into a cylinder like a burrito. Serve immediately.

Serves 4

The Tonkatsu Sauce can be made ahead of time and refrigerated, tightly covered, up to 1 month.

SIZZLER
Steak and Shrimp

SIZZLER FEATURES RIB EYE AND TRI-TIP STEAKS, EITHER BY THEMSELVES OR IN COMBINATION WITH SHRIMP OR LOBSTER. TRY THIS SAVORY VERSION OF SURF AND TURF WITH THE STEAK OF YOUR CHOICE AND TENDER SHRIMP, LIGHTLY POACHED IN A BUTTER AND WINE SAUCE THAT SMOOTHERS THE JUICY STEAKS JUST BEFORE SERVING.

4 (10-ounce) steaks, boneless rib eye or tri-tip
1½ teaspoons kosher salt
1 teaspoon pepper
28 medium shrimp, peeled and deveined, leaving the last shell knuckle intact
1 lemon, quartered
Parsley sprigs, for garnish

White Wine Butter Sauce
½ cup (1 stick) unsalted butter at room temperature
4 large cloves garlic, minced
4 large shallots, minced
¼ cup dry white wine
1 tablespoon lemon juice
½ teaspoon kosher salt
¼ teaspoon pepper
1 tablespoon chopped parsley

1. Light a charcoal barbecue or heat a gas grill to medium. Clean the grate and coat it with vegetable oil.

2. Season the steaks with the salt and pepper. Grill the meat 6 to 8 minutes per side, turning once, or until cooked to your preferred doneness. Set the steaks aside to rest for at least 10 minutes.

3. To make the White Wine Butter Sauce, melt the butter in a medium saucepan over medium-low heat. Stir in the garlic and shallots and let them simmer with the melted butter over low heat until softened.

4. Add the shrimp to the mixture and spoon the sauce over them. Let them cook in the butter for about 2 minutes, then add the white wine and lemon juice.

5. Reduce the sauce a little, then season with salt and pepper and stir in the parsley.

6. Place the steaks on warmed plates and spoon 7 of the shrimp and a portion of the sauce over each steak. Put a lemon quarter on each plate.

7. Garnish with parsley sprigs, if desired.

Serves 4

Sizzler offers a savory rice pilaf with this dish. Whip up your own for a close-to-copycat meal!

SONIC DRIVE-IN
Hickory Burger

WITH 3,500 DRIVE-IN LOCATIONS, SONIC OWNS THIS SECTOR OF THE FAST-FOOD
WORLD. WHAT THEY DO BEST IS BURGERS AND, AFTER MAKING A FEW OF THESE
AT HOME, YOU'LL UNDERSTAND WHY SONIC CUSTOMERS ARE SO LOYAL!

4 ounces ground beef or chuck
½ teaspoon kosher salt
¼ teaspoon pepper
I hamburger bun, split in half
I tablespoon unsalted butter,
  melted

I tablespoon hickory barbecue
  sauce
I tablespoon chopped sweet
  onion
¼ cup chopped green leaf lettuce

1. Shape the ground beef into a patty. Wrap it in plastic and refrigerate at least 30 minutes before using.

2. Light a charcoal barbecue or heat a gas grill to medium. Clean the grate and coat it with vegetable oil.

3. Season the patty with the salt and pepper. Grill 3 to 4 minutes per side, turning once, or until cooked to your preferred doneness.

4. Brush both sides of the bun with the melted butter. Grill both halves until lightly toasted, taking care to not burn the bread.

5. To build your burger, spread the barbecue sauce over the bottom bun and sprinkle with the chopped onions.

6. Pack the lettuce over the onions, then set the patty on top. Finish with the top half of the bun over the patty. Serve hot.

Serves 1

**Feel free to add a slice of American or Cheddar cheese. Pickles,
tomatoes, and onion rings are other delicious options.**

SONIC DRIVE-IN
House Burger

THIS IS YOUR BASIC BURGER DONE REALLY WELL. MELTED BUTTER COATS THE HAMBURGER BUN, WHILE LETTUCE, TOMATO, AND PICKLES PROVIDE FLAVOR AND TEXTURE. AND THEN, OF COURSE, THERE'S THE SIZZLING HOT, JUICY BEEF MAKING THIS THE PERFECT SANDWICH.

4 ounces ground beef or chuck
½ teaspoon kosher salt
¼ teaspoon pepper
1 hamburger bun, split in half
1 tablespoon unsalted butter, melted

2 teaspoons mayonnaise
3 dill pickle chips
1 tablespoon diced sweet onion
¼ cup chopped green leaf lettuce
2 thick slices tomato

1. Shape the ground beef into a patty. Wrap it in plastic and refrigerate at least 30 minutes before using.

2. Light a charcoal barbecue or heat a gas grill to medium. Clean the grate and coat it with vegetable oil.

3. Season the patty with the salt and pepper. Grill 3 to 4 minutes per side, turning once, or until cooked to your preferred doneness.

4. Brush both sides of the bun with the melted butter. Grill both halves until lightly toasted, taking care to not burn the bread.

5. To build your burger, spread the mayonnaise over the bottom bun and arrange the pickle chips on the mayonnaise. Sprinkle with the diced onion over the pickle chips. Pack the lettuce over the onions and follow with the tomato slices.

6. Set the patty on top of the tomato and finish with the top half of the bun. Serve hot.

Don't have hamburger buns? Use whatever is in the pantry. Any type of bread will be enhanced by a coating of melted butter and a few seconds on a hot grill.

SONIC DRIVE-IN
Jalapeño Burger

THE BASIC BURGER JUST TOOK A GIANT LEAP INTO THE WORLD OF HOT AND SPICY. JALAPEÑO PEPPERS COME READY SLICED IN CANS AND JARS, PICKLED OR PLAIN. EITHER WAY, THEY'RE A HUGE ADDITION TO THE FLAVOR AND TEXTURE OF AN ALL-AMERICAN BURGER.

4 ounces ground beef or chuck
½ teaspoon kosher salt
¼ teaspoon pepper
1 hamburger bun, split in half
1 tablespoon unsalted butter, melted
1 tablespoon yellow mustard
6 slices canned jalapeños, or to taste
1 onion, sliced
¼ cup chopped green leaf lettuce

1. Shape the ground beef into a patty. Wrap it in plastic and refrigerate at least 30 minutes before using.

2. Light a charcoal barbecue or heat a gas grill to medium. Clean the grate and coat it with vegetable oil.

3. Season the patty with the salt and pepper. Grill 3 to 4 minutes per side, turning once, or until cooked to your preferred doneness.

4. Brush both sides of the bun with the melted butter. Grill both halves until lightly toasted, taking care to not burn the bread.

5. To build your burger, spread the mustard over the bottom bun and arrange the jalapeños on the mustard.

6. Pack the lettuce over the onions, then set the patty on top. Finish with the top half of the bun over the patty. Serve hot.

Serves 1

Make your mouth go crazy by adding a slice or two of spicy pepper Jack cheese to the burger while it's still on the grill.

STEAK AND ALE
Meat Marinade

FOR THE MANY FANS NATIONWIDE WHO LOVED THE STEAK AND ALE EXPERIENCE, THE STEAK MARINADE IS AN ESSENTIAL PART OF THE FABLED RESTAURANT'S LORE. GONE SINCE 2008, HOPE IS JUST AROUND THE CORNER, IF A CORPORATE ANGEL CAN RESURRECT THE POPULAR BRAND.

3 cups pineapple juice concentrate

1 cup light soy sauce

1 cup Sauvignon Blanc, or other dry white wine

½ cup red wine vinegar

½ cup golden brown sugar

3 large cloves garlic, minced

1. Whisk the ingredients together thoroughly and store in an airtight container, refrigerated, until ready to use.
2. To use the marinade as a basting sauce, bring it to a boil, then lower the heat and simmer for about 20 minutes. The liquid will thicken, making it perfect for brushing over chops and ribs.

Makes about 6 cups

Lean meats such as sirloin and flank need the most time in the marinade, and an overnight stay in this acidic marinade will tenderize them so that they can be grilled over high heat without drying out.

STEAK 'N SHAKE
Frisco Melt

STEAK 'N SHAKE IS AN AMERICAN CLASSIC: DRIVE-THROUGH, DINE-IN, BREAK-FAST, LUNCH, DINNER, AND A SPECIAL KIDS' MENU. ONE OF THE FEW CHAINS TO OFFER A WHOLE SECTION OF MELTS, THE FRISCO IS ONE OF THE MOST POPULAR.

Buttery Blend
¼ cup (½ stick) unsalted butter, softened
¼ teaspoon garlic salt
¼ teaspoon ground white pepper

Frisco Sauce
2 tablespoons mayonnaise
2 tablespoons ketchup
2 tablespoons yellow mustard

2 tablespoons Thousand Island dressing

2 pounds ground beef or chuck
2 teaspoons kosher salt
1 teaspoon pepper
8 thick slices sourdough bread
4 slices Swiss cheese
4 slices American cheese

1. Do ahead: Form the ground beef into 8 equal-sized patties. Refrigerate them at least 30 minutes before grilling.

2. Do ahead: To make the Buttery Blend, whisk together the softened butter with the garlic salt and white pepper. Pack the seasoned butter into a ramekin or cup and refrigerate, covered. Let it come to room temperature before using it.

3. Do ahead: The Frisco Sauce can be made a day or two ahead of time if you wish. Whisk all the ingredients together and refrigerate in a covered container.

4. Light a charcoal barbecue or heat a gas grill to medium. Clean the grate and coat it with vegetable oil.

5. Season the patties with the salt and pepper. Grill the patties for 3 to 4 minutes per side, turning once, or until cooked to your preferred doneness.

6. Spread 1 side of all 8 slices of bread with the Buttery Blend. Grill the bread, coated side down, until toasted, taking care to not burn the bread.

7. To build the Frisco Melt, cover the bottom piece of sourdough, untoasted side up, with the Swiss cheese. Top it with a patty, then the American cheese and then another patty. Spread some Frisco Sauce on the top patty and cover with the top piece of bread. Repeat for all 4 sandwiches.

8. Slice the sandwiches in half diagonally and serve hot.

Serves 4

Make your Frisco Melt extra special by adding sliced onions, tomatoes, and leaves of crispy iceberg lettuce.

SUBWAY

Sweet Onion Chicken Teriyaki Sandwich

THIS SANDWICH HAS A LOT OF FLAVORFUL THINGS GOING ON. THE CHICKEN IS MARINATED FOR HOURS, THEN GRILLED UNTIL TENDER, AND SLICED. THE CHICKEN AND YOUR CHOICE OF TOPPINGS ARE DRENCHED WITH THE TANGY SWEET ONION SAUCE BEFORE BEING ROLLED UP IN A SUB ROLL.

1 (4-ounce) boneless skinless chicken breast
¼ cup teriyaki marinade
1 sub roll

¼ teaspoon black poppy seeds
¼ teaspoon granulated garlic
¼ teaspoon kosher salt
¼ teaspoon pepper

Sweet Shallot Sauce
½ cup light corn syrup
1 tablespoon red wine vinegar
2 tablespoons white wine vinegar
1 tablespoon balsamic vinegar
1 teaspoon fresh lemon juice
1 teaspoon light brown sugar
1 medium shallot, diced

Toppings
Sliced tomatoes
Red onion rings
Provolone cheese, sliced thin
Red bell pepper rings
Carrot, julienned
Iceberg lettuce, shredded

1. Put the chicken breast in a resealable plastic bag and pour the teriyaki marinade over it. Massage the marinade over the chicken to thoroughly coat it. Push the air out of the bag and seal it. Refrigerate the chicken at least an hour.

2. To make the Sweet Shallot Sauce, combine all the ingredients in a microwave-proof bowl and cover with a sheet of vented plastic wrap.

3. Microwave on high for 1 to 2 minutes, or until it begins to boil. Whisk the sauce until it stops boiling and set it aside to cool.

4. Light a charcoal barbecue or heat a gas grill to medium. Clean the grate and coat it with vegetable oil.

5. Shake off excess marinade and grill the chicken 5 to 6 minutes per side, turning once, or until cooked through and no longer pink in the center. Let it rest for 10 minutes, then slice it into long strips.

6. Open the sub roll and arrange the sliced chicken on the bottom half. Spoon a little of the Sweet Shallot Sauce over the chicken, then layer on the toppings of your choice. Spoon more sauce over the toppings and close the sandwich. Any leftover sauce can be served on the side or refrigerated (up to 4 weeks) and used for another sandwich.

Serves 1

You can use a tablespoon of diced sweet onion, if you would prefer, in place of the shallot, and the poppy seeds can be replaced with sesame seeds for the sauce. The corn syrup adds body as well as sweetness, but you can use the same amount of real maple syrup if you'd like.

TACO BELL
Santa Fe Gordita

TACO BELL USES PITA BREAD FOR ITS *GORDITA*—A CLEVER ALTERNATIVE TO THE ORIGINAL, WHICH IS OFTEN MADE WITH FRIED CORN MASA. TOAST A FRESH PITA AND STUFF IT WITH GRILLED CHICKEN AND CRISP VEGETABLES. SAVOR THE CHILI-SPIKED MAYO AND CHEESE THAT COMPLETE THIS HEALTHY OPTION FROM A FAST-FOOD LEADER.

Chili Mayo
2 tablespoons mayonnaise, regular or reduced fat
2 tablespoons chili sauce
1 teaspoon red wine vinegar
2 teaspoons fresh lime juice

Bean and Corn Relish
1 (10-ounce) can black beans, rinsed and drained
1¼ cups frozen corn kernels thawed
1 large red bell pepper, seeded and finely diced

2 tablespoons chopped cilantro
1 teaspoon kosher salt
½ teaspoon pepper
¼ teaspoon cumin

4 (4-ounce) boneless skinless chicken breasts
1 teaspoon kosher salt
½ teaspoon pepper
4 large whole wheat pitas
½ cup shredded Mexican blend cheese

1. Do ahead: Whisk together the ingredients for the Chili Mayo, cover, and refrigerate before using.

2. Do ahead: Toss the beans and corn for the Bean and Corn Relish with the red bell pepper and cilantro. Season with the salt, pepper, and cumin. Cover and refrigerate before using.

3. Light a charcoal barbecue or heat a gas grill to medium. Clean the grate and coat it with vegetable oil.

4. Season the chicken breasts with the salt and pepper and grill them 6 to 8 minutes per side, turning once, until cooked through and no longer pink

in the center. Let the chicken rest 10 minutes, then carve into thin, wide slices.

5. Put the pitas on the grill to heat them through. Make an opening at the top of each one and spread with a tablespoon of the Chili Mayo.

7. Lay the sliced chicken on top of the Chili Mayo, then spoon a portion of the Bean and Corn Relish into each pita. Finish with a sprinkling of the cheese over the vegetables.

8. The pitas are ready at this point, but you may wish to grill them a bit more to heat the fillings and melt the cheese.

Serves 4

Use smaller pitas for a less filling sandwich, or cut 2 large pitas in half for 4 smaller sandwiches.

TEXAS ROADHOUSE
Rockin' Fajitas

EASY TO PREPARE, FAJITAS ARE GREAT FOR A LARGE GATHERING OR A DINNER FOR TWO. TAKE ADVANTAGE OF BOTTLED DRESSING FOR A QUICK MARINADE AND PREPARE THE PROTEIN; CHICKEN, STEAK, AND SEAFOOD ARE THE TRADITIONAL FAVORITES, BUT HOW ABOUT ALL THREE? IT'S UP TO YOU, SO ROCK THOSE FAJITAS!

Fajita Mix
2 tablespoons kosher salt
2 tablespoons chili powder
1 tablespoon cumin
1 teaspoon pepper

Marinade
2 limes, quartered
2 lemons, quartered
1 (8-ounce) bottle Italian dressing
1 cup canola oil
3 large cloves garlic, lightly smashed
1 medium jalapeño, seeded and chopped
2 tablespoons roughly chopped cilantro

4 (4-ounce) boneless skinless chicken breasts
or
4 (4- to 6-ounce) sirloin steaks
or

2½ pounds medium shrimp, peeled and deveined
3 tablespoons canola oil
3 large red bell peppers, seeded and thinly sliced
3 large yellow bell peppers, seeded and thinly sliced
2 large green bell peppers, seeded and thinly sliced
2 large yellow onions, cut into thin strips
4 large cloves garlic, minced
4 large Roma tomatoes, each cut into 8 wedges
Flour tortillas, if desired

Toppings
Pico de Gallo
Sour cream
Guacamole
Mexican blend shredded cheese
Salsa, medium or hot
Jalapeños, seeded and sliced

1. Do ahead: Combine the ingredients for the Fajita Mix in a small bowl. Set aside.

2. Do ahead: To make the Marinade, squeeze the juice from the lime and lemon quarters into a medium bowl. Whisk together the remaining ingredients and pour over the meat, chicken, or seafood. Marinate beef and chicken at least 4 hours; shrimp and fish for 30 minutes.

3. Heat the oil in a large skillet and sauté the peppers and onions until soft. Stir in the garlic and sauté a few minutes more. Take the skillet off the heat and toss in the tomatoes. Season with the Fajita Mix to taste and set the skillet aside.

4. Light a charcoal barbecue or heat a gas grill to medium. Clean the grate and coat it with vegetable oil.

5. Shake excess marinade from the protein. Season the steak, chicken, or shrimp with some of the Fajita Mix. Grill beef 4 to 5 minutes per side, chicken breasts 6 to 7 minutes per side, and shrimp 1 to 2 minutes or until pink throughout. Grill the beef until cooked to your preferred doneness and the chicken until cooked through and no longer pink in the center. Let the meat rest for 10 minutes.

6. Slice the steak and chicken into thin strips. Remove tails from the shrimp and butterfly them.

7. Put the vegetable skillet over high heat and toss with the chicken, beef, or shrimp. When all are heated through, serve the fajitas on warmed plates with flour tortillas, if desired, and the toppings of your choice.

Serves 6 to 8

Put the Fajita Mix in a small shaker and offer to guests at the table. Save any extra to liven up other dishes.

TEXAS ROADHOUSE
Steak Rub

USE THIS WET RUB AS A BASTING SAUCE FOR CHICKEN, RIBS, CHOPS, AND STEAKS. IT CAN ALSO BE USED AS A SPICY DIPPING SAUCE FOR FRIED CHICKEN AND WINGS. FOR A TEX-MEX SURPRISE, MAKE IT THE BASE OF YOUR NEXT BARBECUED CHICKEN PIZZA!

1 tablespoon Worcestershire sauce
1 tablespoon spicy brown mustard
2 tablespoons white wine vinegar
1 tablespoon ancho chili powder

1 teaspoon black pepper
1 teaspoon kosher salt
½ teaspoon cumin
½ teaspoon granulated garlic
½ teaspoon cayenne pepper

1. Whisk together the Worcestershire sauce, mustard, and vinegar. When smooth, whisk in the remaining spices. The consistency should be a thick paste. If too dry, add a little more vinegar or water.

2. Rub over both sides of meat or chicken, coating thoroughly in an even, thin layer.

3. Brush a little more rub over each item on the grill, but don't let it blacken.

Makes about ⅓ cup

The flavors of this rub are very concentrated. Add a tablespoon or two to your favorite plain barbecue sauce for a little variety.

T.G.I. FRIDAY'S
Apple Butter Barbecue Sauce

IT'S NO SECRET THAT THE APPLE BUTTER BARBECUE SAUCE SERVED AT T.G.I. FRIDAY'S IS SIMPLY A COMBINATION OF APPLE BUTTER AND BARBECUE SAUCE. WANT TO MAKE IT SPECIAL? MAKE YOUR OWN APPLE BUTTER AND SAVE MOST OF IT FOR SPREADING ON FRENCH TOAST AND BANANA BREAD!

Apple Butter

2 cups unsweetened applesauce	2 tablespoons apple cider vinegar
2 cups light brown sugar	1 teaspoon cinnamon
3 tablespoons fresh lemon juice	¼ teaspoon allspice

1. To make the Apple Butter, whisk together the applesauce and brown sugar in a small saucepan over low heat. Stir frequently until the sugar dissolves.

2. Whisk in the remaining ingredients and simmer over low heat for about 20 minutes or until thickened.

3. Let it cool, then pour into a container with a tight seal and refrigerate until needed.

Makes 4 cups

Apple Butter Barbecue Sauce

1 cup apple butter	3 cups sweet and tangy barbecue sauce

To make the Apple Butter Barbecue Sauce, whisk the 2 ingredients together and refrigerate, covered, for up to 1 week.

Makes 4 cups

T.G.I. FRIDAY'S
Dragonfire Chicken

THIS DISH GETS ITS NAME FROM THE JALAPEÑOS AND CHILI GARLIC PASTE THAT GO INTO THE MARINADE AND THE KUNG PAO SAUCE SERVED WITH THE GRILLED CHICKEN. A SIDE OF STEAMED RICE OR STIR-FRIED VEGETABLES WOULD MAKE AN AMAZING CONTRAST TO ALL THAT HEAT.

4 (4-ounce) boneless skinless chicken breasts
I teaspoon kosher salt
½ teaspoon pepper

Marinade
½ cup orange blossom honey
½ cup peanut oil
3 tablespoons rice wine vinegar
I jalapeño, seeded and chopped

Kung Pao Sauce
½ cup light brown sugar

¼ cup soy sauce
2 tablespoons rice wine vinegar
I tablespoon chili garlic paste
4 large cloves garlic, minced
1-inch piece fresh ginger, peeled and minced
Water, as needed
4 green onions, chopped
2 large cloves garlic, chopped
2 teaspoons onion salt
2 tablespoons fresh lime juice

1. Do ahead: Combine the ingredients for the marinade in the jar of a blender and process until smooth. Put the chicken breasts in a large resealable plastic bag and pour the marinade over them. Push the air out of the bag and seal it. Refrigerate the chicken for 2 to 3 hours, turning the bag over occasionally.

2. Do ahead: To make the Kung Pao Sauce, whisk together the sugar and soy sauce. Stir until the sugar is dissolved. Add the remaining ingredients and refrigerate, covered, until ready to use. Shake well or whisk before serving.

3. Light a charcoal barbecue or heat a gas grill to medium. Clean the grate and coat it with vegetable oil.

4. Remove the chicken from the marinade and shake off any extra. Season the breasts with the salt and pepper.

5. Grill the chicken for 5 to 6 minutes per side, turning once, or until the chicken is cooked through and no longer pink in the center.

6. Place the chicken on warm plates and spoon some of the Kung Pao Sauce over each one.

* * * * * * * * * *

Serves 4

* * * * * * * * * *

If you prefer to not pour a cold sauce over the hot chicken, either bring it to room temperature before serving, or heat it briefly in the microwave or in a small saucepan over medium-low heat.

T.G.I. FRIDAY'S
Grilled Vegetable Pasta

THERE ARE MANY REASONS OTHER THAN BURGERS TO FIRE UP THE GRILL ANY
DAY OF THE WEEK. THINK GRILLED VEGETABLES—MEATY PORTOBELLO MUSH-
ROOMS, CRISP BELL PEPPERS, AND ZUCCHINI—WITH A LITTLE VINAIGRETTE AND
SOME FRESH TOMATO AND BASIL, AND YOU HAVE THE BASICS FOR A REFRESHING
GRILLED VEGETABLE PASTA.

1 tablespoon Italian dressing
1 extra-large portobello
  mushroom, stemmed
4 tablespoons extra virgin
  olive oil
2 teaspoons kosher salt
1 medium zucchini
1 medium yellow summer squash
1 large red bell pepper
4 large Roma tomatoes

2 large cloves garlic, minced
1 (16-ounce) box spaghettini,
  cooked according to package
  directions
1 cup cherry tomatoes, halved
½ cup shredded fresh basil
1 teaspoon kosher salt
¼ teaspoon pepper
½ cup shredded Parmesan
  cheese, optional

1. Pour the salad dressing on the inside of the portobello cap and let it
    marinate while the grill gets hot.

2. Mix 1 tablespoon olive oil with 1 teaspoon kosher salt and brush the
    zucchini and summer squash with the mixture.

3. Light a charcoal barbecue or heat a gas grill to medium. Clean the grate
    and coat it with vegetable oil.

4. Brush the dressing in the cap all over the portobello and grill it on both
    sides, then set aside.

5. Grill the bell pepper until the skin is charred, then the Roma tomatoes,
    just until the skin starts to blister.

6. Let the pepper and tomatoes cool, then peel or rub the skins off.

7. Grill the zucchini and summer squash until cooked but still firm.

8. Discard the seeds from the bell pepper and cut it into 1-inch pieces.

9. Quarter the tomatoes and discard the seeds and pulp.

10. Cut both the zuccini and summer squash into 1-inch pieces.

11. Heat the remaining 3 tablespoons extra virgin olive oil in a large skillet over medium-low heat and stir in the minced garlic. Add the cooked spaghettini and toss to coat with the garlic.

12. Add the cherry tomatoes and basil to the skillet with the pasta and simmer the mixture over low heat for a few minutes. Add the grilled zucchini and summer squash and toss to warm through. Season the pasta and vegetables with the salt and pepper.

13. Use tongs to place mounds of the pasta on warmed plates or in shallow soup bowls. Place the wedges of grilled tomatoes around the edge of the plate like spokes, with one end in the pasta, the other end at the plate rim.

14. Slice the portobello and lay the slices over the pasta. Sprinkle with Parmesan cheese, if desired, and serve hot.

Serves 4

You can vary the vegetables used in this dish. Look for firm vegetables that will hold their color when grilled.

T.G.I. FRIDAY'S
Jack Daniel's Grill Glaze

THIS IS A WONDERFULLY FULL-FLAVORED SAUCE, PERFECT FOR BASTING STEAKS ON THE GRILL OR FOR SERVING ON THE SIDE. USE IT TO DRIZZLE OVER GRILLED VEGETABLES, BAKED POTATOES, OR CHICKEN WINGS. IT ONLY MAKES ABOUT A CUP, SO YOU MAY NEED TO GO INTO BATCH PRODUCTION TO KEEP UP WITH THE DEMAND!

1 whole head garlic
1 tablespoon olive oil
½ cup water
1 cup pineapple juice concentrate
1¼ cups golden brown sugar
¼ cup teriyaki sauce
1 tablespoon regular soy sauce
3 tablespoons fresh lemon juice

3 green onions, white part only, minced
1 tablespoon Jack Daniel's whiskey
¼ teaspoon cayenne pepper
1 tablespoon crushed pineapple, optional

1. Preheat the oven to 325°F.

2. Cut the head of garlic a half inch from the stem end and trim the root end so it stands up.

3. Put the garlic on a sheet of aluminum foil large enough to tightly cover it and drizzle with the olive oil.

4. Tightly seal the foil and put it in a small ovenproof dish. Bake in the hot oven for 1 hour, or until the individual cloves are softened and easily pop out of their skins. Set aside to cool.

5. Whisk together the water, pineapple concentrate, and brown sugar in a small saucepan over medium-high heat. Stir until the sugar is dissolved.

6. Stir in the remaining ingredients and bring to a boil, then turn down the heat until the sauce is just simmering.

7. Mash the roasted garlic with a fork or the side of a knife until it becomes a paste. Whisk the garlic paste into the sauce and stir until it is well incorporated.

8. Continue to simmer the sauce over low heat until it is reduced by half, about 45 minutes. The sauce should be the consistency of syrup.

Makes about 1 cup

The alcohol in the sauce is eliminated as the sauce cooks, leaving only the flavor.

T.G.I. FRIDAY'S
Jack Daniel's Marinade

HERE'S ANOTHER GREAT USE FOR JACK DANIEL'S, OTHER THAN DURING HAPPY HOUR. USE THIS MARINADE AS A MOP SAUCE OVER RIBS AND PORK, AND AS A COATING FOR SEA SCALLOPS, GIVING THEM A CRUSTY CHAR AFTER A MINUTE OR TWO ON A HOT GRILL. YOU'RE BOUND TO FIND MANY MORE USES FOR IT!

¼ cup Jack Daniel's whiskey
¼ cup light soy sauce
¼ cup Grey Poupon, or other Dijon mustard
5 green onions, minced

¼ cup golden brown sugar
1 teaspoon kosher salt
¼ teaspoon pepper
¼ teaspoon Worcestershire sauce

Combine all ingredients and whisk vigorously, until the sugar is dissolved.

Makes 1¼ cups

Prepare this marinade ahead of time and keep it refrigerated up to 4 days in a tightly covered container. If you are concerned about the alcohol, it will burn off on the hot grill. You can also flame it in a small saucepan and cook it out. Let the liquid cool completely before whisking with the other ingredients.

TONY ROMA'S
Barbecue Baby Back Ribs

TONY ROMA'S HAS BEEN DOING BARBECUE RIBS SINCE THEY OPENED MORE THAN 40 YEARS AGO. MANY RESTAURANTS HAVE ITEMS THAT COME AND GO ON THEIR MENUS, BUT RIBS WILL ALWAYS BE A MAINSTAY AT TONY ROMA'S.

Barbecue Sauce
1 cup ketchup
1 cup red wine vinegar
½ cup corn syrup
2 tablespoons dark brown sugar
1 teaspoon kosher salt
½ teaspoon granulated garlic

½ teaspoon onion powder
¼ teaspoon prepared
  horseradish

2 full racks baby pork ribs
1½ tablespoons kosher salt
2 teaspoons pepper

1. Do ahead: Whisk together all the ingredients for the Barbecue Sauce. Refrigerate in an airtight container until ready to use.

2. Preheat the oven to 275°F.

3. Wash and dry the ribs and pull or cut off the membrane on the underside.

4. Season both racks with the salt and pepper.

5. Set a wire rack or grate in a roasting pan large enough to hold the ribs and add a cup of water. Place the ribs on the rack, bone-side down, and cover the pan very tightly with aluminum foil.

6. Bake in the hot oven for 2 to 2½ hours, or until a knife goes easily through the meat and the meat has started to pull away from the bones.

7. Leave the pan covered while the grill heats.

8. Light a charcoal barbecue or heat a gas grill to medium. Clean the grate and coat it with vegetable oil.

9. Put the ribs on the grill and brush with the Barbecue Sauce. Turn the ribs occasionally, brushing each time until they start to build a crust from the charred sauce, about 20 minutes or less.

10. Divide the racks in half and serve a half rack to each guest, with extra barbecue sauce on the side.

Serves 2 to 4

To make a thicker sauce, bring the sauce to a boil in a small saucepan, then lower the temperature and simmer until thickened, about 10 minutes.

TONY ROMA'S
Blue Ridge Smokies Barbecue Sauce

ONE OF THE MANY SAUCES DEVELOPED AT TONY ROMA'S OVER THE YEARS IS THIS SMOKY SAUCE, REMINISCENT OF WHAT'S TRADITIONALLY PREPARED IN SOUTHERN VIRGINIA AND NORTHERN TENNESSEE.

1 cup ketchup
1 cup red wine vinegar
¼ cup dark molasses
1 teaspoon liquid smoke flavoring

1 teaspoon kosher salt
½ teaspoon pepper
¼ teaspoon granulated garlic
½ teaspoon onion powder

1. Whisk together all the ingredients in a small saucepan over medium-high heat and bring to a boil.
2. Lower the heat and simmer for 20 to 30 minutes, or until the sauce has thickened.
3. Use the sauce to brush on grilled pork ribs and beef ribs.

Makes about 2 cups

If you really like a smoky flavor, increase the amount of smoke flavoring in this recipe. It can be very strong, so it's best to start out using less and build from there.

TONY ROMA'S
Carolina Honey Barbecue Sauce

A VINEGAR-BASED SAUCE IS CENTRAL TO BARBECUE IN THE CAROLINAS, BUT THIS HONEY AND MOLASSES VERSION IS POPULAR EVERYWHERE. THIS IS ONE OF SEVERAL BARBECUE SAUCES THAT IS SOLD BY THE BOTTLE OR SIX-PACK BY TONY ROMA'S ONLINE STORE.

1 cup ketchup	1 teaspoon kosher salt
1 cup red wine vinegar	½ teaspoon pepper
½ cup dark molasses	¼ teaspoon granulated garlic
½ cup clover honey	½ teaspoon onion powder
1 teaspoon liquid smoke flavoring	¼ teaspoon Tabasco sauce

1. Whisk the ingredients together in a small saucepan over medium-high heat. Bring the sauce to a boil, then lower the heat and simmer for 20 to 30 minutes, or until thickened.

2. If not using right away, let the sauce cool, then store for up to a month in the refrigerator in a tightly sealed container.

Makes about 3 cups

If dark molasses is too strong for your taste buds, you might want to try using an equal amount of real maple syrup. Clover honey is fairly light and mild and would blend well with the maple.

WENDY'S

Garden Sensation Mandarin Chicken Salad

WENDY'S HAS A ROTATING SERIES OF GARDEN SENSATION SALADS ON THEIR MENU, OFFERING A FRESH TAKE ON POPULAR VARIETIES: TACO, CAESAR, ASIAN, BLT, AND OTHERS. THE MANDARIN IS ASIAN STYLE, WITH ORANGE, ALMONDS, AND NOODLES TOSSED WITH CHUNKS OF CHICKEN BREAST AND A SWEET AND SAVORY SALAD DRESSING THAT IS POSSIBLY THE BEST THING ABOUT IT. MAKE A LARGE BATCH TO KEEP ON HAND FOR OTHER SALADS, OR EVEN AS A MARINADE.

Sesame Dressing
¼ cup light corn syrup
3 tablespoons apple cider vinegar
2 tablespoons reserved mandarin juice
2 tablespoons golden brown sugar
1 tablespoon rice wine vinegar
1 tablespoon light soy sauce
½ teaspoon toasted sesame oil
½ teaspoon dry mustard
½ teaspoon ginger powder
½ teaspoon kosher salt
½ teaspoon sweet paprika
¼ teaspoon pepper

¼ teaspoon granulated garlic
½ cup canola oil

4 (4-ounce) boneless skinless chicken breasts
1 teaspoon kosher salt
½ teaspoon pepper
4 cups chopped Iceberg lettuce
4 cups baby mixed greens
½ cup slivered almonds, lightly toasted
1 cup crispy rice noodles
1 (11-ounce) can mandarin oranges, drained, 2 tablespoons juice reserved
1 tablespoon white sesame seeds

1. Do ahead: Combine all of the Sesame Dressing ingredients, except the canola oil, in the jar of a blender and pulse until smooth. With the motor running, slowly pour a thin ribbon of oil into the mixture until it is incorporated. Refrigerate the dressing in a covered container until ready to use.

2. Light a charcoal barbecue or heat a gas grill to medium. Clean the grate and coat it with vegetable oil.

3. Season the chicken with the salt and pepper and grill for 5 to 6 minutes per side, turning once, or until no longer pink in the center. Let it rest 10 minutes, then cut into bite-sized chunks.

4. Combine the iceberg and baby mixed greens in a large bowl. Toss with half the slivered almonds, half the rice noodles, and half the mandarin orange segments.

5. Place a portion of the tossed greens on chilled plates and top with equal amounts of the grilled chicken. Drizzle each salad with some of the dressing, then add the remaining portions of the almonds, rice noodles, and mandarin segments.

6. Sprinkle each salad with some of the sesame seeds and serve extra dressing on the side.

Serves 4

It's a good idea to make the dressing ahead of time to give the flavors time to combine. It lasts over a week if kept refrigerated in a closed container.

TRADEMARKS

- A&W is a registered trademark of Yum! Brands, Inc.
- Applebee's is a registered trademark of Applebee's International, Inc.
- Arby's is a registered trademark of Arby's Restaurant Group, Inc.
- Bahama Breeze is a registered trademark of Darden Concepts, Inc.
- Baja Fresh is a registered trademark of Fresh Enterprises, Inc.
- Benihana is a registered trademark of Benihana, Inc.
- Bob Evans is a registered trademark of Bob Evans Farms, Inc.
- Bonefish Grill is a registered trademark of Bloomin' Brands, Inc.
- Buca Di Beppo is a registered trademark of Planet Hollywood International, Inc.
- Burger King is a registered trademark of the Burger King Corporation.
- California Pizza Kitchen is a registered trademark of California Pizza Kitchen, Inc.
- Carino's Italian Grill is a registered trademark of Fired Up Inc.
- Carl's Jr. is a registered trademark of Carl Karcher Enterprises, Inc.
- Carrabba's is a registered trademark of OSI Restaurant Partners, LLC.
- Chevy's Fresh Mex is a registered trademark of Chevy's, Inc.
- Chi-Chi's is a registered trademark of Chi-Chi's, Inc. and Prandium, Inc.
- Chick-Fil-A is a registered trademark of CFA Properties, Inc.
- Chili's is a registered trademark of Brinker International.
- Chipotle Mexican Grill is a registered trademark of Chipotle Mexican Grill, Inc.
- Claim Jumper is a registered trademark of Claim Jumper Restaurants, LLC.

- Copeland's of New Orleans is a registered trademark of Al Copeland Investments.
- Cracker Barrel is a registered trademark of CBOCS Properties, Inc.
- Dave & Buster's is a registered trademark of Dave & Buster's.
- Denny's is a registered trademark of DFO, LLC.
- Don Pablo's is a registered trademark of Rita Restaurant Corp.
- El Pollo Loco is a registered trademark of El Pollo Loco Inc.
- El Torito Grill is a registered trademark of El Torito Restaurants, Inc.
- Famous Dave's is a registered trademark of Famous Dave's of America, Inc.
- Fuddruckers is a registered trademark of Luby's Inc.
- Hardee's is a registered trademark of Hardee's Food Systems, Inc.
- Houston's is a registered trademark of Bandera Restaurants.
- In-N-Out Burger is a registered trademark of In-N-Out Burgers.
- Jack in the Box is a registered trademark of Jack in the Box Inc.
- Joe's Crab Shack is a registered trademark of Landry's Seafood Restaurants, Inc.
- Kenny Rogers is a registered trademark of Berjaya Roasters.
- KFC is a registered trademark of Yum! Brands, Inc.
- Krystal is a registered trademark of The Krystal Company.
- Lone Star Steakhouse is a registered trademark of Lone Star Steakhouse & Saloon, Inc.
- Longhorn Steakhouse is a registered trademark of Darden Concepts, Inc.
- Luby's Cafeteria is a registered trademark of Luby's Inc.
- Olive Garden is a registered trademark of Darden Restaurants, Inc.
- Outback Steakhouse is a registered trademark of Outback Steakhouse, Inc.
- P.F. Chang's is a registered trademark of P.F. Chang's China Bistro, Inc.
- Panda Express is a registered trademark of Panda Restaurant Group, Inc.
- Panera Bread is a registered trademark of Panera Bread.

- Planet Hollywood is a registered trademark of Planet Hollywood, Inc.
- Ponderosa Steak House is a registered trademark of Homestyle Dining, LLC.
- Qdoba Mexican Grill is a registered trademark of Qdoba Restaurant Inc.
- Red Lobster is a registered trademark of Darden Restaurants, Inc.
- Red Robin is a registered trademark of Red Robin Gourmet Burgers, Inc.
- Romano's Macaroni Grill is a registered trademark of Macaroni Grill LLC.
- Ruby Tuesday's is a registered trademark of Morrison Restaurant's, Inc.
- Schlotzky's is a registered trademark of Schlotzsky's Franchise LLC.
- Sizzler is a registered trademark of Sizzler USA.
- Sonic is a registered trademark of Sonic Corp.
- Steak and Ale is a registered trademark of Atalaya Capital Management.
- Steak 'n Shake is a registered trademark of Biglari Holdings.
- Subway is a registered trademark of Doctor's Associates, Inc.
- T.G.I. Friday's is a registered trademark of T.G.I. Friday's, Inc.
- Taco Bell is a registered trademark of Yum! Brands, Inc.
- Texas Roadhouse is a registered trademark of Texas Roadhouse, Inc.
- The Cheesecake Factory is a registered trademark of The Cheesecake Factory, Inc.
- Tony Roma's is a registered trademark of Tony Roma's Inc.
- Wendy's is a registered trademark of Wendy's International, Inc.

RESTAURANT WEBSITES

To find a restaurant near you, please visit:

A&W	www.awrestaurants.com
Applebee's	www.applebees.com
Arby's	www.arbys.com
Bahama Breeze	www.bahamabreeze.com
Baja Fresh	www.bajafresh.com
Benihana	www.benihana.com
Bob Evans	www.bobevans.com
Bonefish Grill	www.bonefishgrill.com
Buca Di Beppo	www.bucadibeppo.com
Burger King	www.burgerking.com
California Pizza Kitchen	www.cpk.com
Carino's Italian Grill	www.carinos.com
Carl's Jr. Carl	www.carlsjr.com
Carrabba's	www.carrabbas.com
Chevy's Fresh Mex	www.chevys.com
Chi-Chi's	www.chichis.com
Chick-Fil-A	www.chick-fil-a.com
Chili's	www.chilis.com
Chipotle Mexican Grill	www.chipotle.com
Claim Jumper	www.claimjumper.com
Copeland's of New Orleans	www.copelandsofneworleans.com
Cracker Barrel	www.crackerbarrel.com
Dave & Buster's	www.daveandbusters.com
Denny's	www.dennys.com
Don Pablo's	www.donpablos.com
El Pollo Loco	www.elpolloloco.com
El Torito	www.eltorito.com
Famous Dave's	www.famousdaves.com

Fuddruckers	www.fuddruckers.com
Hardee's	www.hardees.com
Houston's	www.hillstone.com
In-N-Out Burger	www.in-n-out.com
Jack in the Box	www.jackinthebox.com
Joe's Crab Shack	www.joescrabshack.com
Kenny Rogers	www.kennyrogersroasters.com
KFC	www.kfc.com
Krystal	www.krystal.com
Lone Star Steakhouse	www.lonestarsteakhouse.com
Longhorn Steakhouse	www.longhornsteakhouse.com
Luby's	www.lubys.com
Olive Garden	www.olivegarden.com
Outback Steakhouse	www.outbacksteakhouse.com
P.F. Chang's	www.pfchangs.com
Panda Express	www.pandaexpress.com
Panera Bread	www.panerabread.com
Planet Hollywood	www.planethollywood.com
Ponderosa Steak House	www.ponderosasteakhouses.com
Qdoba Mexican Grill	www.qdoba.com
Red Lobster	www.redlobster.com
Red Robin	www.redrobin.com
Romano's Macaroni Grill	www.macaronigrill.com
Ruby Tuesday's	www.rubytuesday.com
Schlotzky's	www.schlotzskys.com
Sizzler	www.sizzler.com
Sonic Drive-In	www.sonicdrivein.com
Steak 'n Shake	www.steaknshake.com
Subway	www.subway.com
T.G.I. Friday's	www.fridays.com
Taco Bell	www.tacobell.com
Texas Roadhouse	www.texasroadhouse.com
The Cheesecake Factory	www.thecheesecakefactory.com
Tony Roma's	www.tonyromas.com
Wendy's	www.wendys.com

INDEX

Venetian Apricot Chicken, 210–11
vinaigrette:
    Blue Cheese Vinaigrette, 57–58
    Citrus Herb Vinaigrette, 87–88
    Dijon Balsamic Vinaigrette, 100–101
    Sun-Dried Tomato Vinaigrette, 268–69
    tomatoes, Grilled Salmon with Sun-Dried Tomato Vinaigrette, 268–69
    see also dressing

W

websites, restaurant, 335–36
Wendy's, 329–30

Western Bacon Cheeseburger, 109
whiskey:
    Jack Daniel's Grill Glaze, 322–23
    Jack Daniel's Marinade, 324
White Wine Butter Sauce, 301–2
Wildfire Grilled Corn, 86
Wood-Fire Grilled Salmon, 217–18
Wood-Grilled Chicken Breast, 69–70
Wood-Grilled Tilapia in a Spicy Soy Broth, 281–83
wood planks, 8
wrap, Asian Chicken Wrap, 299–300

Y

Yukon Blend Marinade, 157